STAGING AND STAGERS
IN
MODERN JEWISH PALESTINE

Raphael Patai Series in Jewish Folklore and Anthropology

A complete listing of the books in this series can be found at
http://wsupress.wayne.edu.

General Editor
Dan Ben-Amos
University of Pennsylvania

Advisory Editors
Jane S. Gerber
City University of New York

Barbara Kirshenblatt-Gimblett
New York University

Aliza Shenhar
University of Haifa

Amnon Shiloah
Hebrew University

Harvey E. Goldberg
Hebrew University

Samuel G. Armistead
University of California, Davis

Guy H. Haskell

STAGING AND STAGERS
IN
MODERN JEWISH PALESTINE

THE CREATION OF FESTIVE LORE
IN A NEW CULTURE, 1882–1948

YAACOV SHAVIT & SHOSHANA SITTON

TRANSLATED BY CHAYA NAOR

Wayne State University Press   Detroit

Copyright © 2004 by Wayne State University Press,
Detroit, Michigan 48201. All rights reserved.
No part of this book may be reproduced without
formal permission.

Manufactured in the United States of America.
08 07 06 05 04   5 4 3 2 1

Library of Congress Cataloging-in-Publication Data

Shavit, Jacob.
　Staging and stagers in modern Jewish Palestine : the creation of festive lore in a new culture, 1882–1948 / Yaacov Shavit and Shoshana Sitton ; translated by Chaya Naor.
　　p. cm. — (Raphael Patai series in Jewish folklore and anthropology)
　Includes bibliographical references and index.
　ISBN 0-8143-2845-8 (cloth)
　1. Jewish folk festivals—Palestine—History—19th century. 2. Jewish folk festivals—Palestine—History—20th century. 3. Jewish folk festivals—Palestine—Management—History. 4. Popular culture—Palestine—History. 5. Religion and culture—Palestine—History. I. Naor, Chaya. II. Title. III. Series.
　DS113.S425 2004
　394.2695694—dc22
　　　　　　　　　2004000536

∞ The paper used in this publication meets the minimum requirements of the American National Standard for Information Sciences—Permanence of Paper for Printed Library Materials, ANSI Z39.48-1984.

Publication of this book was made possible through the generosity of the Bertha M. and Hyman Herman Endowed Memorial Fund.

"If you want to learn about the soul of a nation,
observe it on its festival days."
—Boris Schatz, "Al Omanut, Amanim, veMevakrehem"
("On Art, Artists, and Their Critics"), 1992

"Festivals also need a homeland."
—Yehudith Harari, *Ben HaKramim*
(*In the Vineyards*), 1:221, 1947

"With the return to the land, with the movement of national revival,
the search for new festivals began."
—H. Wissman-Dizengof, "Hagigat Hag Ha-Hanukkah baGan"
("The Hannukah Festival in the Kindergarten")
Hed haGan 2:42–44, 1937.

Contents

Acknowledgments ix

Introduction xi

PART I

1 Placing the Stagers on the Cultural Stage: Identifying the Stagers 3
2 The Setting: Hebrew Culture, Hebrew "Formal Folk Culture," and the Hebrew Stagers 14
3 Ceremonies and Festivals in Modern Jewish Thinking 21
4 How Do the Stagers Work? The Mechanism of Innovation 29

PART II

5 The Missing Stage of Political Culture 41
6 To Celebrate in the Spirit of the Homeland: Staging School Festivals and Ceremonies 48
7 The Urban Stagers and the Town as an Open-Air Stage 84
8 Festivals in the Kibbutz: Stagers and Staging in a Communal Society 106

Conclusion 125

APPENDIXES

1 First Program for a Commemoration of the First Fruits Festivity, 1929 131
2 Commemoration of the First Fruits: Proposal for a Ceremony, 1934 134
3 Planting on the New Year for Trees (Tu Bishevat), 1930s 148

4	Program for Purim Festivities in Tel Aviv, 1929	154
5	A Citizen of Tel Aviv: A Proposal for the Organization of a Purim Carnival, 1931	159
6	Letter from Members of the Atz-Kotzatz Editorial Board, 1932	164
7	Letter from Yehudah Nadivi Outlining Proposed Preparations for the Tel Aviv Jubilee Celebrations, 1924	168

Notes 173

Selected Bibliography 189

Index 199

Acknowledgments

Professor Dan Ben-Amos (Pennsylvania University) has generously provided guidance and comments during the past years, from the inception of the idea behind the book through the research up to publication. We are enormously grateful to him. The detailed comments of anonymous readers indicated various flaws in the manuscript. These have been remedied, or so we hope.

Mrs. Liat Steir-Livny and Mr. Chaim Cohen helped us throughout the project. We thank them both. We thank Mrs. Chaya Naor for her translation of the manuscript and Mr. Aaron Jaffe for editing it.

Much of the source material was found in the following places: the Festival Archive in Kibbutz Beit HaShitta, the Jewish National Fund Archives (Jerusalem), the Tel Aviv Municipality Archives and Educational History Archive at Tel Aviv University. These archives and their archivists were of great assistance to us.

The research enjoyed the generous support of the Research Institute for the History of the Jewish National Fund (KKL), and we are grateful to the Institute and its director, Dr. Gabriel Alexander.

Introduction

Our interest in the invention of festivals, festivities, and ceremonies stems from our research into the history of Hebrew culture (Yaacov Shavit) and modern Hebrew education (Shoshana Sitton) in Eretz-Israel (Jewish Palestine) that illustrated the key role played by the invention of festivals in both fields of study. When we began our work on this topic, we found that it embraces several fields of research and may be studied utilizing various academic disciplines. We cannot but agree with Roy Strong's words that "Few subjects have suffered so much from the compartmentalization of knowledge as festivals. It has fallen between so many schools, those of the history and of art, literature, ideas and political history. . . . Perhaps the study of festivals can never by its very nature ever be a coherent discipline without distortion."[1]

Indeed, our subject can be approached through different perspectives: as a part of the history of modern nationalism; as part of the processes of the overall cultural planning of a society and within it its festive lore; as part of the creation of national ceremonies as well as of a folk culture;[2] as a case of tradition invention (more precisely, of inventing a new festive calendar[3]); as the dramatization of collective memory; as part of the creation of a civic culture; as a key facet in the creation of an outdoor and indoor public space; and as a tool for socialization, indoctrination, and modernization. All these perspectives, and the insights they provide, make an important contribution to our comprehensive understanding of festivities and illuminate various aspects thereof. All of these approaches have helped us to understand the particulars of our topic.

This study has both a universal and a particularistic aspect. Clearly, the construction of a system of festivals and ceremonies is a universal phenomenon, and not peculiar to the case of the new Hebrew culture in Eretz-Israel. As background material for our research on the latter case, we reviewed a considerable number of studies on the process of constructing festivals and ceremonies in various countries—from Venezuela to Finland, the Soviet Union to the United States and Canada, particularly in the modern era (the nineteenth and twentieth centuries). Of course, there is much similarity between the cases, with regard to needs and motivations as well as the functions of the festivals and ceremonies.

For example, all cases demonstrated complex links between the ceremonial tradition and the festivals, which simultaneously belong both to the religious system and to the modern national and political tradition, which is generally secular in nature. In all cases the creation of ceremonies and festivals is an integral part of nation building and identity shaping. By contrast, the relationships between religion and nationalism in the various cases are marked by quite a few differences, an outcome of disparate historical circumstances.

We looked to various disciplines when reviewing this literature, which describes the festivals and ceremonies and reconstructs their content and the manner in which they were held. As we read, questions came to mind: Who organized and staged these ceremonies? Did the modern ones develop "spontaneously," or were they organized and staged by groups and individuals? Is there any resemblance between the organization and the staging of the festivals and ceremonies in the modern era and those in earlier periods, even in ancient times? Our attempt to answer this question led to the premise that the reconstruction of the processes of creating and constructing a system of ceremonies and festivals in the new Jewish society in Eretz-Israel may serve as more than just a description of such processes in a specific society. Rather, this effort may give rise to general and basic conclusions regarding the manner in which these processes occurred in other societies as well. We believe that the case of Hebrew culture in Eretz-Israel is an important and fascinating test case, not necessarily because there is anything so singular about the contents of its festivals and ceremonies but because it enables us to closely examine the way in which the creators of the festivals, whom we call stagers and whose work we call staging, carried out their activity. Hence it seems to us that even readers unfamiliar with the contents of the traditional and revised Jewish calendar of festivals will be interested in this study, which shows the stagers in action and does not simply present the product of their creativity.

We describe the manner in which a formal popular culture, constituting an integral part of Eretz-Israeli Hebrew culture, from 1882 to 1948, was created and institutionalized in the new Jewish community during this relatively brief period. The study concentrates on the new festive calendar, the manner in which its contents were determined, and by whom. Our major argument is that the creators of the new festive calendar were aware of the functions this new calendar, with its content and symbols, was meant to fulfill. Moreover, they were aware that it was important not only to create a repertoire of texts (and music) for the festivals and ceremonies but also to stage them. This is why we prefer to use the terms "formal (or official)" "popular (or folk) culture."[4] They indicate that the creators and agents of the new folklore and popular culture are identifiable, and that it is characterized by written texts of instructions, telling the participants what to say and how to perform. On the one hand, this culture was official because it was invented consciously and its creators are identifiable, and because some of them over time underwent a process of bureaucratization; on the other hand, it was "popular" because it was intended for the entire public, not just for defined sectors, and all were supposed to take part as either active participants or spectators.

Our study, then, deals with an official folk culture, not with national festivals, for the simple reason that during Turkish rule (until 1918) and the British rule over Palestine (until 1948), the Yishuv found it hard to organize the kind of national festivals that are typically held by sovereign states. It may be said, however, that the celebrations addressed below combined two elements: they constituted a major part of the new folk culture, but were also national festivals (and a part of the new civic culture as well). For example, the Purim carnival in Tel Aviv was not only a folk festivity but also a national and municipal one. The fact that national motifs, symbols, and values took center stage at many various holiday celebrations made these, to a large degree, into national and civic festivals.

In the broader, more general context, we do not intend to propose a new theoretical framework for portraying the role of rituals and festivals in the building of a society, which would differ from that which has already been suggested in the extensive research literature. In the specific context, our main interest is to depict the group of cultural entrepreneurs (the stagers), and describe their modes of activity and creative products.

In other words, the contribution of this research to the various disciplines mentioned above, which are concerned with the various aspects of the ceremony, the holiday, the festival, and the like, is its emphasis on the significant role of the stagers and the importance of reconstructing the staging process. It is our contention that stagers perform a important function in constructing the culture and that the product of their work is evident in a wide variety of public social events that include a distinct performative dimension. We may be familiar with the products of their work—the ceremonies and festivities—but we do not always know who created these products, and even more rarely are we able to trace the process of their work and reconstruct the considerations that guided them in the staging process. This is particularly true in relation to stagers of small events in small social units. However, this also very often applies to well-organized social units, such as urban society, and even to stagers of official state ceremonies. Sufficient documentation has not always been available to enable us to identify the stagers and to reconstruct the process of their work. In some cases, the creators of the texts and the stagers were one and the same, but in many other cases these were two separate groups, each fulfilling a different, defined function in the process of creating and organizing the new culture. However, it is usually more difficult to identify the stagers than the writers of the texts, the composers, the artists or even the performers. Thus, because in many instances the work of the stagers is done behind the scenes, they are anonymous cultural players who somehow vanish from the history of culture. Like the masses of artists, artisans, and builders who have constructed cultural assets according to certain models, they remained anonymous, and we are accustomed to assuming that public events do not have individual creators. The case of Hebrew culture in Eretz-Israel offers a unique opportunity to identify and examine the manner in which the essence of the festivals and ceremonies was understood, and to follow the stagers and reenact their staging instructions. Not many case studies allow us to closely examine the mechanism of the stager's work. Hence we believe that this study can also shed light on the manner in which stagers in other societies have created a national culture (perhaps also in the pre-nationalist era).

STATE OF THE ART

In the thirties, Chaim Nachman Bialik (1873–1934), the Hebrew national poet and perhaps the most important initiator of Hebrew culture, promoted the preparation of a Sabbath book (*Sefer Hashabbat*), which would be a compilation (*kinus*) of various texts connected with the Sabbath. In 1938, *Mo'adim—Seder Sefarim Lechagei Ha'am* (*Festivals—Book of Folk Holidays*) was published, edited by Chaim Harari (whose name will appear later as one of the shapers of the ceremonies and festivals in Tel Aviv). But these two books, as well as other anthologies of the traditions of holidays and festivals in old and new Jewish folklore, focused mainly on the textual side of the holiday, its development and meaning, and less on the manner in which it was staged. Since then, many studies have focused on the development of the verbal dimension—the creation of the new canonical text, written and rhetorical, prose and poetry—and on its contents. Much has been written about the history of the textual corpus (national literature and the literary canon) that shaped and reflected modern Hebrew culture and modern Jewish identity; no less attention was given to describing the genesis of the new set of historical-national myths and their functions.[5] These studies deal mainly with the process by which the new texts were created, which in most cases was a combination of the rewriting and reshaping of traditional texts, interspersed with new elements, some original, some borrowed, in a manner that would provide an expression of the new "organic" national life cycle and the new worldview, its values and symbols.

These studies are concerned mainly with the link between the new collective memory of the Jewish society in Eretz-Israel and its repertoire of myths, on the one hand, and its worldview and value system, on the other. No less attention is devoted to the transition from a religious-traditional system to a national secular system and the link between these two layers, in particular the way in which the latter competed with the former in an attempt to create a new sacred time and a new sacred space as a complete alternative. The changes that occurred in religious rituals in all layers of religious society constituted another focal point, particularly in anthropological literature. Conversely, very little has been written about the concrete, visual aspect of the holiday and the ceremony, namely, the staging. We did not set out to provide a full and detailed description of the festive activity in Eretz-Israel, and certainly not to describe the entire repertoire of each and every festival (in particular the songs, music and dance which were an integral part of almost every performative act). Rather, we focused on the ways the festive lore was organized by the various stagers in the rural and urban Jewish society in Eretz-Israel. Contrary to the prevalent image, the urban Jewish society created a large-scale system of ceremonies and festivals of its own, and had an active group of stagers, even more organized and institutionalized than those in the rural society. It was not only the rural community that perceived festivals as an expression of both its "organic" and "authentic" character; the urban society also perceived it as a major component of its *Sitz im Leben*.

PART I

1

PLACING THE STAGERS ON THE CULTURAL STAGE: IDENTIFYING THE STAGERS

WHO ARE THE STAGERS AND WHAT DO THEY STAGE?

We begin with the somewhat sweeping assertion that every culture is staged, and almost every socio-cultural event taking place therein is staged in one way or another. Many of these events are not "spontaneous" creations, staged without any guiding hand, "emerging out of the collective unconscious of a single-voiced, organic community,"[1] but were created, carefully reconstructed, framed, shaped and disseminated at some time or another by a person or persons, whom we call stagers.

However, the origin of the form of staging and the identity of the stagers are generally obscure. The majority of texts documenting festivals and ceremonies do not tell us who "dramatized," "directed," and "staged" them; they do not tell us who determined the form of the ceremony. Only infrequently do we find the formative version of the staging rules, namely, the wording of the ceremony's protocol and the "stage directions." As a result, the sequence and organization of the festival and the ceremony—the costumes, scenery, movements and gestures—this entire complex and refined structure, which repeats itself with precision and a set rhythm, and is part of an organized public performance, often seems to us a self-evident structure, a collective creation which has existed since the beginning of time. Often it seems as if a certain hidden hand tried to conceal whoever had written and staged the innumerable festivals and ceremonies and ritual etiquette that are an integral part of every mode of social behavior, in order to give the impression of a popular creation. Or perhaps it is because they evolved over time and so many took part in shaping them.

We could accept the latter explanation if it referred only to the innumerable ritual and ceremonial acts, but it is hard to believe that more complex festivities and rites, performed according to a precise protocol and rules of direction, in which the scenery, costumes, movements, and gestures are meticulously repeated, could be a "spontaneous" creation that evolved, as it were, "by itself." William Graham Sumner writes that "Folk-ways are made unconsciously . . . they are not creations of human purpose and wit."[2] In the modern case, at least, folk culture is very often an anonymous creation but seldom is it a spontaneous creation. In fact, modern liturgy, rituals and festivals are always constructed or reconstructed.[3] Indeed, many studies recognize the fact that festivities and ceremonies are planned and orchestrated through the matrix of command[4] and that various organizations and persons participated in such preparation by contributing resources and creativity. However, these studies do not usually divulge the identity of the creators of the festivities and ceremonies; instead, the creating entity is classified as a collective entity.

As a result, in most cases, the creators of the festivities and ceremonies are depicted as a defined but anonymous group which is given various names. Sometimes the creators are described as local leaders,[5] other times as local entrepreneurs. Simon P. Newman, in his book on street parades and popular festivities in the early days of the United States, writes that "It is all but impossible to determine who organized most of these civic festes, but what little evidence there is suggests that militia companies and other groups and societies elected committees to organize the events."[6] John MacAllon writes that "there is no performance without pre-formance."[7] Paul Connerton writes that "all rituals, no matter how venerable the ancestry claimed for them, have to be invented at some point."[8] Robert H. Lavenda writes that small-town festivals in Minnesota were organized by the business people, "with some assistance from those elements of the professional community that are most closely aligned with them," and he notes that it took several months of meetings and coordinated effort to organize a festival.[9] James Clifford writes that in the twentieth century, "Everywhere individuals or groups improvise local performances from (re)collected pasts, drawing on foreign media, symbols, language."[10] Susan G. Davis writes, in her study on parades in nineteenth-century Philadelphia, that street ceremonies (street dramas) "do not seem to have individual creators."[11] Christel Lane, in her study of the Soviet case, calls the organizers of the new public rituals after the revolution "creators/inventors," usually local organizers and administrators of the party, "dramatists or ritual specialists": "those who devise new, or adapt old rituals in order to uphold their definition of social relationship. They are thus distinct from mere 'masters of ceremonies,' although in practice both functions may be performed by the same person."[12] Robert Stites, studying the same case, calls them "ritual designers."[13] Mona Ozouf, studying the case of the French Revolution, calls them "organizers."[14]

In all these examples, none of the dramatists or organizers are identified, and hardly any of the staging instructions are described. In the case described in this book, they can be identified and their mode of work can be described. We prefer to call these people stagers, a term meant to emphasize the fact that they were engaged not only in writing the text (and the music) but also in mounting it on the stage. They chose not only the content of the ceremonies (and perhaps even wrote them) but also the manner of their performance, the costumes, the scenery used as a backdrop, the props, and the gestures to be exhibited. In the narrow sociocultural context, the group of stagers mounts a defined set of festivals, or only one specific festivity, while in a broad sociocultural context, the group is responsible for constructing a large part of the performative dimension of the society and the culture. Although the stagers play an important role in any society, this importance is magnified when the society is in the midst of rebuilding its culture, and when a revolutionary society is trying to construct an entirely new system of ceremonies, totally different from the previous ("old") one. In such transitional societies this role is performed in a conscious and organized manner and efforts are made to create a new canonical corpus of texts, new traditions, new holy sites, new icons, new symbols—and a new festive culture.

In traditional societies, the stagers, as well as the performers, were probably priests, perhaps even special priests (and in the Jewish society of the First Temple and the Second Temple periods, evidently also Levites). In royal courts they were presumably professional masters of ceremony, or artists working in the service of the courts (whose names are often known).[15] In modern "secular" societies, the stagers are usually kindergarten teachers, schoolteachers, members of ceremony committees, and specialists (artists) hired specifically for this purpose. In other cases they are party or state officials. The nature of the stagers and their modus operandi are affected by the character of the society in which they do their work, by the type of stage on which the performance is held, and the character of the performers. The identity of the stagers in a small, intimate society will differ from that of the stagers in a large society, or in a local or nationwide official setting. As the framework broadens and becomes more formal, the separation between the performers and the spectators widens.

We shall see later that as the Jewish society in Eretz-Israel, including its subsocieties, became more institutionalized, the process of creating, planning, and performing festivals and ceremonies became more organized and institutionalized, and a progressively clearer distinction was drawn between performers and spectators. But it is important to recall that this process occurred in a voluntaristic society, and not within the framework of a sovereign society possessing the tools of governance. Moreover, the process of bureaucratization also differed in character in the various social settings: festivals in schools were organized differently than those in small rural communities or in suburban society.

We maintain, as already stated, based on the role of stagers in modern societies, that stagers of one type or another also functioned in organized traditional societies. Even though we have no evidence of their existence or their modus operandi, it is difficult to assume that no one in such societies determined the "stage direction." Our case study may typify the staging patterns of every culture at any given time: a combination of the work of many anonymous dramatizers and stagers along with that of an identifiable group whose modus operandi can be traced.

Festivals and Stagers — Ancient and Modern

Could a ritual, festivity or ceremony come into being without an initiator or stager? Is it enough that every society and every culture vitally needs festivals and ceremonies for these performances to spontaneously appear, seemingly out of nowhere, and to then constantly repeat themselves and become an integral part of society and culture?

We do not mean to say that ceremonies in the various societies had similar functions; we merely suggest that their patterns were all created by some guiding hand, and that in both pre-industrial ancient civilizations and in modern industrial and modern national societies, public rituals and ceremonies were actively planned. We will cite several examples of festivals and celebrations in traditional and modern societies, the precise organization of which indicates, in our view, guidance by the hand of anonymous stagers.

Here are but a few examples:

The order of the Babylonian new year rituals was based on written instructions, which guided the head priest (*sesgallu* or *urigallu*) and told him which ceremonies to perform and which texts to recite, and when to do so, but we do not know when or by whom these instructions were composed.[16] The Bible provides guidelines for the manner in which various holidays and ceremonies are to be held (for example, the consecration of the priests in *Exodus* 29[17] and the offering of sacrifices in *Leviticus* 1–15) or, as another example, the ceremony on the night of the exodus from Egypt (the Passover ritual[18]), but the description of worship in the temple in Jerusalem, for example, given in great detail in *Mishnah Yoma,* is a later construction and not a copy of the original guidelines. The Bible describes in minute detail the construction of Solomon's temple according to a predetermined plan, but it says nothing about the manner in which the priestly rites were determined, and who did so. The Daphnephoria, the day of bearing, which was part of the Apollo cult in Thebes (for which Pindar composed songs), was conducted according to defined rules, but we do not know who set out the rules and when this was accomplished.[19] The public festivals in Athens were organized by state officials (the *hieropoie*) and later by the *athlotheatai*,[20] but we do not know how they were organized in practice; only the results—the festivals and the processions themselves—are known to us. A rare case from ancient times is the unique document from Pharaonic Egypt (Dynasties 28 and 29; the end of the fifth or the beginning of the fourth century B.C.). This document (hieratic papyrus) contains instructions on how to conduct the annual celebration of a king's assumption to power, which was conducted by a master of ceremonies.[21] We do not know who wrote the instructions but it is safe to assume that it was composed by a group of court-stagers in the service of the new dynasty.

Egeria, a nun who visited Palestine during 381–384 A.D., described in great detail the content and patterns of the new Christian liturgy that had recently developed around the holy sites in Jerusalem under Byzantine rule. This liturgy staged a kind of theatrical cycle, composed of fixed texts (prayers) divided into various acts (cycles), as well as a long series of performances—such as processions and ceremonies—that took place at set stations and set times (*apte diei et loco*). "It consists entirely of a record of prescribed movements among ten liturgical centers in Jerusalem and its environs," and there was "a prescribed set of lections that are read to the congregation."[22]

Egeria writes: "And what I admire and value most is that all the hymns and antiphons and readings they have, and all the prayers the bishop says, are always relevant to the day which is being observed and to the place in which they are used. They never fail to be appropriate."[23]

We can reconstruct how this Christian liturgy in Byzantine Jerusalem evolved, how its traditions were shaped, and how its annual and weekly cycles were determined, we can describe its course and the repertoire of behavior entailed in it, and we can explain its world of symbols and values (and the interests underpinning the form it took). But we cannot know who staged it, nor who decided what acts each pilgrim had to perform at each of the stations. Who, for example, shaped the character of the Palm Sunday procession? Egeria writes that "the pilgrims do everything in the usual way," or "follow the same order," but she does not tell us who decided upon these customary patterns of behavior. The form of the Jerusalem liturgy, in which various changes were made over time, is attributed to Bishop Cyril. But is he the one who set out the complex system of stations, texts and rules of performance?[24] Similarly, we can reconstruct the route (or the "circuits") taken by Jewish pilgrims to Palestine during the Middle Ages, as well as the ceremonies they held at the various stations (until the arrival of the Crusaders) in Jerusalem, but we cannot know how and by whom they were shaped.[25] The history of the Holy Land, and of the Jewish, Christian, and Muslim holy sites in it, is a dynamic succession of inventions of traditions and their transmission from religion to religion and from site to site. The tradition is the story of a site and the events or persons associated with it. The ceremony, its content, and the manner in which it is staged, develop after the tradition has been created. But a ritual, ceremony, or festival is not created and performed in every site. In other words, there is a wide range of traditions that are not necessarily linked to ceremonies and performances.

The festivities in Italian cities during the Renaissance were marked by a vast wealth of performative occasions, which included religious and secular holidays: carnivals, triumphal processions (*trionfi*), torchlight processions, and the like. Burckhardt writes that the Florentines were known for their skill as directors of festivals (*festaiuoli*) and consequently were invited to many cities to organize festivals there.[26] In some instances we can trace how the festivals of Italian cities, such as Siena's, emerged and were planned, organized and regulated;[27] yet, while the names of painters, poets, and musicians were generally preserved, those who organized these spectacular shows and performances have remained nameless.

It is not only the manner of staging in distant periods that is obscure. We also do not know the identity of those who dramatized and staged festivals and ceremonies in more recent times. Very rarely do we possess evidence, including the precise stage directions, of a festival, ceremony, or ritual, that enables us to reconstruct the staging process, and only rarely can we describe the stages of ceremony planning, and only rarely do we know the name of an individual "director" who appears in the spotlight. Theoretically, we are given the opportunity to try to reconstruct the processes of staging a complete cultural system when it is created as a result of a revolutionary act, entailing a conscious, planned, and organized attempt to create a new cultural system. The festivals of the French Revolution are a consummate example of invention and organization by semi-official and official bodies, who were assisted by professionals, and saw to every minute part: the site of the event, the scenery, the actors, the text, the music, the costumes, the hairdos, the performance, and so on, nearly down to the last detail, but the identity of most of them remains obscure.[28] The same is true concerning the French Republic, where ceremonies and spectacles were created by state institutions and offices.[29] Avner Ben-Amos describes French state funerals and analyzes the values they reflect and the message they meant to convey, but he too fails to describe the manner in which the various funerals were organized by the committees charged with the task.[30] We also know how Baden-Powell's Boy Scouts developed their performative acts, or how the Nazi parades in Nüremberg were organized and staged. H. T. Burden describes the plans of these outdoor spectacles and the "organization mania" behind them, but gives no details about the organizers and the way they acted.[31] David Cannadine describes the development of English royal rituals from 1820 to 1977, but does not tell us who initiated the changes that occurred during these years.[32]

We may conclude, then, that every unit of performance, ranging from an impressive, widely attended coronation ceremony, or court festivals, to a ritual ceremony with only a few participants, is a set of repetitive artistic acts, in which the participants perform according to rules well known to them. These rules have been passed down from generation to generation, orally or in writing, and intend to create a repetitive, stylized act, namely, to prescribe the permanent order of a performance, that will express the meaning, order, and hierarchy it embodies, preventing any possibility of disorder or spontaneity of an anarchic nature, or any other negative phenomena. The repetition of a fixed, routine pattern expresses and embodies continuity, hierarchy, respect, and sanctity. However, this often results in the anonymity of the creators and stagers of the vast repertoire of ceremonies and festivals.

What Are the Stagers Staging?

We do not intend to discuss the various distinctions among ritual, festival, and ceremony. Since rites, rituals, ceremonies, and festivals are internalized in the complex fabric of human civilization and determine the pace of its life and time, their various functions have been the subject of extensive studies in various disciplines.[33] Various studies suggest different distinctions between ritual, festival, ceremony, rites, and the like, and the different characteristics of their components.[34] Max Gluckman, for example, suggested this distinction within the general field of "ceremonial" between "ceremonious" and "ritual" by taking ritual to be "actions which are often similar to ceremonious actions, but which contain in addition 'mystical notions.'"[35] David I. Kerzer defines rituals as "a symbolic behavior that is socially standardized and repetitive,"[36] while Jack Goody has pointed out that all these definitions and characterizations are quite vague. He also asserted that the same characteristics apply to various social activities that do not fall into the category of ritual, and that in many cases, rituals and festivals reproduce themselves "mechanically," and since the participants do not really identify with the festival and its content, their message becomes vacuous, and the rituals do not fulfill any real function.[37]

In any case, rites, rituals, and ceremonies create a ritual process[38]—or a liturgical order—establish a hierarchy of significance, and dramatize historical events, filling an array of religious, social, or psychological functions. Some are "social dramas,"[39] taking place in public, some in the open air; they are usually public events, well constructed and organized, taking place on a permanent site and on permanent occasions. They reflect the worldview of the society, its power structure, its myths, its memories and images of a shared past, and its hopes for the future. They are intended to create bonds and solidarity within the group, often breaking social and political divisions. The various public events create an annual collective life cycle by specifying special days, marking special historical events by symbolic acts and practices. In other words, they are artistic acts that are an integral part of the fabric of social life and religious and political rituals, and some possess a "cultic force."

Whatever the definitions and descriptions, rites, rituals, ceremonies, and festivals constitute the indivisible part of both the "Great Tradition" and the "Lesser Tradition" of every organized social framework,[40] which include a wide variety of events, and form and construct every social framework, filling them with content and meaning, creating their rhythm of life, shaping their link to a specific space and time, imparting and bequeathing values, producing and disseminating accepted symbols and messages, providing an expression of social relationships (or opposition to them). Some have simple staging, whereas others have a pageantry character. All of them are part of the performative dimension of society and culture,[41] and, hence, they are always performed. "Performance," asserts Roy A. Rappaport, "is the second sine qua non of ritual" (the first is formality).[42]

The question is whether this entire network of performed rituals and ceremonies is the creation of stagers: Did stagers mount only large-scale festivities, parades, and carnivals, and were all ceremonies and rituals with a set structure and rules staged as well? We have no answer to these questions, but clearly the stagers' activity behind the scenes is more important in the case of large, complex events, in which the performance is complicated and orchestrated, involving numerous participants and filling various defined roles.

Words and Performance

By performance we mean acts of narration, singing, speaking, and acting; it is a mode of expressiveness and communication, by verbal or visible means.[43] In

Connerton's words: "Performances are echoed also in a set of postures, gestures, and movements."⁴⁴ The visible means which are employed to tell the story and convey the message include various dramatic techniques, gestures, icons, symbolic items, works of art, and the like, and the performers are either a selected and trained group, or the general public. These events are always conspicuously regulated and repetitive and socially standardized. Obviously, not every social and cultural performance has the same character. Weddings, concerts, and religious rites all have disparate characters, take place on different stages, and are participated in by different actors. The feature common to both groups is that they relate to the "rules of the game" that govern the festival and ceremony as if they are self-evident and are invariably structured to be repeated. The words of Paul Valry, quoted by Johan Huizinga, can be applied to the rules of the game: "No skepticism is possible where the rules are concerned, for the principles underlying them are unshakable." To this, Huizinga adds: "Indeed, as soon as the rules are transgressed, the whole play-world collapses."⁴⁵ A change in these rules reveals the changes that have occurred in the character of the society and culture, on one hand, and reflects these changes, on the other. It is also likely to be expressed in the diminution of their significance or even in their disappearance.

Performances always incorporate an organized program of activity, whether this program is fixable or fixed, conscious or unconscious, consensual or conflictive, or, as is the case, a little of each. In open-space performances, the open space is constructed as a public sphere in which the participants—the performers and the audience—know their part in the event. Public events shape the public sphere. They express control over the public sphere, by reshaping it for the special occasion and by sacralizing it. As such, public festivals are indeed "cultural performances par excellence."⁴⁶ In stating the above, we also note that dramatized social events, such as ceremonies and festivals, tend to exaggerate some (selected) elements, and thus do not necessarily reflect the structure and content of the social, cultural and political lore.⁴⁷ Often they may represent a distorted image of it.

The performative activity addressed herein was guided by ideology and by the recognition that words alone—a canonical corpus of texts, including ideological writings, literary works, myths, popular songs—cannot create a national culture, but words need the support of visual symbols and icons,⁴⁸ as well as rituals and festivals. Thus verbal components constitute the public performative dimension of society and culture only when enhanced by a formal ordering of rituals, ceremonies, and festivals. The relationship between a corpus of texts expressing a worldview, on the one hand, and rituals and festivals—that is public (religious, or secular) performances dramatizing the worldview, myths, and symbols—on the other, is a key motif in the development of every culture and religion. As a result, it is also a central topic in the study of the origin and development of cultures and religions, and of the manner in which they function and operate. The very extensive literature on this subject reflects an intense debate and diverse views on the origins of myths and rituals and on the different ways they operate, both separately and in collusion. In the case of modern society, the verbal dimension does not consist simply of myths (defined by Clyde Kluckhohn as a "system of word symbols") alone,[49] but a far more complex system of both "words" and "acts."[50] The texts and rituals are frequently associated not only with myths and beliefs (religious or historical) but also with texts that are concerned with such issues as social order, attitude toward nature, environment, and political goals.

In the modern case, particularly in national movements and nations, it is the textual-verbal dimension that came first. The new ideological creed, and its set of values and norms, its lore of mythologies, icons and symbols, its national literature (which includes prose, poetry, and drama) was the first to appear and to be formulated; the ritual-ceremonial followed in the form of ritual actions, ceremonies, festivals, processions, parades, and commemorative events. In due course, various texts become integrated into the ceremonies and festivals, some of which were selected from an existing repertoire (occasionally altered to make them more suitable for the ceremony), while other texts (as well as music) are specially written for the specific occasion. In our case, writers and composers were invited (and paid) to write a large corpus of songs, short stories, short plays, and legends specifically to be incorporated into the various festive occasions.[51]

In the case of the new Hebrew culture (as in many other cases), a precise distinction between festival, ceremony, and ritual is not possible, nor is it important, for we are presented with a combination of all three. What is important is that these were social events performed before an audience, which sometimes participated actively, and that the events were planned in advance based on a clear-cut ideology. They were held in order to introduce a performative element into the verbal element and to fulfill all the functions of festivals and ceremonies as described above. The rituals, festivals, and ceremonies addressed in this book can be defined as civic, national, and secular, even when many of them originate in religious tradition.[52] This is because they were not celebrated within the framework of a religious society, and the changes in their structure and content were made by those who can be defined as "free thinkers," or "traditionalists," and not by observant orthodox Jews. All the festivals and ceremonies we describe (with the exception of a brief discussion of ceremonies, such as weddings and funerals) are of a distinctly secular nature, and both men and women (as well as children) took an active part in them. There was no separation of the sexes, neither in the (non-religious) schools, nor in the rural or urban communities.

Jewish society had a long, very rich tradition of festivals.[53] How, then, are we to understand why a void existed in modern Jewish society, in this particular realm? And if a new tradition was created, what connection did it have with the old tradition? To answer this question we have to first define the nature of modern Hebrew culture (and modern Jewish society) in Eretz-Israel.

2

The Setting: Hebrew Culture, Hebrew "Formal Folk Culture," and the Hebrew Stagers

> National celebrations connected to the land, some of which have been in practice since ancient times and others recently reinstated, are appropriate only here [in Eretz-Israel].
> YIZCHAK BEN-ZVI, *ha-Achdut* 21, 1913

The Setting of Hebrew Culture

From the discussion in the previous chapter it is clear that there is nothing new or unique about the invention and internalization of new traditions as a product of the emergence of nationalism and its imagined communities and an integral part of every process of nation-building.[1] Newly reconstructed societies, particularly revolutionary societies, very often try to break their links with the old traditions, including old traditional rites, ceremonies, festivals, and their repertoire. Thus an important part of their creative efforts was devoted to the creation (invention) of new national ceremonies and new folk cultures. In fact, this is a common mechanism which operates in every cultural system (in religious and traditional cultures as well[2]). One example from modern Jewish history is the appearance of the Reform movement in Judaism in Germany during the nineteenth century, which involved the invention of new religious traditions.[3] When the performative dimension is part of a newly invented national tradition, as in the Hebrew case, the events aim to traditionalize the new tradition, and their content and style are both a manifestation and expression of new values, newly constructed collective memory, and national narrative. Whenever a new culture is structured, or reconstructed, a system of rituals, festivals and ceremonies must also be formulated. This was the case of the modern Jewish (Hebrew) society in Eretz-Israel.

The relevant time span, 1882 to 1948, covers the years in which the new Jewish society in Eretz-Israel was constructed and its culture—known as Hebrew culture (or Eretz-Israeli Hebrew culture)—took shape. These formative years, particularly the period of the British Mandate (1920–48), saw intensive activity in the invention of traditions, the creation of a new formal (official) popular (folk) culture or official national folklore. Eretz-Israeli Hebrew culture was a culture of immigrants, some of whom wished to break away from the religious tradition and the way of life prevalent in the Diaspora, and to create a new culture that would imbue the new society with its identity. However, the Jewish immigrants brought with them ideas about the desirable cultural content of their society; they had a historical worldview, values, symbols, and cultural models. Moreover, their deliberate abandonment of many of the elements of the traditional cultural system compelled them to rapidly create a complete alternative cultural system, which would reflect cultural perceptions, including the link to the country and its landscape, and would, to the extent possible, perform functions similar to those filled by religion in the traditional society. The immigrants came bearing a long tradition of festivals, which provided the high points of their calendar, but the festivals' traditional content was religious in nature, and had to be rejuvenated in the context of the newly born society in Eretz-Israel. The new society lacked a folk culture, since the traditional Jewish folklore that existed in the Diaspora was regarded as outdated, or religious in nature. Hence, while newly organized European national cultures could preserve, revive, and utilize various layers of their traditional folk culture, the new Jewish society in Eretz-Israel lacked "folkloristic" materials that could be employed in the new setting. As a result, many elements of its folk life had to be improvised. Hence a new folklore had to be invented, one that would suit the character of the new society and its different manifestations—rural and urban communities, kindergartens and schools, and political culture. New folk songs,[4] folk dances, and the like had to be invented,[5] folk culture embodying the society's new image of the world, and encompassing its symbols, heroes and value system.[6]

The deficiencies in the new sociocultural system necessitated prompt replenishment with original creations, translations, and adaptations of songs, music, and dances from other cultures. As for the festivals, the problem was ostensibly a simpler one, and it was possible, according to Gellner, to use a folk or traditional culture to forge an operational high (national) culture.[7] However, the inventors of the new festivals and ceremonies injected new content into the traditional calendar, based in many instances not on the folk-religious tradition but on (partly imagined) models from earlier periods, that is to say, the First Temple and Second Temple periods, during which "the people were settled on their land." Thus a great emphasis was placed on national myths, memories, legends, and symbols, on the one hand, and on the immediate natural environment, including the regional landscape, on the other. This was done in order to create an emotional link not only to the entire homeland but also to the immediate landscape, and it was aimed at instilling local identity. This was achieved by underscoring the specific features of the local vicinity and its historical background and by cultivating *Heimat* folklore.

To understand how the Hebrew stagers went about their work and the problems they faced, we must first briefly characterize the essence and content of Hebrew culture. It was, in many ways, a new beginning in Jewish history, one that created a new and comprehensive cultural lore. "Hebrew culture" refers to the new national culture, which comprised two interrelated, complementary layers. The first is the new—national and "secular"—definition of Judaism, and the values and symbols that express and represent it. The second layer is the creation of a broad repertoire of cultural components as part of the national culture. These components were perceived both as essential cultural assets of every nation of culture (*Kulturnation*) and as elements that are—or ought to be—an expression of the nation's heritage and unique character. For our purpose, it is important to stress the basic assumption: that Hebrew culture, like any modern national culture, should encompass all those components of culture that are highly regarded. This was particularly true with regard to the Hebrew culture in Eretz-Israel, which was a culture developing within an autonomous society and a territory that was perceived as a national-historical motherland. Hence the history of the new Hebrew culture in Eretz-Israel can be depicted as a "filling-in" process; various agents of culture created all the missing components, and as a result of their activity the cultural system was filled in. This process emphasized those components defined as belonging to "high culture": language, belles lettres, theater, plastic arts, textbooks, and the like, and largely dispensed with those defined as components of "popular culture."

Thus cultural initiatives were simultaneously imperative in almost every field. Although this process took place in a relatively small society with a common ideological and cultural base, it was necessary from the outset to construct institutions and to invent traditions—all the result of a conscious action, initiated and organized by agents of culture and various other bodies. The creation of the new Hebrew culture involved the creation of a new system of values, beliefs, habits, lifestyle and rhythm of life, and etiquette, a new corpus of texts (including myths), as well as a new popular culture with its repertoire of songs and dances, and a new public culture, including a new mode of leisure time. In other words, creation of the new Hebrew culture was an all-embracing activity, which involved staging the many layers of this new culture.

Hence the invention of a new performative language was part of a very dynamic, rapid and intense creative endeavor. Nonetheless, we are faced with a paradox: the cultural programs included plans for "cultural work" in many fields: education for children and adults, science institutions, libraries, and the like. Many programs reflected the need to foster the romantic dimension of the link to the territory and to the soil. But in most of the official cultural programs there was hardly any expression of the need to revive, or to invent a popular (folk) culture, one that would include ceremonies and festivals.[8] There were even radical groups that saw ceremonies as a mode of old "formalism," oppressive and artificial (usually of the "bourgeois culture") that they contrasted with the "organic nature," "freedom," and "spontaneity" of the new culture. However, an innovative culture, even a revolutionary one, that aspires to utterly destroy the formalism of the old culture, cannot do without a fabric of holidays, ceremonies, and customs. It also senses that its life will not be complete without the dimension of sacral time, whose absence fills it with *horror vacui*. The new culture was therefore compelled to invent festivals and ceremonies, in a variety of ways, and to stage them.

As we will see later, this process had two contradictory aspects: on one hand, the new tradition became so well internalized that it almost seemed to have deep historical cultural roots, and its source became so obscure that it is often difficult to reconstruct the circumstances of its appearance and acceptance. On the other hand, some parts of the tradition had a defined and short-lived existence—mainly during the society's formative period—and these dwindled, and even disappeared after some time.

The stagers of the new Hebrew culture were cultural entrepreneurs, who served the cultural elite and the common ideology and were acting in various frameworks, both official and unofficial. This group included teachers, writers of children's books, children's songs and school textbooks, publishers, composers, choreographers, painters, art designers, and many others. All these entrepreneurs played a significant role during the formative period of culture. They were aware of the missing components in the cultural lore and cultural repertoire, and they took the initiative to fill that void. They did this because they assumed that these lacunas (particularly within the context of a national culture), would create an incomplete and ill-functioning cultural system. This was in fact a consciously cultural enterprise constituting an essential part of the more general project of nation-building in modern Eretz-Israel. The creators and stagers were well aware of their role, the origin of their borrowed models, and the nature and meaning of their innovations.

Emergence of an Open-Air Public Sphere

A major element in the new historical setting was the open-air nature of the public culture. Many of the festivals and ceremonies at issue were public events and took place outdoors. This was possible because Jewish society and polity in Eretz-Israel controlled at least part of its public sphere. This was a new phenomenon because in the Diaspora, Jewish popular culture—including its institutions, various customs and rituals—was primarily part of the Jews' own private sphere, and its boundaries were, by and large, the family and the synagogue. Jews did not hold regular processions in the city or village streets and squares, nor did they conduct public ceremonies. There also were, of course, ceremonies held "outdoors," in places having an autonomous Jewish character, or, for example, at pilgrimage sites and sacred places. The Jews of Morocco, for one example, had a custom they followed on the last day of Passover; when the prayer service ended, they would leave the synagogue in a festive procession through the streets of the Jewish quarter, carrying sheaves of wheat in their hands.[9] A. S. Hirschberg (1858–1943), a religiously observant member of Hovevei Zion, and a *maskil*, who visited Eretz-Israel in 1900, was very impressed by the rituals of the Sephardic community in Jerusalem, which were conducted partly in the courtyard, and partly in the streets of the Jewish quarter.[10] The modern "lesser tradition" invented by the Jews of Germany was manifested primarily in the creation of popular literature, or in the new staging of performances in the private sphere (synagogues, clubs, schools), but not in the general public sphere. American Jews, on the other hand, occasionally conducted public events, such as funerals and parades in city streets.[11] However, there was a salient difference between the situation in both Germany and the United States, on one hand, and the situation in Eretz-Israel from the beginning of the new Jewish settlement there, on the other. In Eretz-Israel a whole modern Jewish cultural system was created, which for the first time in centuries was an open-air public culture, in which the public space was controlled by Jewish society in the towns, cooperative settlements, and villages, in the schools, and in other organized settings.

The new set of ceremonies and festivals was a vehicle for the transmission of old traditions,[12] which at the same time, followed current historical events and assigned special status to some of them (as well as a notation on the calendar). Moreover, the mode of staging expressed the new attitude vis-à-vis the natural environment and the changes in the patterns of interpersonal relationships. These changes affected the texture of the staging: the dramatization, the participants, the costumes, and the movements and gestures.

THREE MAIN PUBLIC SPHERES OF HEBREW CULTURE

Three public stages, different in nature, will be the focus of our discussion: the educational system, the rural community, and the urban community. To a certain extent, the methods of staging for these three settings were documented. The modern Jewish educational system created the need to develop a system of new and revived ceremonies and national holidays, which would then form an integral part of the education and socialization (and the indoctrination) of the young generation. They were created and disseminated in the authoritative setting of the kindergarten and the school, and we know the identity of the writers and stagers: the kindergarten teachers and schoolteachers wrote the plays and their staging instructions and also described how the staging should be performed. As to the rural communities, they could not follow any existing agricultural folk traditions, except, of course, those of the Second Temple period, which were reflected later in the Talmudic (Sages') literature. The new Jewish rural community, particularly the intimate community (especially the cooperative settlements), felt a compelling need for a system of ceremonies and holidays both to express its new system of values and symbols and the life cycle of the agricultural seasons, and group intimacy and solidarity. The Hebrew village was apparently a modern village insofar as its modes of production and its social structure were concerned, but it tried to create a traditional layer too, in the form of community agricultural festivals, like those of old, well-established farming societies. The modern urban society also wanted to create for itself a layer of urban festivals similar to those of traditional European cities. The Jewish community in the cities in the Diaspora had no tradition of public urban culture. This tradition was first created in Eretz-Israel. It was much more difficult to stage public culture in an urban setting, since an urban society is by nature stratified and anonymous. Nonetheless, from its inception (in 1909), Tel Aviv urban society consciously nurtured an open-air culture through its municipal institutions and established committees to determine the content and form of various ceremonies, ranging from public funerals and formal receptions to Purim carnivals. While it is commonly believed that the rural-agricultural setting was the ground in which the new ceremonial dimension emerged and grew, our study will show that the urban community played a central role in it.

These three public spheres constitute an important segment of the public forum of Jewish society during the Yishuv period. In the absence of a government-sanctioned public stage, with its ceremonies and rituals, like the one created after the establishment of the sovereign state, these three stages were the most central and the most active. Stagers, with a quasi-formal status, engaged in their work in all three.

Two main models of outdoor festivals inspired many planners and creators of the performative dimension of the new culture: the East European village, with its "organic" rhythm of life, and the European city, with its well-organized ceremonies and festivals, on the one hand, and the Jewish society in Eretz-Israel during the First and Second Temple periods, on the other hand. These last two historical periods served as a model of inspiration not only because a territorial, in part also sovereign, Jewish entity then existed, but also because of the cycle of holidays celebrated almost entirely in the public sphere, centering on the Temple and the festive assemblies held in it during the holidays, as well as the pilgrimages to Jerusalem. Modern Hebrew literature depicted the life of the ancient Hebrew village as an organic form of existence. In fact, the image of the biblical era and the East European village were combined into a single model.

Few open-air events took place in the public sphere of Palestine (Eretz-Israel) prior to 1882: the Arab-Palestinian society performed seasonal popular festivals (first among them, the Nebi Mussa festivities, held at the same time as the Greek Orthodox Easter week); processions and pilgrimages to the graves of prophets and saints were held, and Orthodox Jews celebrated the traditional holiday rituals on Mt. Meron on Lag Ba'Omer. These, however, did not serve as the models of emulation for the new Jewish society insofar as staging holidays and ceremonies in the public sphere were concerned. Nor did the shapers of the new ceremonies draw most of their inspiration from the neighboring Mediterranean countries, noted for their lively outdoor activities, so vividly and richly staged, and where, in several instances, a completely new nationwide system of holidays and ceremonies had been instituted (one example is the colorful spectacle of the well-organized and officially sponsored carnivals and festivals held in the small Mediterranean island of Malta beginning in the nineteenth century[13]). As we will see later, they preferred to draw on the festive tradition of certain European cities.

3

Ceremonies and Festivals in Modern Jewish Thinking

Herzl's Conception of Ceremonies and Their Functions

We face an intriguing paradox: the new Jewish society had an urgent and immanent need for folk culture and public festivals; however, most, if not all, of the thinkers of modern Jewish nationalism and modern Hebrew culture, including those who wrote a great deal about the desirable content of the new Jewish-Hebrew culture, even about its material and aesthetic aspects, paid scant attention to the nature of popular culture in the future Jewish society and to its ceremonies and festivals. They generally perceived the "popular" aspect as equivalent to folklore. What they generally defined as "popular Jewish culture" was comprised of customs of a religious or traditional nature (some of them borrowed from neighboring cultures).

Moreover, even those who could be expected to be aware of the need for festive lore and full-range folk culture and to perceive culture as an "organic cosmos" uniting all spheres of life,[1] neglected the performative dimension of the new Hebrew culture and wrote nothing about it.[2]

Benjamin Zeev (Theodor) Herzl (1860–1904), the founder and leader of the Zionist movement, was one of the very few political Zionist leaders and thinkers who were aware of the essential role of the performative dimension in the organization of a political movement or in that of a new national society. In the former context, as we shall see later, Herzl himself was a stager and tried to imbue the Zionist congresses (in particular, the First Congress held in Basel in August 1897) with a dramatic, distinguished quality by meticulous staging. Herzl was conscious of the importance of an orderly system of ceremonies and festivals in the life of a modern national society. In relating to the performative dimension of the new Jewish society to be established in Eretz-Israel, Herzl referred to two facets of creating festivals and ceremonies: on one hand, this dimension would be marked by a yearning to create an "organic society" from scratch, in which festivals and ceremonies develop from "below," are indivisible and a constitutive "intimate" part of life and its rhythms, and, on the other hand, by the notion that festivals and ceremonies must be planned and directed from "above."

On June 8, 1895, Herzl wrote the following thought, near the beginning of his diary: "Folk festivals with an artistic character, *éparpillé* throughout the land, organized so that the throngs will not be crowded into a single space, where they will feel miserable during their festivities (*Festen*). But there will also be national festivals (*Nationalfeste*) with wonderful attractions, colorful costumes, and the like."[3]

Herzl foresaw the performative facet of the future new Jewish civic and national culture in Eretz-Israel as a combination of uniform folk festivals held throughout the country and national festivals dramatic in nature. According to Herzl's vision, not only the official national ceremonies, but also the supposedly spontaneous folk festivals, would be centrally organized, as if an "invisible hand" were pulling all the strings. In that way—and only in that way—would a uniform, popular, national culture, common to all segments of the public, be created.

We have no way of knowing whether the inspiration for this idea came to Herzl from European folk festivals, which he certainly must have seen, such as those celebrated by European peasantry, but in our view he was far-removed from German romanticism and its concept of *Volksmunde* and *Volkskunde*.[4] We also do not know if Herzl was aware of the utopian plan for the future Polish state, written by Jean Jacques Rousseau in 1771 (*Confédération sur le gouvernment de Polania*), which proposed, inter alia, the creation of civic festivals and the reinforcement of solidarity and national character. What we do know is that Herzl was closely acquainted with the theatrical aspect of modern political life in Europe, both in the royal court and in the street,[5] and that he was quite impressed by the organized official ceremonial facet of public life in the French republic, as well as by the fact that the festivals were "amusement for the masses."[6]

On September 22, 1892, for example, in the *Neue Freie Presse,* the Austrian liberal newspaper for which he wrote, Herzl colorfully described the centennial festivities of the French republic. The French people love this holiday, he wrote, and "you can see this in the special movement throughout the city . . . the holiday procession that was announced appeals to the imagination and the curiosity of the Parisian people, who so adore changes that the Republic is compelled to decide to be amusing." However, Herzl concludes: "It might have been possible to arrange this entertainment-spectacle with more taste and more imagination; in any event, the goal was achieved: they wanted to entertain the people, and the people were entertained." Two years later, on July 2, 1894, Herzl penned a vivid report of the mourning procession and the state funeral of the assassinated French president, Carnot, which he described as a "festival of mourning."[7] These ceremonies witnessed by Herzl in Paris of the 1890s, in addition to the ostentatious, elaborate official ceremonies held in the court of the Viennese emperor, may have fired his imagination. His diary contains other flashes of imagination in which he depicts several ceremonies to be held in the future Jewish state.

Herzl's flights of imagination can serve as a good introduction to our discussion. First, because they reveal an appreciation of the important role of national festivals in shaping national culture, and an awareness of the immense value of the meticulously staged, ceremonial-theatrical dimension of festivals, and second, because Herzl did not expect festivals and celebrations to arise spontaneously and naturally in the new Jewish national society. He believed instead that both national and popular festivals had to be planned and organized as an integral part of the planning and organization of the new culture. His itemized report on the arrangements of President Carnot's funeral, for example, is a description of a public show organized down to the last detail. The guiding hand of a "director" was at work behind the scenes of this funeral and of the centennial celebration of the republic, and it staged them on the Parisian stage. This work involved more than just creating the "text" of the festival; it was also necessary to invent its "texture." In other words, this invisible "director" staged the performances of both the participants and the audience.

These excerpts from Herzl's diary may also serve as one of the many illustrations of his fertile imagination, or as evidence of his profound grasp of the nature of the political life of modern mass society, in which the symbolic dimension and its manipulation play such an important role. Herzl gave more thought to the content and organization of the "elite" culture and its esteemed assets, particularly theater and opera, and far less to the content and organization of popular culture and its repertoire. He tried to influence the staging of the official political culture of the Zionist movement, and made a significant contribution to its aesthetics and its respected status. And yet his awareness of the importance of the ceremonial dimension of political culture, and of culture in general, as well as of the impact of "official public culture" on the general public and its power to excite and move that public, did not lead him to produce a well-formulated program covering the entire scope of the ceremonial and visual dimension of the future new Jewish society and culture. What is the reason behind this lack of interest by the majority of the cultural elite in the development of both popular culture and public performances? This near-indifference toward the functions of popular culture should surprise us because the cultural (and political) elite was fully aware that the intention of Zionism and the Hebrew revival was to create a new cultural universe, and within it a new tradition. We can assume that this indifference stems from the fact that all components of popular culture (except for several items that were regarded as part of religious tradition, i.e., *yiddishkeit*), were thought to be an inseparable part of life in the Diaspora, and hence to have no place in the new Jewish society. This attitude perceived the old folkways of East European Jewry and its customs as a collection of outdated, even "primitive," customs, usually those of a peasant society. It may have also stemmed from a narrow idealistic conception of culture; they were interested mainly in "high culture." In the case of festivities, many considered ceremonies an expression of the formal, stagnant society, and ceremoniousness was seen as the very antithesis of the spontaneity, vitality and freedom of imagination and action that characterize a revolutionary society. As a result, festivals and ceremonies were not mentioned by the ideologues of Hebrew culture as part of the total lifestyle that had to be "Hebraized." Ceremonies and festivals were not included in the list of required cultural assets.

From this standpoint, the ideal modern Jewish society and modern Hebrew culture were seen as aspiring to be a society and culture without folkways and popular culture; with no folk holidays, no ceremonies, no popular beliefs. It seems that the chief spokesmen of the idea of a Hebrew culture were not caught up with the folk-mania, as the Russian literary critic, Vissarion Belinski (1811–48) termed it in his description of the enthusiasm and ardor of the Russian Slavophiles.[8] In the eyes of the ideologues, the utopian portrait of the new Hebrew culture was one of a full and complete cosmos, although at the same time it lacked the dimension of popular culture.

Only a few thinkers and writers drew a vague picture of a future folk culture. In 1914, Aharon David Gordon (1856–1922), the spiritual mentor of the Zionist labor movement, and one of the few Zionist thinkers who gave any thought to this subject, stated that it is impossible to create national festivals "based on logical arguments and arithmetic—for is that not like making poetry to order? What is a holiday, if not the essence of the poetry that exists in the profane?"[9] From this romantic-organistic vantage point, Gordon apparently failed to understand the vital and urgent need to fill the void, without having to wait for the "natural" development of the popular festival. Gordon also pointed out the paradox in which an ostensibly spontaneous society, like the kibbutz, had to invent and stage holidays in a planned and contrived manner.[10] The author Yaacov Fichman (1881–1958), in an article titled "Popular Culture," wrote that the negative attitude of Zionists and Hebraists to folk culture stemmed from the fact that they perceived it as a symbol of life in the Diaspora. Fichman acknowledges the difference between "high culture" and "folk culture," but he views the latter as a culture that emerges and grows out of "real life," and inspires both "high culture" and national culture. In every Jewish workshop, folk songs and folk legends were created as "indigenous natural art," not "art for its own sake." His conclusion is that the new Hebrew culture cannot exist without an authentic folk culture (which he believes can emerge only in rural society), based on the ancient foundation of biblical culture. Fichman, in any event, did not explicitly mention festivals and festivity as part of the future folk culture he believed was needed.[11] The author Eliezer Steinman (1880–1932) also felt that modern Hebrew culture would be incomplete as a cultural system without the existence of folk and popular culture, which would create a distinct lifestyle—"from the kindergarten to high school; from the market to the work table and the ballroom,"[12] or, in the words of teacher and educator, Dr. Nisan Torov (1877–1953), "from interior decorating to mourning customs."[13]

Secondary Thinkers and Entrepreneurs

If leading men of letters, thinkers and the key figures engaged in cultural affairs within the Zionist movement and Jewish society in Eretz-Israel did not regard "popular culture" as an important part of the new Hebrew culture and thus felt no need to plan it, how does one explain the fact that "popular culture" was nevertheless created and became a central feature of cultural life in Eretz-Israel? The answer is that local and secondary entrepreneurs were usually the ones engaged in this broad domain of creating rites and festivals, as well as all the other dimensions of popular culture. They were those who sensed the void, especially the lack of a festive and ceremonial dimension in the Hebrew culture. These secondary cultural agents, rather than the central cultural or political figures, were the ones who were engaged in the creation of folk songs and dances, ceremonies, and processions.

In order to explain what motivated the secondary agents of Hebrew cultural to act "from below" to produce and invent new festivals and ceremonies, let us try to imagine a Hebrew teacher at a school in one of the Jewish settlements established in Eretz-Israel after 1882. Such a teacher would have been confronted by several voids: he had to teach in a language (Hebrew) that was usually acquired by the students at schools. This was a language lacking many words and technical terms that had to be created; there were no textbooks in Hebrew and the teacher had to determine the curriculum in keeping with the dominant national ideology; he had to cope with the absence of songs in Hebrew as well as with the absence of any school festivals and ceremonies. The traditional system of festivals, which was religious in nature, did not suit the new content of the modern Hebrew school; hence it either had to be altered through the introduction of new elements or given entirely new content.

In such circumstances, teachers could not wait for some central institutionalized bureaucratic framework (according to Herzl's vision) to provide the traditional festivals with new content; they had to initiate this change themselves and do so based on various familiar models or their own inventive skills.

There was not only one such anonymous teacher; there were many, and there were other entrepreneurs who produced festivals and ceremonies in other social frameworks—both in the rural settlements and in the cities, where the need was felt "from below" for such a new system. As a result, the initiative came "from below," until it took on a more institutionalized and organized form. This void was strongly felt in small rural communities, where rituals, folk songs and dances, children's songs, and celebrations were regarded as an "organic part" of social existence, as the glue that held it together and created an intimate link between it and its natural environment. In this setting the void was perceived as an egregious lacuna resulting in an incomplete, flawed social framework.

Here is how a member of Gedud Ha'avodah (a commune of young workers known as the Yosef Trumpeldor Labor Legion, which existed between 1920 and 1928), sensed this void:

> Who among us has not often felt depression and abysmal emptiness, in the absence of those things that always bring light and joy into the lives of the group and the individual everywhere, the birth of a child, hope for the future continuation of our endeavor, marriage and holiday, *in particular, the holiday* [our emphasis]. Where is the divine inspiration that infused us with an "additional-soul"[14] while we were still in our parents' home? Where is the song and poetry that so pervaded our holidays?
>
> Everyone admits this, but there are many among us who belittle any initiative in this regard, and even among those who give some thought to this question, there are many who place their trust in the future. They believe that a way of life will come into being on its own. And they have some basis for thinking so, for a cultural lifestyle is not created artificially, as if in a laboratory.

Indeed, a way of life is not created by force of arguments and decisions. But our situation is unique. We have lost the thread that connects us to the past. We are starting from naught. Neither our work nor our lifestyle is a continuation of what existed previously. We have begun from "Genesis," the very beginning, after having cast off the past. To Eretz-Israel we came as newborn babes.

And life—our lives—as deeply as we may delve into them, will not, and cannot make do with "one pocket for us all" and "one pot shared by all" or any lofty and abstract idea. A member of the group, like any other human being, will always have, after a day's work, empty corners in his life that he will want to fill. There are hours when a man kicks at his loneliness, and longs for outside contact and impressions, to attach himself and merge with those around him.

Our situation is urgent and does not allow us to wait for the mercies of the future or its transformations, just as one cannot command a hungry man to wait until the fruit ripens on the tree. It may be somewhat semi-formed, we will feel there is something artificial about our cultural life at first, there will be faults and flaws, and things that will not much impress us insofar as their full festivity is concerned, but it is impossible to leave everything to the fortunes of time. And the planning, which we follow in our agricultural work, must also apply to our cultural life. We must create it and direct it with thought, at first in light of the scope of our endeavor. And if there is any need for a motto, let it be: "We shall create a style!"[15]

The awareness of *horror vacui* reflected in this text is particularly acute, and the absence of a "popular culture," which gives expression to "festive time," calls for a lifestyle that exists beyond "profane time," dispels loneliness and creates a psychological and experiential glue that binds the members of the group, and an intimate link between them and their environment (the soil, the land, the natural landscape) is perceived as a profound emptiness on both the individual and the group existential planes. The writer underscores the consciousness not only of a grievous lack of holidays but also of family celebrations of births or marriages. The reason for this is that the social group in question had abandoned the traditional religious ceremonies, and hence believed it had to quickly invent or create new ceremonies in their place. They could not wait for the spontaneous development of a lifestyle, but had to plan one, even at the cost of viewing it as artificial and semi-formed. In very small groups (*Gemeinschaft*), there was a longing to create a "shared spirit"—a gemeingeist—whose outward expression would be conversation, song and dance, even the shared "dinner table," whose rules had to be determined. After about a decade during which communal life had developed, and after beginning as a group employed in public works had become a stable cooperative agricultural settlement, the writer could point only to a specific development. The yearning for a "Sabbath atmosphere," for an "additional-soul," had found a partial answer in the organization of a new version of the Passover seder, but not a satisfactory one. He writes that in the humorous version of the seder that had been introduced, there was neither a connection nor a psychological relationship between the symbol and the object it symbolized. Only the settlement's *Rosh HaShanah* festivities were somewhat successful.

Eliezer Shochat (1874–1971), one of the heads of the moderate socialistic HaPoel Hatzair party, explained the inherent problem: "In all the countries we came from, we had certain lifestyles with many negative as well as many positive sides. We came here and found no lifestyle at all. We have to create one, and in the meantime we are hanging in thin air. We live a barefoot life, we have no set customs of etiquette."[16]

The new society, then, could not wait for the spontaneous-organic growth of a new pattern of folk life. For some at least, even in the framework of the intimate society, there seemed to be a vital and urgent need to create all the components of ceremonial culture, including the special *Sitz im Leben*. They believed it was impossible to maintain a society without holidays and ceremonies, without rules and formula, that is without staging. The official popular culture, created from the 1880s in the Jewish village and city, tried to fill this lacking dimension.

The above demonstrates that even in an intimate sub-society, like the communal kibbutz society, the process of inventing festivals and rituals and internalizing them as an integral part of the community's life did not occur rapidly and was attended by a search for the correct form of the festival and the most suitable content.

We see, then, that the role of filling the void in the new cultural system fell to the "people in the field"—teachers, kindergarten teachers, creators in various fields of art. The inevitable result was that they too could not simply produce the texts required for the festivals and ceremonies; they also had to fashion the patterns of their performance, and hence to become stagers themselves.

4

How Do the Stagers Work?
The Mechanism of Innovation

Three Main Mechanisms

As we have seen, there was a basic difference between Herzl's view concerning the need to build a national system of celebrations and ceremonies, and the view held by members of the intimate and communal kibbutz society.[1] Both recognized that ceremonies are an organic part of society, but the latter were concerned mainly with their function as part of the organic life of an intimate society—not of a nation, or a state. Whereas Herzl was occupied with organized festivity on a national scale, members of the new communal agrarian community were concerned with the way ceremonies would develop "from within" on a local level.

We have seen that all the entrepreneurs of the festive culture in Yishuv society began their work after sensing the absence of festive culture. While some simply felt that festivals and ceremonies were lacking as an integral part of the setting in which they were active (for example, the schools), others assigned an existential significance to these events.

In reality, three main mechanisms were employed. They were: *replacement* (or *adaptation*), *integration,* and *innovation*. By replacement we refer to the process of replacing a significant part of the traditional structure and of the content of a festival or ceremony with new form and content. By integration we refer to the process of adding selected new elements into the traditional structured performance. By innovation we refer to the creation of both a new structured form and a new repertoire. While during the early years, integration (adaptation) and replacement were a result of "spontaneous" and anonymous creativity, in later years, the planning of large-scale and public-held events involved a selection of the many replaced, integrated or innovated elements. This selection was intentional, well planned, and guided by a clear conception of both the content and the form of the new festive lore and of the function and message of every element within it.

These mechanisms have been implemented throughout Jewish history from its earlier periods. Jewish cultic and festive tradition was always dynamic and diverse in nature; for example, dozens of marriage customs were practiced by German Jews in the Middle Ages.[2] Adopting customs from the surrounding cultural environment and adding them to religious ritual and, even more so, to family or folk celebrations, was a virtually unavoidable, common practice in religious tradition and Jewish folkways, and some of the traditions were regulated in writing. The basic difference between the Jewish experience in the Diaspora and in the emerging new Jewish society in Eretz-Israel was that in the last case an overall set of festive activity was intentionally created and introduced into culture.

The inventors of the new festivals and ceremonies in Eretz-Israel, including those from the radical secular sectors, were well aware that it was extremely difficult to create an entirely new calendar of such events, and in particular to make them an integral part of the cultural and educational system.[3] Thus they first devoted their efforts to replacing traditional elements with new ones and to integrating new elements into the traditional structure; however, they also created entirely new festivals. Thus the new performative scene was an admixture of traditional elements, on the one hand, and new ones that were added to them, or replaced them, on the other.

The need to keep the traditional festive calendar was justified by the claim that festivals preserve historical continuity. Hence it is preferable to replace major elements thereof rather than to create entirely new ceremonies: "It is strange how an ancient custom, unaware of its own origin, greets the recent arrival of a new form."[4]

Changing the Traditional Form

In the early stages of forming the new Jewish society and culture, new elements were introduced into the traditional form of a ritual or a ceremony. The main mechanism used was that of replacement and integration, and only in the second stage of development did a large-scale replacement and innovation become the dominant mechanism. Here are a few examples of "spontaneous" integration and replacement in the early years of the new Jewish society and its new patterns of social-cultural behavior:

The first is the ritual of installing Torah scrolls at the synagogue in Rishon Le Zion in the early 1890s. When the procession marched along the road from Rishon Le Zion to Gedera (a distance of some 17 kilometers), people rode on horseback and in wagons, gunshots were fired into the air, and there was music and singing.[5] These were totally new elements, despite precedents such as the use of gunfire in the German-Jewish folkways at the end of the Middle Ages, lighting bonfires and firing gunpowder on *Succoth* and *Simchat Torah* (apparently in emulation of Johanes Feuer[6]). More likely it was an adaptation of the Arab *fantaziah* ("shooting in the air during wedding celebrations"), which the new settlers had observed up close. In any case, the procession, the riding display and the firing were possible because the public space in the *moshava* and its surroundings was open and free, and because gunfire was seen as an integral part of rural life.

A second, more striking example of the introduction of the new custom of shooting into the air as part of a religious-traditional ceremony is the wedding ceremonies held in the *moshavot* in the 1880s. The arrival of the bride and groom was accompanied by shots fired, or, in other cases, a volley of shots fired after the ceremony of the seven blessings. Rifles were included in another manner in wedding ceremonies held in cooperative settlements, which were characterized by a radical social and cultural ideology: the wedding canopy was held up by rifle barrels, and fireworks, torches, gunshots, bonfires and riding displays took place.[7] A wedding canopy supported by rifle barrels at the wedding in 1909 in Meshcha (Kfar Tabor) in the Lower Galilee, was, according to testimonies, deliberately intended as an innovative, symbolic act. In other ceremonies, agricultural elements were often added (a wedding canopy entwined with sheaths of wheat and barley and held up by pitchforks instead of rifles), along with new songs and dances.

It should be noted, that from a radical-secular point of view, the new elements that were introduced into the traditional wedding ritual were perceived as expressing an anti-formalistic attitude and a protest against, even derision of traditional ritual. In most cases, however, commitment to at least part of the traditional ceremony was preserved — (the wedding canopy, rabbi, breaking of the glass, the seven blessings, and so on) — and newly introduced elements were intended to give symbolic expression to the new values. This combination of the traditional framework with new elements is described as "a mixture of customs — ranging from strict Orthodoxy to the most extreme renunciation of all tradition."[8]

A third example is *kabbalat shabbat* (the Friday night ceremony welcoming the Sabbath) which took place in the moshava of Rosh Pina, in the Upper Galilee in 1890.

> When we returned from the synagogue, the house was glowing with the light of flames, the table was set with a white cloth, and on it shining candlesticks were placed; the children were freshly bathed, the woman of the house wore her best Sabbath dress—all these constituted a picture of a delightful and festive Friday night in the home of a Jewish family. . . . When, during the intervals between courses, it came time for the traditional *nigunim*, the children, on a signal from their father, burst into a Hebrew song that was on everyone's lips in Eretz-Israel: "We have not yet lost our hope . . . to return to the land of our forefathers."[9]

The singing of *nigunim*, or *zmirot* (traditional songs) during Friday night dinner was a prevalent custom in Jewish culture and it was common to write words and music composed for this purpose.[10] The innovative nature of introducing the national song (the future national anthem, *HaTikvah*), as part of the *nigunim*, was that in this case it was a national song.

A fourth example is the Passover seder at the moshava of Rehovoth in 1916, when national songs were added to the *Haggadah*. The narrator summarizes what he observed as follows: "No laborious effort was made to create new forms or to renew them—[but] there was a natural change that developed out of its own vital essence."[11]

A more radical process of introducing new elements is the version of the traditional Passover seder as celebrated by a group of workers in the moshava of Sejera in the Lower Galilee that same year:

> We began the seder with song and wine, as usual. The sadness in which we had been immersed during that period slowly dispersed. . . . Happiness grew with every new song, and our fervor grew with every glass—a mixture of chasidic devotion and sweet yet wild excitement prevailed at all the workers' festivals in Eretz-Israel. The songs were accompanied by dances—unrestrained dances that had neither rhythm nor measure, which we accompanied by clapping our hands in time with the dancing.[12]

As the moshava took shape as a rural (and semi-urban) community, and as life in the rural communal settlements (kibbutzim, moshavim) became institutionalized (and, inter alia, schools were established in them)—so the need to develop a new system of ceremonies and festivals grew, along with the need to endow traditional festivals with a new, homogeneous character. Processes of introduction and replacement became more comprehensive, complex and spontaneous. The guiding hand of the dramatists or stagers became ever more palpable. Even if their identity was unknown, their presence and imprint were felt.

The last example is the "fire ceremonies" that developed in all the youth movements. Tamar Katriel devotes a special study to the pyrotechnic display in the form of "messages in flames" that were used as a rhetorical-ceremonial vehicle. She considers at length the question of the degree to which these fire ceremonies were an expression of cultural continuity (namely, to what extent they were based on the symbolic role of fire in Jewish tradition). We believe she exaggerates in her conclusion about the degree of continuity, since fire is a universal motif and symbol, and since the context in which it was used in the youth movements differs from the traditional use of a candle, a torch, or a beacon. In any event, "fire ceremonies" were organized around one central symbol and meaning. Unlike a holiday ceremony, in which several symbols were combined and which includes organized dramatic activity, the fire ceremony does not have much of such activity. Usually the collective performance consisted of a dramatic procession or assembly, in which the fire takes various forms: bonfire, torches, "messages in flames," and serves as a setting for a swearing-in ceremony, based mainly on the recital of texts.

Katriel, however, does not tell us how the fire ceremonies came into the cultural system, how they were organized in the early stages, and how they became institutionalized. Her description suggests this was a "spontaneous" entry into the system of an element deeply rooted in Jewish culture. This explanation seems inadequate, and it is very likely that anonymous secondary cultural entrepreneurs introduced this ceremonial event and disseminated it by means of instruction material.[13]

Birthday Celebrations—A Case of an Innovation

Birthday celebrations are a unique example of the combination of the spontaneous and planned innovation of a new social rite, with its rich repertoires of songs, dances, and games. Only in modern times have birthday celebrations become an inseparable part of kindergarten life and of childhood culture (and later, also of adolescence) in Jewish society.[14] Thus the process in which birthday celebrations were introduced and the manner in which they were so quickly adopted and became one of the formative social ceremonies also illustrate how it is often difficult to trace the first appearance of a new rite. It seems that birthday parties were first celebrated in the modern Hebrew kindergartens, then moved from there to the family unit (the extended family and friends), and afterward became a social institution. In many respects, the process in which the society in Eretz-Israel and in Israel became middle class and was exposed to various cultural fashions is reflected in the manner in which the nature and content of birthday celebrations have changed.

The Jewish and Hebrew kindergarten, as a part of the modern educational system, is a twentieth-century development. The kindergarten is an institutionalized framework underpinned by a consummately educational outlook, and administered by a clearly specified group of usually female kindergarten teachers.[15] The kindergarten teachers needed to create, relatively quickly, a repertoire appropriate to the traditional cycle of festivals, including songs and dances that would function as *Sitz im Leben*. Birthday celebrations were a new element that served as a catalyst for creating a suitable repertoire.

Children's birthday celebrations originated from the German Kinderfeste.[16] Adults' birthdays were celebrated in various ways, but an annual celebration for children was a social and cultural innovation that began in German urban bourgeois society, and developed through the perception of time and of the child as an individual.[17] This custom was probably brought to Eretz-Israel by kindergarten teachers sent to Germany between 1909 and 1911 by the Jewish-German "Ezra" (*Hilffsverhein der Deutschen Juden*, the German-Jewish philanthropic organization, founded in 1901) for advanced studies in the Berlin kindergarten teachers seminary, Pestalozzi-Froebel Hause (founded in 1873), or by those who had studied there in previous years. The Ezra Society also gave courses in Jerusalem based on the Froebel method. The first Hebrew kindergarten in Europe based on Froebel's method was established in Warsaw in 1909. In Eretz-Israel the first kindergarten was established in Jerusalem in 1901 in the Rothschild School for Girls, while the first Hebrew kindergarten was established in 1898 in the moshava of Rishon-le-Zion, followed by all the moshavot. In 1919, there were 32 kindergartens in Israel, with 2,525 children enrolled.[18]

Birthday celebrations may have taken place in Hebrew kindergartens in Eretz-Israel after 1911, but there is only a single testimony about one such celebration held in a kindergarten in Jerusalem. It was organized by Hasia Feinsod-Sukenik (a kindergarten teacher who studied in Germany) in 1921 to celebrate the fourth birthday of her second son, Yigal Sukenik (later Yigal Yadin [1917–84], the renowned archaeologist and statesman who was also the Israel Defense Force's second Chief of Staff). According to this testimony, the child, sitting on a chair, was lifted into the air four times, and then games were organized in which the children played in circles of four. This birthday celebration became a model for emulation. According to another, later, testimony, other mothers asked their children's kindergarten teachers to arrange celebrations for their children's birthdays too, and the new custom spread throughout the country. While the first celebrations may have been spontaneous, the repertoire eventually expanded—birthday songs were written, dances were choreographed, and games were designed—and birthday celebrations were staged in a structured manner with varied repetitive patterns. The ceremony usually included the following elements:

> The children were assembled in the classroom or in the yard, adorned with wreaths of flowers, and led into the hall to the sound of piano playing. There were various rhythmic games and finally the "birthday" children recited pieces, and if they were too young to do so, others, older than them, did so for them. After the recitations, the birthday children stood on chairs placed in the middle of the room and contributed to the JNF, dropping into the collection box the same number of coins. Then they were raised into the air the same number of times, plus one time "for the next year," and everyone clapped their hands. When the birthday children sat in their places, they were given gifts, as the pianist played, by the children who had participated in preparing them.[19]

The custom of raising the birthday child, seated on a chair, into the air apparently originated in Eretz-Israel, perhaps borrowed from the traditional custom of doing so for a bridegroom.[20] It is no wonder that the new ritual caught on so quickly, first in the kindergarten, later in the school and family, and ultimately as a public event, or that its repertoire and staging was so rapidly created, first in urban society. The process was rapid and successful for at least two reasons: First, because kindergarten teachers were an organized professional group with a special educational outlook, who kept in close touch (through professional literature as well); kindergarten teachers were recruited to write birthday songs—or recruited others to write them—and wrote instructions for conducting the celebrations. The popularity of birthday celebrations is evident from the kindergarten teachers' pedagogical journal, which, from the 1930s onward, offered instructions and suggestions on how to organize such celebrations. Second, because the individual child was accorded an important position within the framework of modern Jewish society. It is true that birthdays were frequently celebrated as a group event, and that symbolic elements and national motifs were introduced. Nevertheless, the very fact of relating to the individual, and the shift of the birthday celebrations from the formal framework—the kindergarten and school—to the family framework as well, is proof that the consummately individualistic dimension was intrinsic to the Eretz-Israeli collectivist society (certainly in the urban society), and birthday celebrations and their attendant repertoire of songs and games reflected the special attitude toward every individual, to every child.

The guidelines for organizing birthday celebrations in the kindergarten, published in 1940, include elements such as a blue and white flag and a crown, and making an album of the children's drawings and arranging a basket of flowers. A table covered with a blue tablecloth, with flowers on it, is placed in the center of the kindergarten, and chairs are arranged around it. Alongside it there is a second table, bearing the refreshments. The children get into a line with the birthday child, who, wearing a crown and holding a flag, is at its head. To the sound of a march or the song "Chag, chag, chag ha-yom" ["Festival, festival, today's a festival"], the children enter the hall in a procession, walk around in a circle several times and sit on the benches and chairs. The birthday child or children sit on the sofa which is decorated with greenery. According to the guidelines, the children sing a few songs and then the birthday child comes to the middle of the hall, walks around in a circle several times and then is raised into the air on his chair. Then the children and guests sing birthday songs and play organized games. Finally, the refreshments are served, with the piano playing in the background all the time. Sometimes there is also a short play or a puppet show.[21]

This was, then, a new tradition of a ceremony that was created, spurring the constant development of a repertoire of songs and games. Moreover, the kindergarten teachers were not satisfied with a simple ceremony but kept embellishing it by means of stylized staging.

Birthday celebrations and holiday ceremonies in the Hebrew kindergartens provide an illustration of the two facets of the patterns of festivity in this early educational setting. On the one hand, these events began as a local initiative "from below," and on the other hand, given time they took on a uniform character, nurtured by the Kindergarten Teachers Association and its professional literature.

Although the new Hebrew kindergarten emphasized the importance of childhood as a special chapter of life and encouraged the children's individuality—each child was allocated a place of his or her own, and game playing and aesthetics were encouraged—this individualistic dimension was combined with the national-collective dimension, in which the major nationalist contents and symbols occupied the center stage. This dualism also continued after the establishment of the state. In fact, it is arguable that the kindergarten was the setting in which this combination was sustained even after it was significantly weakened in other places.[22]

The kindergarten, of course, was not only the source of birthday celebrations but also of the creation of further expressions of official popular culture.

However, we lack sufficient evidence about the process by which its major innovation—birthdays—was created. Despite all our efforts, we have not succeeded in tracing how this custom became popular in Eretz-Israeli society or how birthdays became a well-staged ceremony to which many new elements were added over time.

It seems then that our inability to describe the emergence and evolution of such a major rite of passage clearly demonstrates the difficulties involved in tracing the origins and of rites of passage even in modern societies. This fact supports our claim that very often a new custom, ceremony, or festival is so completely absorbed, that it and its newly invented repertoire are perceived as a traditional and self-evident custom, an integral part of the cycle of life, that needs no explanation or legitimization.

Up to this point we have described the infusion of individual elements into the system of ceremonies and holidays. From the 1920s onward, more general models guided the stagers in their efforts to festivalize the new Hebrew culture and to create a new Hebrew folk culture.

PART II

5

THE MISSING STAGE OF POLITICAL CULTURE

THE ABSENCE OF STAGERS OF POLITICAL CEREMONIES

Political rituals are instruments of propagating political myths, creating a sense of solidarity, expressing power, and recruiting public support. In the new setting of the Jewish society in Eretz-Israel, a modern polity guided by an all-embracing ideological platform (the Zionist idea) and by partial ideologies (those of the various political movements), one would expect to find a performative political culture, including political cults, commemorative days, and political parades. One would expect the political open stage to call upon stagers to plan the pattern of public political events.[1] Moreover, it would stand to reason that in the life of the Zionist movements and in the political culture of the Yishuv in Eretz-Israel, as is the case in modern political parties elsewhere, ceremonies and parades would play a key role. Such events significantly contribute to the creation of internal solidarity among the members of the movement (or the party), by mobilizing them in support of the movement's objectives, and imparting messages and symbols to the entire membership.

In reality, the political performative dimension was not assigned an important status. Of course, there were committees and rallies, and parades were held, but insofar as the performative life of a political party was concerned, no attempt was made to shape public political activities. The absence of public political performative lore in the Jewish polity during the period of British rule may be explained by the fact that this was not a sovereign political framework. Hence state ceremonies, such as the coronation of a monarch, the inauguration of a president, the festive opening of the first session of a recently elected parliament, military parades, and state funerals could not be held. Only after independence, in May 1948, was this void rapidly filled through the planned staging of the ceremonial dimension of the new state.[2] Another reason was the fact that the political partisan-ideological split in the Jewish political community interfered with the creation of public political ceremonies that would have been accepted by the entire Jewish community.

In spite of all this, there were a few successful attempts at staging open-air political events during the period of the years of British rule. These attempts expressed the political-ideological struggle to gain control over the Jewish public sphere by demonstrating a physical and symbolic presence. This presence took the form of parades, torch processions, marches, and widely attended gatherings in squares or in open areas. Participants in the marches and parades wore uniforms representing their party affiliation and political beliefs. In apolitical ceremonies such as the opening of the Maccabiah games (the "Olympic" games of Maccabia, the international Jewish sports organization), public events were planned and staged as both a symbolic and a concrete demonstration of the strength of the Yishuv, and to demonstrate unity and physical capability ("muscular Judaism").

Opening Ceremonies of Political Events

On September 3, 1897, after returning to Vienna from Basel, Herzl wrote the following entry in his diary, describing the First Zionist Congress: "One of my first ideas, months ago, on how the Congress should be conducted was to have swallow-tails and white tie obligatory at the opening session. It worked out admirably. Full dress has a way of making most men feel rather stiff. The stiffness induces a measured, deliberate tone—one not so easily come by in light summer suits or travel wear—and I spared nothing to heighten this tone in the pitch of solemnity."[3] Herzl, who, as we have already seen, was very conscious of the symbolic and metaphorical value of ceremony as a vital part of the renewal of the political dimension in Jewish history, made meticulous preparations prior to the Congress. From the flights of imagination he recorded in the pages of his personal diary, he moved in August 1897 to the firm ground of realistic politics and political theater—the dramatization and staging of the first constitutive political ceremony in the history of modern Jewish nationalism. He tried to stage the First Zionist Congress as a political ceremonial drama, with procedural arrangements similar to those of the most respected of parliaments.

The staging of the Zionist Congress in Basel was intended to impart a sense of real substance to the abstract notion of a Jewish state, turning a screenplay into a live performance, so to speak. And as Herzl himself explained to his associate Max Nordau (1849–1923), the aim was to accustom the Jewish public to viewing the Zionist Congress as "the loftiest and most festive thing."[4] Incidentally, Nordau, who wore a frock coat on the day of the opening, refused to wear it on the second day of the Congress, and this was the reasoning Herzl used to convince him.

The festive-ceremonial staging of the opening sessions of the First Zionist Congress was not repeated at the following Congresses. Until the state of Israel was established and state political ceremonies, including their protocol and etiquette (such as the inauguration of a president, the swearing-in of a new Knesset [the Israeli parliament] and others) were created, there were no obligatory rules for conducting ceremonies in the official political culture of the Zionist movement and of the Yishuv, and these ceremonies were neither grand nor festive. Of course, procedures for debate and rules of protocol were laid down, but rules governing ceremonies were not.

On October 7, 1920, the first session of the first elected assembly of the Yishuv was convened in Jerusalem. This was an important political event, one that expressed formal recognition by the British government of the political autonomy of the Yishuv and its representative institutions. The organizers of the event decorated the dais, on which the honored guests would sit, with symbols of the twelve tribes of Israel, photographs of King George V and Benjamin Zeev Herzl, and bedecked the walls with greenery. But there were no trumpet blasts, no horns were blown, no doves were released; there was only the "usual"—festive speeches and greetings.[5] We do not know of any instructions given to the participants in connection with the need to arrive dressed in a manner befitting the occasion. To Herzl, an opening so lacking in grandeur might have seemed a deplorable failure to use the opportunity to express the symbolic status of the occasion through a more impressive performative event. On the other hand, the organizers of the event could have defended their action by noting that 1920 was not the appropriate time for festive occasions and that the Yishuv, faced with so many serious problems, could hardly afford to take time to plan ceremonies.

The formal institutionalized system of the Jewish polity was too weak and too preoccupied to serve as a platform on which a political liturgy could be staged. As a matter of fact, hardly any political events were held for the general public, which could serve as such a stage. This role therefore was left to the political parties and movements.

Chapter 5

STAGING LEFT AND RIGHT

Dov Ber Borochov (1881–1917), the ideologue of the left wing Zionist Marxists, wrote that the Jewish labor movement ought to learn from the bourgeoisie how to conduct public ceremonies expressing majesty and profound emotions,[6] and to celebrate the workers' holiday in similar majestic fashion. It was mainly in the new political setting of Eretz-Israel that the labor movement could organize distinctive May Day parades. These parades, which marched through the streets of the cities, were a demonstration of the solidarity, affiliation, and power of the organized workers in Eretz-Israel. It reflected their desire to control the open-air arena of the Jewish public and to place their symbols in it. That is also the reason why the May Day parades aroused terse opposition from the liberal middle class, and even greater, more belligerent opposition on the part of the right-wing Revisionist movement.[7] The holiday was celebrated in a format similar to the May Day parades in other countries, but sometimes there was also dancing and gymnastics displays. The labor movement in Eretz-Israel did hold other rallies and conventions, but they were almost completely devoid of a ceremonial dimension. At the most, important political gatherings were accompanied by choral singing, but until the 1990s they almost completely lacked any ceremonial characteristics of the kind that are an integral part of important political meetings in various countries, for example, the United States.[8]

Unlike the labor movement, the right-wing Revisionist movement declared its intentions to carry on Herzl's view of ceremoniousness. Zeev Jabotinsky (1880–1940), the founder and leader of the movement, regarded ceremonial rituals as an important demonstration of renewed national life. He believed that aesthetically constructed rituals and ceremonies expressed the new Jewish essence, which he called *hadar* ("grandeur"). This "grandeur" should be an integral part of both the private sphere (nobility, dress, cleanliness, manners and customs) and the public sphere (uniforms, quasi-military parades, and processions). Jabotinsky declared: "I have made what was for me a great discovery—that nearly three-quarters of true culture is composed of ritual and ceremonies. Law and political freedom rise or fall by way of ritual and parliamentary procedure, and the entire life of social groups would degenerate into benightedness were it not for the rites of passage of culture and customs."[9] According to this view, the organized ceremony, with all of its rituals, was important because it transformed the many individuals comprising the public into a cohesive entity. The ceremony, Jabotinsky wrote, is more than just an "external form"; it is an expression of individual and collective inner essence.

Since Jews in the Diaspora were unable to maintain a civic society or hold public ceremonies demonstrating inner grandeur, Jabotinsky attributed much importance to the ceremonial, festive character of the new public sphere, viewing it as a salient expression of the national (in his mind, also the existential) revolution of the Jews. Unlike his critics from the Left, who regarded the rituals of ceremony as little more than the vain follies of a stultified, artificial formalism, lacking in spontaneity and creative force, and the like, Jabotinsky defined these rituals as an integral part of daily life.[10] The same held true for the military arena, since an army's strength and influence also stem from its magnificence, from dress uniforms and parades with all their rituals.[11]

The labor movement viewed this ceremonial, formalistic facet of the Revisionist political culture as a consummate reflection of its nationalistic show-off character, focusing on the formal aspects of political activity, particularly the rhetorical and declarative aspect. Its attraction to ceremoniousness was perceived as further evidence that it belonged to the romantic-conservative realm of the European right-wing movements. Professor Joseph Klausner (1874–1958), a prominent thinker and historian closely associated with the Revisionist movement, responded to this criticism by stressing the fact that:

> He [Jabotinsky] has been accused of ascribing importance to external things like uniforms, flags, ceremonies and slogans. I think even in this regard his understanding was loftier than that of his accusers, as lofty as the heavens above the earth. The Torah of Israel, the foundations of which are faith in God and morality, knows the great value of the deed, of the ceremony and of external glory in educating the nation, in particular in educating the youth. One does not need God in order to sit in the Succah, to perform the water libation, or to wave the willow, one does not need the High Priest wearing his breastplate encrusted with precious stones or the gold bells of his clothing. But there can be no national education without deeds, without ceremonies and symbols, without slogans and festive acts.[12]

In reality, while the Revisionist movement had a strong presence in the public culture of the Jews in Eastern Europe (particularly in Poland), its presence was weak in the public sphere in Eretz-Israel, and mainly took the form of political parades. The ceremonial activity was carried out primarily by members of its youth organization, Betar (the Yosef Trumpeldor Union) who wore uniforms and held quasi-military parades and processions (sometimes torch processions), usually in the cities, which sometimes aroused violent reactions among the left-wing parties.

Although the Revisionist movement assigned so much importance to festivals and ceremonies, it did not develop new patterns for traditional holidays. In this context, it displayed conservatism and a lack of imagination, as well as loyalty to tradition. Moreover, in contrast to the labor movement, the Revisionists did not have appropriate social frameworks in which to reshape holidays.

Open-Air Memorial Ceremonies

Memorial and mourning ceremonies serve as a meeting place for the general public. An attempt was made in the Yishuv to turn some of these into memorial days celebrated in the open air by the entire community, but this met with very little success.

The debate on the nature of public mourning in the Yishuv began two years after three Jewish workers were killed by Arabs in the Lower Galilee. It focused on the issue of the historical symbolic status that ought to be assigned to the deaths, and whether the deceased should be sanctified as martyrs. The debate centered mainly on the content of the texts (in particular their connection with traditional texts), which would be included in the "Yizkor" Book, to be published in 1911.[13] But the debate never touched on the issue of what form the funeral ceremonies would take. This ritual aspect received no attention at all in the debate.

Tel Hai memorial day was the first case in which a memorial ceremony, national and political in nature, was staged. Two political movements claimed proprietorship, each stressing different aspects of the incident. It was the first memorial ceremony designed in Eretz-Israel, and was held to commemorate the victims of the violent Arab attack on Tel Hai, a small settlement in the Upper Galilee, on the 11th day of Adar (March 1, 1920). Chief among the defenders of the settlement that day was Yosef Trumpeldor (1880–1920), who became the first national hero-martyr of Jewish society in Eretz-Israel. Much has been written about how the legend of the heroism of the Tel Hai defenders was spun, about the "myth of Tel-Hai" and about the ethos embodied in the story.[14] But hardly anything has been written about the manner in which the rival Zionist movements—the labor movement and the Revisionists—shaped the public ceremonies to mark the 11th of Adar at the site of the event—Tel Hai in the Upper Galilee.

The victims killed in the attack were first buried at nearby Kfar Giladi in 1924, and later reinterred at the commemoration site established at Tel Hai. In 1934 a large memorial statue known as the "Roaring Lion," by the sculptor Abraham Melnikov (1892–1960) was erected there. The locale has become a symbolic site, but the memorial ceremonies held on the 11th of Adar at Tel Hai courtyard during the Mandatory period were not a widely attended public event, mainly because of the difficulty of reaching the settlement. Yael Zerubavel, who follows the various transformations of the Tel Hai myth and notes the importance of Tel Hai as a site of secular pilgrimage, does not describe the ceremonies held there. This is not only because she focuses on the development of the "myth" and its message, and not on the performative aspect, but also because there are very few descriptions of the ceremony; it was not constructed in a manner that left an impression on the participants.[15]

As we will see later, the 11th of Adar became an important date in the new Hebrew calendar, and was celebrated in ceremonies in Hebrew schools. Special texts were written for this purpose, accompanied by detailed, orchestrated staging.

Other days of mourning to mark the death of Zionist figures, first and foremost Herzl and Bialik (in August), became common public commemorative events in the schools, and occasionally in the urban community as well.

Thus, although the importance of political ceremonial and celebrative public lore did not go unnoticed, and despite the centralized structure of the political movements, which allowed them to plan, initiate and stage political events, they created no formal entities charged with undertaking this responsibility. Unquestionably, some of the various ceremonies held during political events or intended to mark historic events, were planned in advance. But we have no documentation telling us how this task was carried out.

Neither the Yishuv as an organized polity, nor the labor movement and the Revisionist movement (or other political movements) succeeded in creating a new organized public lore of national-political ceremonies. Hence the performative dimension contributed very few elements to the political culture of the Yishuv. The performative arena was more a scene for public political conflicts and confrontations than a demonstration of common values. The creation of the ceremonies and festive lore of the Jewish community was largely left to the stagers in the rural and urban communities and in the Hebrew schools. They were the ones who took up the role that the political organization of the Yishuv and its political parties were unable to assume.

6

To Celebrate in the Spirit of the Homeland: Staging School Festivals and Ceremonies

The Hebrew Educational Network and the Jewish National Fund

As far back as the 1890s, the Hebrew schools in Eretz-Israel served as the venue for the first experiments in organizing festivals and ceremonies. We have already seen that the schoolteachers were the first group to feel the lack of a new calendar of festivals, one accompanied by ceremonies, and were the first to begin creating and shaping such a calendar. These were isolated experiments until the 1920s, when teachers embarked on an organized and institutionalized endeavor to create a common, uniform system of festivals and ceremonies to be celebrated in all the Hebrew schools throughout Eretz-Israel.

The school that opened in Jaffa in December 1892, for girls aged 7 to 14, was the first Hebrew school in Palestine, and its teaching staff produced a group of cultural entrepreneurs and stagers. While another school that opened the same year in Jaffa—a boys' school—was run by the Alliance society, the girls' school was run by the Hovevei Zion movement, and hence had a national-Hebrew, moderate-secular character. It was a center of Hebrew speech and education of the new Yishuv, and existed within the Jewish society in Jaffa, which was religious in nature. By early 1920, 267 girls were enrolled in the school, and its teaching staff included some of the pioneers of Hebrew education and members of the teachers' organization in Palestine. Four of the teachers—Mordechai Krishavsky (Ezrachi, 1862–1951), Yosef Ozravokitch (Ezariyahu, 1872–1945), Yehiel Yehieli (1866–1937) and Haim Arye Zuta (1868–1939)—played an important role in shaping the Hebrew educational system, by creating various texts (textbooks and belles lettres) and organizing festivities within the school setting.

The school archives have been preserved, enabling us to reconstruct certain discussions that took place in 1908, 1909, and 1913 among the active teachers. These discussions related to the contents of the festival and the organization of festival ceremonies—in particular Chanukah and Tu biShevat. These teachers regarded the school festivity as an essential and effective means of imparting values and symbols, which were molded and given expression in the new corpus of texts. Hence they devoted much attention to the performative character and venue of the festivities. The proposal for the structure of the Chanukah ceremony has been preserved. It is composed of several key elements: candle lighting, the creation of a "living menorah" of students, intended to add an impressive visual element to the ceremony, the singing of a choir accompanied by movement, a short play connected to the festival, and musical pieces. The program describes in detail how the "living menorah" should be constructed: "Eight boys or girls, dressed in white, adorned with flowers and greenery, arranged in a semi-circle, which is not too round. The tall ones—in the middle, and the short ones—at both ends, so that the heads create a sort of arc. A crown rests on each head with a candle in it. Behind the menorah, slightly higher than the others, a boy or girl will stand—as the 'sun.'" Discussions were also held regarding the nature of the planting ceremony on Tu beShevat, where it should be held, and what type of trees should be planted. The planting ceremony, which first began in the moshavah of Zihkron Yaakov in 1890, was celebrated for the first time in 1904 in an urban school, and was adopted as a simultaneous expression of the link to the soil and to spring. Another innovation was the introduction of the almond tree, that blossoms before its leaves appear, as the harbinger of spring and the symbol of the festival. The tree was given a feminine name in Hebrew (*shekedia*) and in later years, songs and poems were written about it, making it one of the symbolic trees in the new Hebrew culture.

The culture entrepreneurs in the girls school in Jaffe were pioneering stagers in Hebrew education in Eretz-Israel and perhaps in Hebrew culture in general. They served as the pathfinders for Hebrew teachers from the 1920s and for the organizers of public festivities in Tel Aviv. But it was the Teachers Council (TC) for the Jewish National Fund (JNF) that played the most prominent role in organizing, planning, creating and staging the ceremonial and festive lore in modern Jewish society in Eretz-Israel. It produced a uniform calendar and a broad repertoire of rituals, festivals and ceremonies based on a common formula. As a result, the Hebrew schools became the main stage of Jewish public culture and the major locale in which a well-organized culture of festivals was created. This culture was intended to give concrete, dramatic expression to the national values and symbols, to disseminate and internalize them as an integral part of the collective experience.

The Hebrew educational network in Eretz-Israel was undoubtedly one of the most impressive achievements of the Yishuv during the British mandate. It was this educational network that was primarily responsible for molding the character of the young generation, and making Hebrew the language (written and spoken) of culture. It encompassed the greater part of the population of Jewish pupils; in 1926 about 19,000 pupils were enrolled, in 1945, 55,471, and by 1948 the number had grown to 75,000.[1] Until the 1920s, the school system suffered from an insufficient budget, organizational weakness and a dearth of learning aids—textbooks in particular. Its curriculum and methods were also a constant target of public criticism. The Hebrew Teachers Federation of Eretz-Israel, founded in 1903, was also hampered by organizational problems, and found it difficult to meet the needs of the pedagogical system. The education department of the Zionist Federation, and later the education department of the Vaad Leumi (the autonomous government of the Jewish community), charged with the responsibility for Hebrew education in 1932, were preoccupied mainly with funding and administration, and could not always take the time to shape an institutionalized national-popular culture in the framework of the schools. And that was precisely where the lack of such a culture was felt most keenly. Moreover, the Hebrew educational network in Eretz-Israel was divided into three streams (*z'ramim*): the general "liberal" stream, the Labor socialist stream and the Mizrachi national-religious stream. Each had its specific ideological and educational orientation.[2]

Jewish society had very high expectations of the Hebrew schools, as in almost every modern society. The schools were expected to produce a new generation molded by the values laid down by national ideology. The teachers were called *mechanekhim* (educators). They were judged and evaluated not only by their ability to pass on knowledge but also by their ability to transmit values. It is no wonder, then, that the schoolteachers and kindergarten teachers were more aware than others of the lack of the performative dimension, and hence became its most important creators and stagers. They had a great advantage; having the capacity to mold a society of children (ages 6 to 14) more successfully than other stagers in other, less formal and hierarchical frameworks. They were also helped in this task by a strong and influential Zionist organization that provided them with the required means and resources: *Keren Kayemet le'Israel* (Jewish National Fund, or JNF). Menahem Mendel Ussishkin (1863–1941), the chairman of the JNF, and the man who initiated the establishment of the Teachers' Federation, supported the TC because he regarded it as a vehicle for promulgating his national approach and his concept of the status Hebrew culture should be assigned in the national revival. This status, in his opinion, called for the creation of an agreed-upon cultural basis that would bridge the political and ideological divides in the Yishuv. The organizational and financial support the TC received from the JNF was an important asset in ensuring its success.

The JNF was founded in 1901 by the Fifth Zionist Congress as the Zionist financial body responsible for raising funds for the purchase of land in Eretz-Israel. From 1907, the JNF became the major financial tool of the Zionist Federation, and the lands it purchased belonged to the nation. But from the outset, it expanded the areas of its activity and became what Yoram Bar-Gal recently termed an agent of Zionist propaganda in Eretz-Israel.[3] It engaged in nationalist propaganda on behalf of the Yishuv by issuing stamps, producing magic lanterns and short films, publishing textbooks, periodicals and maps, printing calendars, and most importantly, placing at the center of all this activity the familiar tin Blue Box—a collection box, first designed in 1924, as a kind of modern version of the traditional *tzdakah* (charity) box. In blue and white (the colors of the Zionist flag), it had a map of Eretz-Israel and a Star of David on the front. The box took on a symbolic status, and the collection of donations in various settings, including the school system, in Eretz-Israel and the Diaspora, made it an object at the center of a national cult.

In return for the JNF's cooperation and assistance, the TC placed the JNF and its ideology, focusing on the central role of agricultural settlement in Eretz-Israel, at the very core of Hebrew education. The very act of collecting JNF donations took on the characteristics of a national *mitzvah* (praiseworthy deed), an expression of readiness to recruit financial support for the development of the Jewish Yishuv in Eretz-Israel and *ge'ulat ha'aretz* ("redemption of the land"). But it was also an expression of ideological and spiritual identification with Jewish settlement activity and the process of nation building.

As a result, the combined efforts of the teachers and the JNF succeeded in constructing a orderly set of festivals and ceremonies within a short time, thereby creating a large part of the Hebrew official popular culture. The teachers active in the council soon became a dominant group in the school system and worked to introduce the uniform curriculum into the various schools. The TC commissioned textbooks and texts from teachers, writers and poets, and distributed them to the Hebrew schools in Eretz-Israel and abroad. It initiated the publication of *Sifrei HaMo'adim* and also brought out various publications, including *Shoreshim,* in which most of the programs for the festival ceremonies cited here were printed. Moreover, in many instances, the council expanded its activity and promoted student participation in the organization of holiday ceremonies in the various towns and settlements.[4]

In other words, what we have here is a process of centralized bureaucratization. Local initiatives in various schools induced the TC to organize on a nationwide basis, with the assistance of the JNF, a centralized institution, possessing many resources and representing a central ethos and symbolic asset in the history of Jewish settlement in Eretz-Israel, i.e., the acquisition of land. Only through this kind of cooperation were the teachers able to become the most important creators of the festive culture in the new Jewish society. This resulted in a peculiar state of affairs, in which the very same public institution that was backing the initiative became a key motif thereof.

THE TEACHERS' COUNCIL AS A STAGER: OBJECTIVES AND METHODS

The TC for the JNF was first organized as a voluntary apolitical pedagogical teachers association in 1925. The council introduced new emphases in education and adapted new teaching methods, stressing the importance of the visual, experiential methods, and also composed textbooks and learning aids. In doing so, the council created an educational basis common to all elementary schools. To a certain degree, this common basis blurred the ideological differences between the three educational streams. In the context of the Hebrew schools in Eretz-Israel, at least, one could say that Herzl's wish to see unified national ceremonies was realized in the Hebrew elementary schools from the mid-1920s onward. The council succeeded in creating an array of festivals and ceremonies and imbuing them with the content and messages it found appropriate. The TC produced not only a new corpus of texts—it also accompanied them with detailed staging instructions.[5] It was a key vehicle in the socialization and indoctrination of pupils in schools—the foundry of the nation—and through them influenced the entire society of the Yishuv.

The composition of the TC was only partially representative of the community of elementary schoolteachers in Eretz-Israel. All of its members were males; the percentage of female teachers in 1928 was about 30 percent, all either native-born or immigrants from Europe (the percentage of teachers from Islamic countries was about 2 percent). These figures indicate the stagers' cultural agenda—the combination of a national-secular interpretation of religious tradition with a European inspiration. The impact of the TC's creativity and activity was evident even after the establishment of the State of Israel (in 1948). It resulted in uniformly celebrated festivals and ceremonies in all parts of the country.

According to the educational conceptual framework of the TC, education ought to instill the main Zionist values and symbols. It was a combination of Jean Jacques Rousseau's concept of education as an engaging system, and John

Dewey's civil-liberal concept of education (rejecting Dewey's view that the child should be treated as an individual personality, and that the educator should be satisfied if he has created a good environment for the child's growth). The core content of the "national pedagogy" of the TC was underpinned by the view that *moledet* (local geography and history) studies, emphasizing the link between national history, territory and landscape according to the Zionist interpretation, were the focus of education. It also held that this nation-oriented approach ought to be transmitted not only through formal studies, in which all subjects should be taught from a national and territorial point of view, but also through organized emotional activities.

The focus on the formulation of a new Hebrew calendar resulted in a new cycle of ritual and ceremonies whose role was to turn the school into a performative space cloaked in an atmosphere of awe and sanctity, and the pupils into active performers. This was meant to express the view that the school is a social institution even more important than the family; an institution shaping the youngsters' outlook, imparting notions about the world and creating their concept of time.

School festivals and ceremonies, then, were perceived as events that connected the children to the nation and its culture and instilled shared habits and a deep sense of communality. They were perceived as creating an esthetic dimension and an artistic sense, enriching the children's imagination and their emotional world. To accomplish all these goals, a single festival would not suffice; there was a need for a structured cycle of festivals, repetitive in nature, with a fixed repertoire. It was the fixed organized performative acts that exemplified the central metaphor of the ideology of national revival, that of the deep link between the "old" (the revived) and the "new," which became the embodiment of this metaphor.[6]

In 1926 the Art Committee of the TC began to publish, in Hebrew and in various languages, pageants which included long ceremonies and staging instructions. These pageants contained songs, recitations, dramatic selections, choreographic performances, and forms of different processions, performed by soloists, a choir, individual singers, and the audience.[7] The meticulously planned cycle of festivals and ceremonies was based on a set of visual symbols and icons (such as flags, soil, trees, fruits, torches, decorated gates, and the like), which were a tangible expression of the ethos and the symbolic system of Zionist ideology.

The texts relate a master-narrative of the history of the Jewish people in Eretz-Israel, and with it a new national mythology, its new pantheon of heroes and martyrs, and its new attitude toward the landscape. They were accompanied by detailed staging instructions. These were instructions and guidelines put into actual practice in most schools, at least during part of the period addressed here.

Needless to say, from a historical perspective this was a sophisticated system of indoctrination and propaganda, which could only function in the framework of the school system, utilizing its organizational facilities and its authority. From another historical perspective, the texts and the staging seem to be replete with heroic pathos, dull, even ridiculous, an example par excellence of the attempt to create a uniform pattern of thought directed from above. However, between 1925 and 1948, these ceremonies were accepted with hardly any criticism and they characterize the formative period when the Jewish national society was coalescing in the framework of the Jewish political community in Eretz-Israel.

It is hard to assess the degree to which participants identified with the ceremony, to what extent theirs was only a formal participation, imposed by the system, and how many of them really had a deep emotional experience and internalized the messages that the ceremony embodied and strove to transmit. The testimonies of pupils at the time are not necessarily reliable, since they were written according to conventions, while later testimonies are marked by nostalgia, leading to the idealization of the festivities, or by criticism, which leads the speakers to depict them as rigid formalistic events. As far as we are concerned, the important point here is that these festivals and ceremonies were continually performed, to a great extent in a uniform manner, within the society of schoolchildren.

What looks, in retrospect, like unified indoctrination was regarded at the time as an excellent national-educational act for which a national consensus existed. What may look somewhat pathetic or even ridiculous, when divested of its original meaning, was at the time perceived as representing shared values and symbols. Hence while the decline of this cycle of school ceremonies might be perceived by some as one more manifestation of the decline of Zionist ideology, to others it might be seen as an expression of liberation from the indoctrination aimed at imposing ideological collectivism.

It should be noted that studies of the collection of myths in modern Jewish nationalism have dealt mainly with a selected group of such "myths," and viewed them as a reflection of the changes that have occurred in the national-historical worldview. In fact, the repertoire of festivals and ceremonies was much larger, and the lore of the "myths," symbols and values they expressed was far richer and more diverse than that reflected by selective formative myths of the collective national memory.

THE STAGERS AND THEIR PRINCIPLES OF STAGING

The members of the TC, who were quite aware of the role they were filling, wrote programmatic articles in which they enunciated the ideas underpinning their activity. The TC's first programmatic publication, in May 1928, was a pamphlet called: *Chagim uMo'adim leChagigot veNeshafim Bikhlal uleLag b'Omer befrat* (Holidays and Rituals for Festivities and Parties in General and for Lag B'Omer in Particular) in both Hebrew and German. In the following years, from 1937 to 1942, the head office of the JNF published five collections titled *Sifrei mo'adim* (Holiday Books) which achieved great success and were reprinted many times. Their chief editor was Dr. Chaim Harari (Blumberg, 1883–1940), a teacher at the Herzliya Hebrew gymnasium in Tel Aviv, who was also active in organizing festivals and ceremonies in Tel Aviv and served as the head of the committee for promoting festivals. Harari, who studied at the Sorbonne and in Geneva, wrote a dissertation titled "Literature et Tradition" and published various articles about the nature of popular (folk) culture.[8] Others who participated in this activity were Shmuel Navon (Kligman, 1904–96), a teacher in the Labor stream of education, who performed in an amateur theatre and was involved in cultural affairs in Tel Aviv.[9] Dr. Baruch Ben-Yehudah (Leibowitz, 1894–1991), also a teacher at the Herzliya gymnasium (and from 1941 its principal for many years); Eliezer Shapira (1900–1985), a teacher active in public affairs, who served as the committee's secretary, Abraham Arnon (1887–1960) a teacher involved in public affairs, and others.

These key figures active in the TC had a clear-cut, well-defined concept of the place and role of festivals and ceremonies in the social and cultural life of the community, and were aware of the urgent need to reconstruct a new Hebrew calendar and folk culture. Harari thought that "culture" encompassed "every popular manifestation" and he advocated the establishment of centers for the study of popular Jewish culture, including: "clothing and food, accent and voice, hand gestures and facial expressions." "With the aid of photography and recordings," he believed, one could document the entire scope of everyday life.[10]

In his introduction to the book devoted to the Chanukah festival, Harari wrote that the purpose of the collection was: "To provide material for holidays and festivals for the young generation and for the people, for the schools and for dramatic groups, in connection with the arrangements for festivities and parties marking memorial days in Israel." But for Harari it was not enough to provide a corpus of texts. In his introduction to the anthology book on Hanukkah, he wrote that "the greater part of the material is directed mainly to the *ear*, namely to be *read aloud to the audience, as well as to the eye, to be presented on the stage*" (emphasis in the original).¹¹ This view was shared by Shmuel Navon who wrote:

> We have restored to the people the ground under their feet, the soil upon which the festivals were born, and now we have to labor to create the spiritual soil—the festivals. Fortunately, we have a loyal partner to help in reviving the holidays—the child. The child, who is free of our reaction against life in the Diaspora and the well-known forms of the holidays is the one who can help. He has grown up on the soil of the homeland, its national language is on his tongue, and he is umbilically connected to Hebrew culture and creation in Eretz-Israel. He is capable, perhaps more than we, of being a pioneer of the festival in the land. Of course, and I must stress this, with our help: the help of the kindergarten, of the school and of the home. And the essential nature of the festivals will be all the more evident if we recognize the child's link to the festival and the educational value inherent in fostering the holiday in the life of the child.¹²

Navon quoted the national poet, Bialik, who had reacted to the claim that "a festival is not made by hand" by stating that a festival *had* to be made. Explaining the guidelines of the planning of the Shavuot festival in Tel Aviv by the artistic committee, he wrote:

> There are three basic elements to this holiday: folklore, ceremony, nature. Three or four central places must be determined for a pilgrimage and these must be out in the open landscape. We have to prepare a gateway and a stage and place the first fruits upon it. Carts, camels and donkeys will carry the first fruits. In addition, we will bring the children's tools, even the ploughs. All those bringing the first fruits will be adorned with olive branches. *The form and the act are the main feature in this festivity* [emphasis in original], and this is the place to develop the activism of each and every one.¹³

In another article, "The Festival in the Educational Work of the Jewish National Fund," he wrote:

> Zionist education can only succeed if it finds concrete ways to inculcate [its teachings] so they will leave a deep impression on the child's mind. Abstract explanations will not achieve the goal. The festival, however, incorporates a series of concrete manifestations and symbols (which

also take on a concrete expression) which have an immediate effect on all of the child's mental faculties.

The festival, then, has a twofold value: to further Zionist education and to serve as an educational tool to achieve Zionist aims. A quick look at the value of the festival from the viewpoint of the child will clearly show the role the festival should play in the framework of this education.

Just by skimming through the spontaneous facets of the child's life one immediately comes across the field of popular games, such as: hide and seek, skipping rope, hopscotch, pick-up-stix, etc.,—games that pass from one generation of children to the next without the intervention of adults, in other words, a popular cultural asset. These games contain vestiges of ancient beliefs and customs, even from idolatrous periods of time, that continue to linger in children's games in various countries among different peoples. For example, in the game of hopscotch, which children are so fond of, researchers of popular folklore have found vestiges of an ancient belief, according to which a person's soul, after his death, passes through several sections until it finds its rest in heaven. The stone, which is used in the game, symbolizes the soul passing the squares (the sections) until it reaches the upper arch usually drawn on the ground or the pavement and which the children call "heaven."

The thing that denotes this traditional popular asset is that within the forms of the games and the rhymes that accompany them (syllables devoid of content, in which the vestiges of mythological oaths and customs have been identified), children in every nation devise their own popular creation introducing into it the changes that are appropriate to the spirit of the people, the place and the time.

In this creation of a popular asset, which is the sole property of the world of children, there are two elements—tradition and a popular creation at the borderline of the tradition—two elements that attest to parallel creative forces in the child's psyche. And when we introduce the festival into the children's lives, we can base our activity on these two traits of the child's psyche, which are fundamental to the creation of a system of festivals.[14]

Navon suggested the order in which the festival should be held and what costumes the participants should wear.[15]

Dr. Baruch Ben-Yehudah, head of the TC, was deeply involved in the daily work of the Art Committee and the Literary Committee of the TC, and wrote both text and staging instructions. In his article *HaKeren haMechanekhet* he wrote:

Chapter 6

Festivals in the School

New elements in children's festivals: Many of the committee's meetings have been devoted to this problem. In them, the members considered at depth the festival experience in the lives of children, analyzed each and every aspect in detail, criticized everything being done until now and sought new, appropriate ways for the movement. They did not rush to arrive at any clear-cut conclusions in their discussions nor were they hasty in raising new proposals. With much hesitation, for the first time, they submitted to the Executive Council a proposal for a revived celebration of the Festival of the First Fruits.

Thus several festivities were held with the dedication and deep confidence of their organizers. And each time, much self-criticism was voiced about every festivity, and various opinions were voiced, until finally a comprehensive approach to the role of the festival in Zionist education was formulated. A year or two later, this approach was brought before an expanded nationwide council of teachers in the form of a comprehensive lecture, in which the new elements in children's festivities were delineated. The lecturer put forth two objectives for the festivities: artistic education and emotional education. He sharply criticized what has been done in this area until now, which failed to develop any ability for artistic appreciation among our children, any tendency toward style or grace in our lives, any true attitude toward the emotions. The lecturer cited examples from both the domain of joyfulness—festivities held in the schools on holidays—and the domain of sorrow—the participation of our pupils at funerals—and called for a change of values. In his view, these are the essential elements of our festivities:

1. The active participation of the children themselves, not of adult artists, for whom the children would serve as a passive audience. Every festivity must avoid passive fatigue which rules out any possibility of emotionally affecting the children. Only active fatigue will provide any benefit. This element necessitates preparations over a rather long period of time. The teacher can and should be assisted by an artist, but during the festivity itself, only the children should perform. The number of adults at the festivity should be as small as possible.
2. The festivity is a major goal of the school. The teacher should devote more hours to it than are allocated to art studies. In the school, there should be an atmosphere of preparations for a festivity. It should serve as a project for all the work of the school. The

ancient custom of proclaiming a festival, such as "On the first day of Adar, proclamations are made regarding the shekalim," or "Questions are asked and lectures are given on the laws of Passover for 30 days before Passover," should be revived and observed by us regularly.

3. In each festivity, there should be a minimum that is repeated each year, at least at the beginning and the end. This makes it necessary to have a permanent ceremony and settings, which we have suggested at every opportunity. Of course, each time the festivity should be replete with many new elements and it can also end with spontaneous entertainment, such as games, folk dancing, and the like.

4. Regularity, exactness and seriousness should prevail in every festivity, first and foremost among the adults who are engaged in organizing it.

5. It would have been possible to organize processions, if we could ensure precision and a limited number of participants. But since, at this time, we are not confident of their success, we ask that the processions be cancelled.

6. Speeches at the festivities should be cancelled, at least for the present. The large number of speeches and their length have a detrimental effect.

These opinions have become a dominant element in the members' approach to festivities in the schools. During recent years, the Teachers Council has carried out quite a few exemplary festivities and this has influenced all the schools in the country to follow these guidelines.[16]

Another teacher and stager, A. Tubenfliegel, suggested two main principles of staging:

And now, regarding the ways of implementation. The proper and complete implementation depends on two basic principles: 1.The festival as a central life endeavor; 2. Active self-implementation.

The first principle corresponds totally to the place and function of the festival in its fullest sense: the festival must serve as a result and a point of coalescence for the entire Zionist-educational activity, carried out during the time when the festival occurs. The Sabbath has no meaning unless it is preceded by the first six days, during which the work of Creation was carried out. The same is true of the festivals. All of the theoretical and practical activities that accompany the period of time and encompass the subjects of nature, local geography, Jewish history and the Zionist precepts, should lead to one central point—to the expression concentrated in the festival.

The very essence of the festival demands that it not be celebrated as an artistically enjoyable episode or a surprise that is prepared externally. Rather it should be at the very center of the time period as a life endeavor in which all the creations of the present and the past are concentrated.

The second principle is related to the first and is fundamental to the pedagogy of the festival: the children and the youths must be regarded as faithful participants in implementing the festival endeavor. There is no need to prove the child's affinity to the festival. Every educator knows, sees and feels it. And experience has often shown that the children are far better at achieving the aim from the standpoint of Eretz-Israeli originality than the adults who tried their hand at it. But the children must not merely fill the function of advising or expressing their opinions. They must be active in the implementation, which includes all the work and activity in preparation for the festival. The intent here is that the child must feel that he is acting independently and must have an inner sense of involvement and an inner connection to the festival. And this can be achieved by giving the child the opportunity of a direct and constant contact with the various links in the chain of the festival endeavor, and by giving the children's society the responsibility, with the instructor's help, of organizing the festivity. And it is preferable to compromise somewhat on the perfection of the outward artistic form in order to allow the children to feel that the fruit of their creation is their own spiritual property and the product of their own work.[17]

There were others who contributed ideas on how to plan and conduct the ceremonies, many of whom we were unable to identify. One of these "anonymous" stagers, A. Ben-Hillel, proposed how the stage should be built: "An important principle in artistic education in the present-day school . . . the performance on the stage, the movement, the speech, serve as a direct means of expression for the child, like painting and sculpting, education has the task of raising children who will know how to talk, to move, to create from within their own resources."[18] The TC produced instructions on how to build a stage in the school, how to decide where to place it, guidelines for the scenery, lighting, and so forth.[19]

These people active in the TC had a clear-cut, well-defined concept of the place and role of festivals and ceremonies in the social, cultural and educational life of the community in general and of the schoolchildren within it, as well as of the urgent need to reconstruct a new Hebrew calendar and folk culture. They were, in fact, those who supplied the school teachers with both texts and staging instructions. The principles underlying the organization and institutionalization of the new cycle of festivals and ceremonies in the schools were as follows:

1. A major prerequisite for the success of the festivities is the "organization of the participants and the preplanned, meticulous management of the festivity, down to every last detail."
2. All of the children must actively participate in the preparations and the performance.
3. The festivals and ceremonies are not held separately in the classes but in the larger framework of the entire school.
4. The special nature of each festival is emphasized through its unique content and manner of staging.
5. The festivals and ceremonies are structured according to preplanned formulae, and no room is left for spontaneous creation.
6. Every festival must include three components: a ceremony, a party, and entertainment.
7. In every ceremony, a dialogue is created between the active performers and the audience, or between the chief actors and the children who play the role of a chorus.
8. An attempt will be made to avoid excessively long ceremonies.

Every festival and ceremony included a written text, music adapted to it, visual elements (posters, drawings, costumes), a stage, scenery, and staging. The official ceremony was usually followed by dancing and organized games. The great value ascribed to staging and to visual imagination was also manifested in the attempt to stage the small units of the festival. For example, poems were not merely recited but also dramatized.

The artistic committee and the TC as a whole held many discussions before planning each of the festivals, as well as after the events, to find out which components and items were well received, and which were not and had to be replaced.

Therefore, the modus operandi was as follows: a small group of entrepreneurs of festive culture wrote booklets containing texts and staging instructions and distributed them in the schools, where they were generally used by the teachers assigned to organize the festival ceremonies. The fact that this small group enjoyed the backing of an institution as prestigious as the JNF cannot explain why the group was so successful in creating a festive culture common to all the schools. The major reason was the fact that both teachers and principals keenly felt the lack of a festive culture and were aware of the role such a culture was meant to fill. The TC helped to fill this void, and hence its directives were accepted.

The groups of school stagers created the content of the new system of holiday festivities by combining traditional elements, renewing such elements and inventing new ones, which reflect the dominant national ideology and its major values. The manner in which this was accomplished is discussed below.

Staging Festivals in the Kindergartens

We have discussed the reinstitution of birthday celebrations in the Hebrew kindergartens.[20] Here we will discuss it as a location for a system of festivities, reflecting the general system, adapted for very young children.

The kindergarten is the formative institution of modern education. As we noted, kindergartens first appeared in Jewish society as a central feature of its acculturation and modernization, when the concept of childhood as a distinct period in human life was adopted, as were the teaching methods of European progressive preschool education. At its inception, the kindergarten was conceived as a substitute for the parental home, where the young child does not receive experiential enrichment and aesthetic education, and in Europe it was viewed as an institution that would provide the missing "national environment."[21] In the words of the Hebrew kindergarten teachers, the goal of the kindergarten is to instill national habits in the children, thereby contributing to the unification of the nation.[22] According to this view, this new primary national environment should be constructed in an organized, uniform manner. Thus it became imperative to create an overall repertoire of games and songs for every special occasion, including ceremonies and festivals.

Indeed, there were those who claim there is "too much indoctrination, completely cut off from the everyday life going on around them, thus creating an unhealthy rhythm of life in the kindergarten with the main emphasis placed on festivities, which require great effort on the part of the teachers and the children, causing tension and fatigue." The critics also claimed that it is impossible to formulate a complex system of ceremonies for small children, whose ability to perform had to be taken into account, and the number of festivals celebrated in the kindergarten should be reduced.[23]

Consequently, ceremonies in the kindergarten were planned and staged with easily performed elements. For example, the Feast of the First Fruits was held in the kindergarten's yard; the children were dressed in white, with wreaths of flowers on their heads, and they carried baskets filled with fruits and vegetables.[24] Some festivities were staged in a more artistic way, depending on the teacher's ingenuity and artistic-dramatic talent. The religious kindergarten run by Zipora Wolfson in Tel Aviv in the mid-1930s, for example, was known for its artistic festivities in which a "successful attempt was made to develop and perfect the children's skill in the art of theatrical presentation specifically for children." This was accomplished through a combination of the various elements (dramatic presentation, recitation, song and dance).[25]

During the Feast of the First Fruits the doors symbolized "gates" to the various parts of the country and were adorned with palm branches and sheaves of wheat.

> In the middle of the room there was a stage painted brown and green—earth and vegetation—decorated with the seven species . . . on each side opposite each gate stood a charming little girl, and together, each one alongside her gate, they met the pilgrims walking in a Yemenite manner, slowly, with bent knees, singing: "Hallelujah, Hallelujah." And the pilgrims answered, lifting their heads, "Hallelu." Each girl turned to face her gate and they replied in unison to the pilgrims, "Blessed be the entire people of Israel!" And they began to move, supposedly to Jerusalem, to bring and offer the first fruits.[26]

As we mentioned, there were some who favored "spontaneous" festivities in the kindergarten, and were opposed to organizing the children, requiring them to rehearse and memorize texts,[27] but the quasi-organized pattern was dominant and over time became the uniformly accepted framework.[28] The TC helped the kindergarten teachers by preparing programs for the various festivals, based mainly on the dramatization and staging of holiday songs. In the 1930s and 1940s, the Hebrew kindergarten teachers had at their disposal both a corpus of texts and staging programs. When a graduate of a kindergarten reached grade school, he was already familiar with part of the new calendar of festivals and some of the repertoire.

Staging Festivals and Ceremonies in Schools

Until 1925, Jewish festivals were celebrated in Hebrew schools in a haphazard manner, mainly by putting on various shows ("spectacles"), with the participation of the parents, and sometimes of the community at large. For this purpose, a small repertoire of plays in Hebrew, generally historical plays, was created. In addition, festivals were celebrated by torch and flower processions. It was the TC that, within a short time, created a new Hebrew calendar and made the festivals an inseparable part of the school curriculum. It included the following events: welcoming the Sabbath and the new month, an end-of-the-school year festivity, and in order of appearance on the new calendar: Balfour Declaration day, Hanukkah, the 18th day of Tevet (the "birthday" of the JNF), the 15th of Shevat (Arbor Day), the 11th of Adar (Tel Hai day), Purim, Lag ba'Omer, the Feast of the First Fruits, and the memorial day for Herzl and Bialik. The festivals of Succoth (the Feast of Tabernacles) and Passover were not celebrated in school.

Each month of the year, at least one large festival, with a standard structure, was celebrated in the school. However, it is important to note that the TC created a new priority among the festivals in which the two most important festivals were the 15th of Shevat and the Feast of the First Fruits, and these in fact were given the most elaborate staging.

All the parts of this new calendar were redesigned by changing the traditional format, adding new elements, or creating new holidays. The new visual-symbolic elements were: marching in processions, flying flags, lighting torches and blowing bugles, decorated gates, releasing doves, and the like. Costumes, which were supposed to represent Hebrew culture, were designed especially for the festivals. We will now describe how some of these festivals were staged, in the order of their appearance in the calendar.

The Festival of the New Month

The principle underlying the festivities to mark the new month was to adapt the content and the staging to the special nature of the festival—the month, the season of the year, the agricultural season, or a historical event connected with it—which were reflected in the fixed artistic program.

The festivity marking the end of the month of Nisan (the beginning of spring and the Passover festival), for example, was staged in the following way:

> First an announcer appeared, wearing a costume suggesting the season, and holding a metal placard bearing the sign of the zodiac for that month. His appearance was accompanied by a trumpet blast. Then the pupils came into the hall and took their places. The announcer went up to the podium while the trumpeters remained at the foot of the podium on either side of it. The announcer waved the placard and when the audience rose to their feet, he greeted them: "Members of the school community! The month of Nisan welcomes you today: May the hands of all our

brethren showing favor to the riches of our land be strengthened [the opening line of Bialik's poem "The Blessing of the People"]. The audience replied in unison: "Strong and true."

After a trumpet blast, the announcer removed a scroll from its case and read a text in honor of the events of the month. The text included a mention of the season of the year based on verses from the Song of Songs, a description of the work of the farmer in the agricultural season, and of the Exodus from Egypt. Now a kind of rite, national in character, commenced. The JNF box, containing the pupils' donations, was emptied in front of the audience. The treasurer then proclaimed: *"The land shall not ever be sold, for the land is mine. And in all the land you possess, you shall grant a redemption of the land."*

The audience of pupils rose to their feet and repeated the last line.

Now, the JNF delegate in the school announced the total sum of the donations of each class and the announcer raised his placard and declared the sum contributed by the entire school.

The ceremony ended with a trumpet blast to mark the change of zodiac signs. The announcer for the next month entered, carrying his placard. Both announcers met in front of the table, on which the JNF box was placed. They waved their placards and the announcer for the month that had ended proclaimed the beginning of the new month. The latter went up to the podium and greeted the pupils, who answered him in chorus. Then everyone sang the national anthem, "HaTikvah."

The texts include quotations from and allusions to the Bible and modern Hebrew literature. The trumpet fanfare was intended to create a festive ritual effect, and the dialogue between the announcer and the audience (the chorus) provided the sense of partnership and sanctity.

Welcoming the Sabbath (Kabbalat Shabbat)

The ceremony welcoming the Sabbath, which was intended to replace the traditional religious ritual, included Shabbat songs, the lighting of candles and the reading of the Portion of the Week. In the religious schools, a girl said the blessing over the candles, while in the secular schools, they simply lit them. Before blessing the candles, the girl dropped a donation into the JNF box. Afterward, one of the teachers delivered a "sermon" on a key event in the life of the school, or of the town or village. The staging here was simple and the main point was the dialogue between the "cantor" and the pupils, who served as a chorus, and the communal singing. The ceremony, then, was a secularized form of the traditional ritual of welcoming the Sabbath, with the addition of a national element—the JNF donation. The major innovation was in the content of the texts.

Balfour Declaration Day—the 17th of Cheshvan

Balfour Declaration day, marking the November 2, 1917 declaration by the British Foreign Secretary, Lord Arthur Balfour, of Great Britain's support for the establishment of a Jewish national home in Palestine, was a new holiday on the calendar. The ceremony combined biblical and national texts, and was staged as follows:

The children gathered in the school hall were seated in front of a folded map of Eretz-Israel. At the opening of the ceremony, a pupil read aloud God's promise to Abraham in Genesis 12, and another pupil read a description of the boundaries of the promised land from *Joshua* 1:4. At the same time, another pupil, using a pointer, indicated the boundaries on the map. Afterward pupils went up on the stage, each in turn representing various entities of the Zionist movement and its operations—a representative of the Zionist Federation, a representative of the JNF, representatives of agriculture, immigration, defense, art, etc. Each of the "representatives" read out several sentences connected to his/her "operation." The representative of the Zionist Federation, for example, read the Balfour Declaration, while another marked the boundaries of the British mandate with colored chalk. Between each representative, a story or a short poem connected with the subject was recited. Finally, a child placed a Bible next to the national flag and declared: "The land shall be ours, and we shall be among its builders." The other children repeated the words after him, and then sang HaTikvah and left the hall.

The way this new ceremony was constructed shows its novelty and political character. It was composed mainly of readings and rhetorical declarations, and the stagers tried to add at least some performative elements, in which the pupils took an active part.

Hanukkah

In the Jewish tradition, Hanukkah (Feast of Light) was celebrated primarily by lighting eight candles, one for each of the eight days of the festival.[29] Over time, popular customs were added in different countries, but the first attempt in the Diaspora to give it the form of a public celebration were few in number. Hanukkah parties were held, and plays were put on, but only in Eretz-Israel could there be open-air performances, such as lighting of torches in the center of villages or lighting up the main streets of the cities. In due course, Hanukkah took on a new form, comprised entirely of new textual and performative elements. Light played a key symbolic role, as in the traditional holiday, but could now be expressed by means other than candles, and also took on a new significance.

Hanukkah became a central festival in the modern Jewish calendar and was assigned a more important status than it had in the traditional Jewish system of festivals. From the inception of the Hibbat Zion movement in the 1880s, this holiday was endowed with a national character, marking the heroic struggle for the liberation of the homeland and the defense of the national culture. The texts that were composed in honor of the festival utilized traditional symbols translated into the national master narrative. These expressed the tension between the religious-traditional dimension of the festival and the national "secular" message imposed upon it.[30] The Hebrew schools had already begun, at the end of the nineteenth century, to make it a central festival on the calendar, and invested much effort in preparation for it. They held large parties and put on dramatic shows, usually based on the Books of the Maccabees, which at the time were introduced into the historical-literary canon, a status they had not previously enjoyed.

The first one to introduce Hanukkah festivities into the classroom in Eretz-Israel was the teacher, David Yudilewitch (1863–1943) in the moshava of Rishon-le-Zion. In 1905, Dr. Judah Leib Matman-HaChoen (1869–1939), a teacher who would later found the Herzliya gymnasium in Jaffa in 1906, stated that lighting candles was not enough; a procession with the Zionist flag should be held instead. In Rehovoth, in 1907, the participants at a Hanukkah party went out into the street, rang the moshava bell and lit torches. This practice of lighting torches in the streets spread quickly.

At first, the staging was simple and its central motif was processions of children carrying torches or candles. In the course of time, the custom of preparing paper crowns with a Hanukkah candle in the middle for the children became popular. Soon enough it was recognized that for the new Hanukkah ceremonies, more was needed than the lighting of candles or the traditional game with a top (adopted from the medieval German folk culture). As a result, a whole new repertoire was constructed around these two elements. The TC laid down the structure of a festive ceremony that revolved around the lighting of candles and the singing of Hanukkah songs, but also included the national flag and the Blue Box, followed by the performance of a play connected with the festival. After the ceremony, there was dancing in the schoolyard or in a hall. Here too, no room was left for spontaneity, and the dances were fixed and staged according to precise guidelines. Writers, poets, playwrights and songwriters were enlisted in creating the new repertoire, and over time many texts, stories, plays and songs were written, some of them especially commissioned by the TC.

The important point as far as we are concerned is that this new repertoire was accompanied by the staging of the entire festival, as well as of each of its units.

Here, for example, are the 1936 staging guidelines:

> Four groups of children are arranged like the spokes of a wheel. Each child in a group holds the child next to him by the belt and they turn around the 'axis,' a large pupil standing in the middle, leaning on a rod, a large lamp in the shape of a top on his head. The child in each of the four groups who is on the inside holds on to him, as they all turn and dance to music played on a harmonica.[31]

And these were the staging instructions for kindergarten children, to the song "*Chag HaNitzachon*," described as a "play-song," an adaptation of the famous choral song "See, the Conquering Hero Comes" from the oratorio *Judas Maccabeus* (previously included in the oratorio *Joshua*) by George Frideric Handel, to words by Levin Kipnis (1894–1990), a writer who made the greatest contribution to the creation of a repertoire of Hebrew children's songs:

> The song is performed by a chorus of boys and girls, messengers, soldiers and dancers. The chorus waves flags and torches, and the dancers perform with drums and cymbals. When Judah the Maccabee enters the stage, accompanied by his soldiers (the Maccabees), bearing a flag, the dancers place a victor's wreath on his head [it is very ironic that a victor's wreath, a Greek custom, is used here to adorn the head of Judah the Maccabee, the hero of the Jewish war against the Seleucid empire, but this is not the only "Greek" pagan element introduced into the Hanukkah festivities]. Two new verses were added to Handel's song, telling how the lamp was lit in the temple and the temple was purified, sung with the refrain: "*Hakh, hakh, batof/hakh, hakh batof!/yom zeh lanu/hu yom tov!*" (Ho, ho, play the drum/ ho, ho play the drum/this is our day/and it's a holiday!)[32] The ceremony included quasi-military elements—the trumpet, flags, a procession to the sound of marching songs.

Another proposal from the late 1930s suggested the following program:

On the roof of the school or in a nearby open area, representatives of all the classes, each holding a flashlight, are placed at predetermined distances from each other. Holding flashlights, they are arranged in a U or in a double semicircle. When they hear the blast of a trumpet, the other children leave their classrooms, each child holding a colored candle, and arrange themselves around their representative. Upon hearing a second trumpet blast, the children stand at attention, and the Zionist flag appears accompanied by guards of honor bearing torches. The flag bearer and his attendants pass before the classes until they are standing in front of all those present.

A child from one of the higher classes reads several verses from relevant texts (the Book of Maccabees, for example). Special ushers from each class light the candles held by the children. The torch bearers disperse when the candle lighting ceremony begins, two from each class.

When the festival director gives the order, all classes move to one side and march in a procession of lights behind the flag. As they march, they sing Hanukkah songs and marching songs until they reach the hall where the festivity is held. The flag, its attendants and the torch bearers fall back.

The procession continues into the hall and surrounds the tables, accompanied by piano playing or by singing, so that each class finally arrives at its designated table and each pupil stands behind his/her chair. The pupils take their seats when the homeroom teachers give them a sign, and then each pupil sticks his candle in the sand that has been placed in the candlestick before him.

A musical note is heard. The large menorah is lit. The pianist (or a group of musicians) play an appropriate musical piece to add to the festive mood. When the last note is heard, one of the homeroom teachers recites a legendary story connected with the facts or the ideas of this festival.

All the lights and candelabra are lit at once and everyone joins in singing a Hanukkah song.

The JNF committee proclaims: "Such and such class is donating its Hanukkah money to the JNF." A representative of that class comes forward and hands over a bag holding the donations of his classmates. A member of the JNF committee announces: "Such and such a class will recite its verse!" and the class, at a sign given by the homeroom teacher, recites its verse. This is repeated for all the classes.

When the collection of donations is completed, a song is sung relating to the idea of the JNF. A festive meal is served. Between each course, the classes sing, alternately or in unison. When the meal is over, ushers carrying baskets filled with *dreidel* appear and hand them out while everyone sings the "*dreidel* song." A general game is played with a *dreidel*. . . . The leader of the game spins the *dreidel*, and when it falls, a representative of each class (sitting in the front row) points to one of the walls, the leader lifts the *dreidel* and calls out the letter on which it fell. The classes, whose representative points to the correct wall, win one point. The class that wins 8 points is the winner.

Dances. Finally, the anthem is played.[33]

Another example is the staging instructions for the Hanukkah ceremony from the booklet of the "Gordonia" Zionist youth movement, printed in Lvov (Poland) in 1935:

The curtain opened to reveal the dark blue backdrop of the stage on which there is a large silver menorah. Eight girl scouts stand on the stage wearing colorful paper dresses, their heads adorned with ribbons of gold or colors matching their dresses, and in their hands they hold unlit colored candles. The scouts stand in a straight line . . . to the right there stands a small boy scout wearing a gray shirt and holding a lit white candle—he is the *shammash* [the ninth candle on the menorah, from which the other candles are lit].

The choir bursts into a song in honor of Hanukkah and the *shammash* passes before the row of candles and lights them. A dramatic conversation develops between the *shammash*, the "candles" and the audience.

In the center of the next act, there is a large JNF box made out of cardboard, around which there is also a sort of dialogue, not in rhyme, between the participants and the audience, on the subject of the redemption of the people and the land. At the end of the act, the children raise the JNF box and hang it on the wall. Afterward, a group of children on the stage perform the martyrological story of Hannah and her seven sons.[34]

The staging of Hanukkah festivities made extensive use of the motif of light. The torch procession ["the procession of the lights"] had a key role. Children bearing torches and moving through the schoolyard, or through the city streets served as a tangible expression of the metaphor that Hanukkah symbolizes the coming of light [redemption], fulfilled by the national revival movement in Eretz-Israel. The fact that in Eretz-Israel the Jews could hold processions in the public sphere was also underscored:

Our hearts are troubled as we think upon the thousands of Jewish children in the Diaspora, who were not privileged to take part in this procession of lights. And we, the adults, who have gathered here from all the Jewish dispersions, did we have such processions? In the snow-covered winter nights of our childhood, we would return from the *cheder*, holding kerosene lamps, darkness all about us. And what were the sounds that reached us from the vaulted church of the Christians, shrouded in mystery? Were those not the voices of the *shkutzim*, the gentile boys, who would pelt us with stones? Let us hurry to run away! . . . And now? Here? Look and see these tots marching proudly, heads held high, we cheer jubilantly in the fresh air, the air of Kislev, in the Hebrew city.[35]

The act of staging the festivity in the public sphere was, then, more than a public visual celebration of the holiday. It was a consummate expression of the new staging of the entire Hebrew culture, in fact, of the new Jewish existence in Eretz-Israel.

The 18th of Tevet—The Birthday of the JNF

This was an entirely new festival, one clearly propagandist in nature. Short plays or pageants (ceremonies combining dramatization and songs) were written in its honor. These always centered on the blue JNF box, which served as a type of altar, while the children participating were priests and Levites.

In the play commissioned by the TC and written by the poetess Anda Finkerpeled-Amir (1902–81) in 1939, the heroes are the JNF boxes, representing the various countries of the Diaspora, and various species of trees, symbolizing the forests being planted in Eretz-Israel. The play describes the "ingathering" of the blue boxes, each of whom tells the audience about the Jewish community it represents. Afterward, the trees come to congratulate the JNF, and each one presents the story of its locale.

In the text, the boxes and trees were personified. The staging instructions stated that each child would hold a tree branch—pine, apple, cypress, acacia, eucalyptus, and the like—and specified how they were to wave these branches. Here the trees took on a symbolic status, which reflected their status in the worldview of Jewish settlement in Eretz-Israel as a symbol of renewal, the redemption of the land, settlement, a link to the country, and the like. Other texts dramatized scenes of settling the land and working its soil.

Tu biShevat, 15th of Shevat—The New Year for Trees

In ancient Jewish tradition, the 15th of Shevat marked the new year for trees. The Kabbalists, from the sixteenth century onward, observed the festival by eating special fruits; the Chasidim celebrated with a special prayer on the etrog (citron); and in various communities, other customs developed. But the day was always celebrated by a ceremony of some kind.

Tu biShevat festivities were first held at the moshava of Yesod Hama'alah, in the Upper Galilee, in 1884, and included the planting of hundreds of etrog trees. But the man remembered as the initiator of this planting festival is the teacher and historian Ze'ev (Wolf) Jawitz (1847–1924), who, in 1888, organized schoolchildren to go out and plant trees. This new ritual was adopted after 1904 by teachers in the other new colonies (moshavot) and spread to the cities as well. Within a short time, Tu biShevat was given a much more central place in the Hebrew calendar as an expression of the Zionist ethos. It is no wonder, then, that the ultra-orthodox perceived Tu biShevat festivities as one more expression of the tendency of Jewish nationalists to convert religious festivals into festivals of nature. For example, Rabbi Yehiel Michal Tukchinsky (1872–1955) in his book *Lu'ach etz chayim* (Jerusalem, 1914) described a large holiday procession and with irony called the new festival: "A festival of tree planting, a pagan festival of beauty and nature," which heralded the victory of nationalism in Jerusalem. In contrast to all the other festivals, a major part of this festival was celebrated primarily outside the school. The trees were planted in a grove or a forest, further away. Tu bi-Shevat festivities were held not only by the schools but also by Zionist youth movements in Eretz-Israel and in the Diaspora, and by the various towns and villages.

In the early 1930s, the festival committee of the TC decided to reinforce the element of tree planting. A circular from the national committee of the TC, dated January 30, 1930, suggested the following ordering of the ceremony:

> This is how we picture the program for the day: a planting festivity inside the school or in the schoolyard; the children arrive adorned with flowers and wearing ribbons in their school colors. The festivity begins with songs related to planting, the reading of suitable selections, etc. At a given moment, all the children (from grade 3 and upward) walk in a procession to the site where the planting is to take place, and plant their trees in a fixed ceremony and predetermined order.[36]

To underscore the message of the festival, the TC wanted the ceremony to include more than just the planting of trees, and directed the procession to the planting site and the act of planting itself into a ceremony constructed according to a fixed formula. Texts and staging instructions for plays were also written and disseminated. Here, for example, is the formula of a 1937 planting ceremony: The pupils (the planters) dressed in khaki pants and white shirts walk in a procession wearing straw hats. The "chief planter" walks at the head of the procession, holding a hoe. Opposite them, on a decorated stage adorned with the saplings, stand the members of the "planting guard," dressed in white with green wreaths on their heads. Between the two is the "elder of the guard," attended by four children representing the four seasons. Behind them is an ensemble of flutists wearing striped shirts with skullcaps on their heads. They are flanked on one side by an orchestra, or a choir, and on the other by a group of trumpeters wearing robes and golden ribbons on their heads. The ceremony itself included: handing over the saplings to the planters, proceeding to the planting, reading a pact, the version of a prayer, and the planting itself. The planting procession was accompanied by the waving of palm branches, the ringing of bells, the striking of wooden hammers on a metal plate, and the like. All the movements and gestures during the procession and the planting were precisely fixed.

Clearly, the planners and stagers of the ceremony introduced elements from various sources into it. The procession was a combination of an allusion to the procession on each of the three yearly pilgrimages to the Temple and an allusion to the Greek theatre; in other words, a combination of a Jewish religious ceremony and pagan elements. The use of palm branches was borrowed from the Succoth festival, but recalls (perhaps unknowingly) the Christian Palm Sunday procession on the Via Dolorosa in Jerusalem.

Another version of the Tu biShevat planting festivity, adapted by A. Shapira, secretary of the TC, and edited by the council's artistic committee, laid down the following formula:

> The head of the guard, costumed as a palm tree, leads the procession, accompanied by four attendants representing the four seasons of the year, who wear long white cloth robes with wide sleeves and over them colored cloaks in the spirit of the time of year. In one hand, they hold a long rod, in the other, a scroll containing the (biblical) portion of the day. They are accompanied by flutists playing flutes, dressed in striped shirts with skullcaps on their heads, and a group of dancers dressed in long white cloth robes, adorned with greenery and flowers, and wreaths on their heads.
>
> Other participants are: *1.* A group of announcers—four boys and girls—dressed in white, hoops on their forehead, and wearing a winged headdress made of gold-colored cardboard. They hold branches of almond blossoms in their hands, and others are strewn around the stage. *2.* Four or five girls carrying baskets of flowers and fruit on rattan trays, wearing belted white cotton robes and wreaths on their heads. *3.* A group of drummers and trumpeters. *4.* An orchestra and a choir.

The order of the festivity was as follows: The announcer proclaims the coming of Tu biShevat. The company of trumpeters and drummers enters the field playing the melody of the song "The Almond Tree is Blooming." The audience moves in two sections around the edges of the field. The field itself is decorated with appropriate symbols and drawings. The group of dancers enters followed by the announcers bearing branches of almond blossoms. They descend to the first step of the stage and read out a fixed text. The trumpeters respond and the national flag is flown.

Then comes the rhetorical part of the ceremony with the audience's participation. Afterward, the planters move toward the planting site and a group of girls comes toward them with palm branches that they wave in greeting. The planters walk in three columns and the chief planter goes up on the stage to the sound of a trumpet blast, carrying a shovel on his shoulder. The sapling is handed to him and he reads the text of a vow (*Isaiah* 41:19) and then plants the sapling. When he has finished, the other planters commence planting to the sound of the music. They place the saplings on their shoulders, encircle the planting site, the girls bearing fruit swing their trays, the planters move to the sound of the song "Thus the Planters Walk" and plant the saplings in the holes that were prepared in advance.

The sanctification of the holiday in the modern national culture was given its fullest expression in this planting ceremony.[37] The trees symbolized both Jewish resettlement in the country and the victory of "culture" over the "wilderness." After the Arab Revolt of 1936–37, when the Arab marauders burned Jewish fields, destroying many trees, the ceremonies became "memorial" ceremonies, lamenting the destroyed trees.

The planting site took on a sanctified status while the ceremony itself was perceived as a ritual of sealing a sacred covenant between the children and the land. The landscape, the trees, the birds, the flowers, the fruits—all were personified and represented by the children-performers. An attempt was made to make the ceremony festive and colorful by means of the costumes and the musical accompaniment. Verses from the Bible and from Hebrew poetry were inserted into the text, which was performed as a dialogue between the audience and the participants, with the audience responding after the declarations by the announcer and the participants. Branches of the almond tree, whose white blossoms symbolized the festival, were added to the palm branches; these were used in other ceremonies as well.

A rich repertoire of folk songs was written and composed for the Tu biShevat festival, some of them commissioned, expressing the *Sitz im Leben* character of the holiday and its message. The TC published a collection of extracts from the Jewish literary tradition about trees and new songs that were written for the occasion. The children's poet Zeev (Aharon Zeev, 1900–78) wrote:

> I did not sing to you, my country,
> I did not glorify your name with acts of heroism,
> with battles galore.
> My hands have merely planted a tree
> A tree I planted
> On Arbor day
> In my small garden, I bent down to the earth
> And speaking softly, said:
> You and I
> Are linked forever
> In the fragile seedling
> May it sprout and grow.

In the city, too, tree planting was regarded as important not merely because of the dominant ideology of the "return to the land," "to nature," and rural life. Tel Aviv, in the eyes of its founders, was thought to be a "garden city," or "city of gardens," a city that attributed importance and value to its greenery—gardens, parks, and boulevards. The municipality and the school system did their utmost to nurture the urban green space. Here, for example, are two popular (folk) songs written for this purpose:

> I planted a tree in Tel Aviv opposite the sea and the light
> And my blessing to it says
> Make a branch, spread shade about
> And I will pray: Dear Lord
> Protect the tree and the city.

> In the city and the village
> Awake child, get up
> Go out to the valley and the hill
> With green seedlings

It seems that Tu biShevat, perhaps more than any other national holiday (except the Festival of the First Fruits [Shavuot]), expressed the changed attitude of Jewish society to open space. Not only did it symbolize the new bonds to the land, soil, and landscape but it also reflected the fact that Jewish public space existed outside the synagogue, or the restricted Jewish quarter, and that Jewish society controls this public space and reshapes it.

Chapter 6

The 11th of Adar—Tel-Hai Day

As we saw earlier, this holiday marking the death of Yosef Trumpeldor (1880–1920) and his comrades at Tel-Hai in the Upper Galilee on March 1, 1920, was the first national memorial day to emerge in modern Jewish Eretz-Israel. In schools it was observed by a cultic ceremony that endowed the death of the Tel-Hai defenders with a symbolic meaning, expressing Trumpeldor's place in the new national pantheon of heroes and making him and his comrades the first new martyrs and the chief martyrs of the national movement.[38] The story of the incident at Tel Hai became an heroic legend, even a myth—an event that symbolized and embodied the ethos and the historical narrative of modern Jewish colonization.

As to the performative side of the ceremony, it included a memorial service, during which the participants stood on a dark stage, lit only by a single red candle, symbolizing the place of Tel-Hai on the map of the country. The performers mounted the stage, with torches and sandbags (symbolizing defense) and read several texts (including the "lamentation of David"). Then a trumpet blast was heard, the flag was lowered to half-mast, memorial candles were lit and black ribbons were placed at their feet. Then the entire audience stood for a moment of silence.

The second part of the ceremony included a short play in which one character represented Tel Hai and another a *shomer*, a defender of the land; they both conducted a dialogue with the audience, which evoked the attributes of a vow. The main symbols at the ceremony—other than the model of the "Roaring Lion" monument and memorial candles—were sandbags, a rifle and a shovel—symbolizing the combination of the military and work on the land.

The artistic committee of the TC suggested various versions for this ceremony in an effort to overcome the limited possibilities of dramatizing and staging the event and the messages it conveyed. Here is another example from a 1946 booklet written for the Labor stream of education:[39]

> Now for the ceremony itself. The parents and children assemble in the first room where they spend time viewing the material and looking through books quietly and soberly. A flute is heard (as the signal for the start of the ceremony). The children and parents arrange themselves in pairs. To the music of the flute, they proceed to the donation and insignia table. Each pins on the insignia and makes a donation to the Tel Hai enterprise. When the donation is completed, they stand at attention. The first pair receives the two flags (blue-and-white and red) in silence. The teacher recites a pledge, such as:

> We shall go and build,
> Make music and defend—
> Like Joseph the hero!
> Or:
> We shall grow a little bigger
> And heroes learn to be;
> To the Galilee we shall go,
> Jewish villages to build—
> Like Tel Hai!
> May it be so!

The children repeat the teacher's pledge, followed by the parents. Teacher: "The day has come, we are going to Tel Hai to build and protect it." The doors open, and a flute plays: "In the Galilee, at Tel Hai, Trumpeldor fell." Two by two, the children walk in and sit down to the music, followed by the parents (the children on the front benches and the adults behind). Only the children bearing the flags remain standing, one at each side of the picture of Trumpeldor standing beside a building at Tel Hai. At the signal, all stand. The parents sing the words of the popular song. When the song ends, the children place the flags in their stands beside the picture and take their seats. The teacher announces: "We have come to Tel Hai. . . . Let us listen to what the stone lion has to tell us."

What elements of the story will be told at the ceremony? Joseph's arrival in Palestine, Joseph's heroism, the rebuilding of Tel Hai. As a rule, the children greet each high point in the story with interjections and spontaneous singing of the appropriate song.

The story is followed by a dramatization by the children: settling, plowing, guarding, defense and construction (see the material for dramatization or games of movement and building in the pamphlet). When the children tire of their activities and construction—they sit down to rest. At this point, it is worthwhile to introduce a second opportunity for parent-child cooperation. One parent (there may be someone who was among the guards at Tel Hai and knew Joseph personally) should be prepared to relate his memories of that time in brief, simple words. This concludes with a song such as "From Eilat to Metulla," and everyone joins in singing. Silence. The teacher continues to explain the next step. She brings up the table on which the small gift pictures have been tastefully arranged on a platter or tray. To the music of one of the songs of the Galilee, each child comes forward and receives a picture of Joseph. The teacher adds a few words on how important it is to take good care of the picture as it is precious to us—"Try to be like him." They all return to their places. At the signal, all rise, hold up their pictures, and repeat the pledge in the same manner as before. With this, the ceremony concludes.

Purim

In the new Hebrew culture, the festival of Purim was given the form of a carnival and masquerade. As we shall see, it became the most important festival in the city's open-air arena. The TC did not develop a special form of festivity for Purim, since it regarded it as a part of Jewish life in the Diaspora. In contrast to Hanukkah, for example, which represents national heroism, Purim was perceived as representing the passiveness of Judaism in the Diaspora, always at the mercy of rulers and awaiting a miraculous redemption. Therefore the TC merely recommended that masquerades be held in schools.

The Passover Seder

Passover was also perceived by the TC as a Diaspora holiday, in the sense that in it too, the nation was redeemed—the Exodus from Egypt—through a miraculous act. However, it was impossible to overlook the central place this festival enjoyed in the Jewish calendar, symbolizing now both the Exodus of the Jewish people from slavery to freedom (analogous to the Zionist revolt against the Diaspora and immigration to Eretz-Israel, as well as the beginning of spring).

The TC did not propose that the schools hold a special collective Passover seder, and hence it did not initiate a new version of the *haggadah* for schools. Its celebration was composed only of pageants reconstructing the exodus from Egypt, in which a group of pupils took an active part as performers.[40] Besides the ideological inhibition, another reason for this is the fact that the traditional Passover seder is conducted around set tables and thus the options for new staging were very limited in the framework of the schools.

Lag Ba'Omer

In the Jewish tradition, this festival may have marked the start of the Jewish revolt against Roman rule (55 A.D.). In the sixteenth century a mass festivity at the grave of Rabbi Shimon bar Yohai in Meron near Safed, became a major event in the Jewish popular religion in Eretz-Israel. During the 1880s, the custom of lighting bonfires began there, commemorating the lighting of flares to signal the outbreak of the revolt. In the twentieth century, it was attributed to the outbreak of the Bar Kochba revolt against the Romans (132 A.D.) and was celebrated mainly by hikes outside of the towns and villages and by making toy bows and arrows and playing games with them. In the course of time, it became a folk festival celebrated spontaneously by groups of children.

The development of the festival in Eretz-Israel is connected with the new place—corresponding to the historical event—that the Bar-Kochba revolt gained in the modern historical collective memory. Together with the wars of the Maccabees, this revolt against Roman rule became a pillar in the national narrative. It was perceived as a national heroic event which, rather than the destruction of the Second Temple, symbolizes the end of Jewish statehood in Eretz-Israel. A rich repertoire of stories and songs was written for it, centering on the figure of the leader of the revolt—Shimon Bar Kochba.[41]

The TC turned Lag Ba'Omer into a memorial ceremony, conducted outside the school, or in the schoolyard. The pupils came to the site in a line carrying torches, with which they lit the bonfire. Once it was lit, the pupils stood at attention, a memorial service was held, followed by the pupils dancing around the bonfire. During the dancing, the "dance of the wall," was carried out, in which the children held each other's hands, to depict a "wall" [the defensive wall] as a symbol of national unity.

Again, it is quite clear that in contrast to the central place that was assigned to the myth of Bar Kochba revolt, it gained importance in the realm of the texts and not in the performative realm. Its cultic ceremonies were mainly spontaneous acts and not organized staged ceremonies.

The Festival of the First Fruits [Shavuot]

In Jewish tradition, this festival was celebrated in the Temple in Jerusalem as part of the pilgrimage on Shavuot. It was associated with the bringing of the first fruits (bikurim) to the Temple. The Sages linked it to the Giving of the Law and it became the Festival of the Giving of the Law.[42] This festival had no ritual expression in tradition after the Destruction of the Temple, but over the ages various customs became associated with it in folk culture: the eating of dairy meals, decorating the home and the synagogue with greenery, and the like.[43]

In modern Eretz-Israel, the festival lost its religious meaning and became an agricultural festival par excellence; an innovation opposed by the religious circles. The festival was adapted to the agricultural season (the time of the harvest) and its symbols were linked with nature and agriculture. In the texts written for this festival, its link to the giving of the Torah was noted, but the ceremony itself expressed only its connection to nature. The festival was celebrated in the schools as well as in the general local public space—and the ceremony was conducted before a large audience in both rural and urban settlements. One of the innovations of the Hebrew school in Eretz-Israel was the study of agriculture, which included the school garden, tended by the pupils as part of their agriculture lessons. Much effort was expended to grow the first fruits for the festival in the school garden, but in most cases the children brought these from their homes.

The 1929 TC staging instructions prescribed that the ceremony be held outside in a natural setting. Every settlement decided where its "first fruits field" would be located, and a large gate, decorated with greenery, was placed at the entrance to that field. The schoolchildren came carrying baskets of fruits and vegetables, dressed in festive clothing, their heads adorned with wreaths of greenery. A choir of pupils stood on the stage, which was decorated with greenery. The ceremony commenced with a trumpet blast and the singing of the choir. Then the children waved their baskets of fruit and recited a suitable verse. Afterward, the baskets were placed at the foot of the stage to the sound of trumpet blasts.

A more elaborate version was developed in 1937: In the middle of the "first fruits field" a stage was constructed, on which there was a tower with a flagpole, decorated with flags and the seven species. Around the stage there were seven gates adorned with greenery and symbols of the seven species. The children were divided into several groups; "the bearers of the first fruits," dressed in white, wearing white skullcaps and adorned with wreaths of greenery and flowers. Every pair of children carried a basket filled with first fruits. Children wearing striped robes and holding shepherds' staffs, walked at the head of each group of "bearers of first fruits." The "arts" welcomed the bearers of first fruits, wearing colorful dresses. The girls carried drums and symbols. Standing on the stage were: the "priests," recipients of the first fruits, a group of trumpeters decorated with flags of the seven species, dancers ["the daughters of Zion"], each holding a sickle and a bunch of sheaves of wheat, and each wearing a belt of greenery and flowers. The director of the ceremony and the choirmaster also stood on the stage and a scout stood on the tower.

The ceremony had sixteen parts: the bringers of the first fruits enter, accompanied by choral singing, drums and cymbals, the first fruits are carried up to the gates, the first fruits are handed over. The ceremony is accompanied by dances, meticulously choreographed, the reading of texts by the chorus, and so forth.

The purpose of this staging was to give the ceremony a serious and festive nature, but the texts were long and flowery and the staging cumbersome. Consequently, this version of the ceremony was not very successful. Other, more successful ceremonies had a simpler structure. In these, the children came to school dressed in white, with wreaths of flowers on their heads, holding baskets of fruit. The procession of bringing the first fruits took place inside the school, in the hall or in the classrooms.

The plays written for the festival contained distinctly pagan elements, including a sort of "ritual dance," and a reconstruction of the harvest time based on the Book of Ruth. But the main message was the triumph of the Jewish spirit over the spirit of idolatry and the social significance of the Torah laws.

The public character of the festival was manifested in the ceremonies organized by the TC in the various cities, towns and villages. In Tel Aviv, for example, they were held in a large public area, with the participation of thousands of schoolchildren. A new custom was added to this ceremony: white doves bearing various greetings were released into the air to symbolically convey greetings from the Yishuv in Eretz-Israel to the Jews of the Diaspora. The instructions stated that the "delivery ribbon" would be a narrow strip of cloth, about 15 centimeters in length, tied in a loop around the dove's neck, and that a greeting would be written on the ribbon with an ordinary pen. The doves were freed, as the senders called out to them to fly to the Diaspora. They represented the Jewish people, the redemption, and the dove that Noah released from the ark, and were asked to return from their flight to the Diaspora, bringing all the Jews with them to Eretz-Israel.

It is interesting to note the important function of the gates in organizing the stage of the spectacle. The gate was a clear allusion to the gates of Jerusalem and the gates of the Temple and their role in the pilgrimages (as well as in Psalms). The gate was intended to symbolically separate temporal space from festive space.

The 20th of Tammuz—Memorial Day for Herzl and Bialik

The memorial ceremonies for the founder of the Zionist movement, Benjamin Zeev Herzl (who died on the 20th of Tammuz, 5664 [1904]) and the national poet, C. N. Bialik (who died on the 21st of Tammuz, 5694 [1934]) were held on the 20th of Tammuz, which became the memorial day for the fathers of the national and cultural revival. The ceremony was held in the schoolyard at dusk. Enough wood for two bonfires was piled up, and between the two piles there was a flagpole flying the national flag. The ceremony opened with a trumpet blast and the declaration that it was a memorial day. The flag was lowered to half-mast, and after the singing of HaTikvah and Yizkor, two pupils, holding a torch in one hand and a book (Herzl's *The Jewish State* and Bialik's *Collected Writings*) in the other, came forward and lit the bonfire. By the light of the fire, excerpts from the writings of the two men were read aloud, "vows" were proclaimed, and the ceremony ended with a trumpet blast and the raising of the flag to full mast.

The verbal aspect of the ceremony combined traditional texts (including the Kaddish prayer) and modern texts with new visual elements: a bonfire, torches, a flag, trumpet blasts, and standing at attention.

The Functions and Meaning of the Schools' Ceremonies

We have presented only a few of the various versions proposed as a basis for the staging of the festival ceremonies in kindergartens and schools in Eretz-Israel during the Mandatory period. The short history of the implementation of the new calendar along with its new texts and the staging rules designed for it, shows that whenever an attempt was made to stage long, complicated texts, this was met with only partial and brief success. Over time, many elements disappeared, leaving a core of simple staging. This core was to a large extent shared by all children in the Yishuv.

The festivities and their ceremonies were intended to create an alternative to the traditional festivals while still based on some parts of these, on one hand, and creating new festivals, on the other. The Bible and modern Hebrew literature were a centerpiece of these ceremonies. Even in ceremonies held in the cities, agricultural symbols were given a central status. The organized, stylized, formalistic nature of the festivals in schools was deliberately intended as an antithesis to the unplanned aspect of Jewish society, and was also meant to realize the ideology according to which the new Jewish society should have compulsory order and rules of behavior and avert anarchy and division—the negative aspect of spontaneity. This principle was also countered by criticism that the formalistic nature of the ceremonies spoiled the simple joy and experience of the people, and hence would prevent the festivals from becoming a popular asset.

The critics preferred short, simple ceremonies. The TC, in contrast, believed that the ceremony and its quasi-ritual dimension would become an emotional experience, imprinted in the students' memory, and would convey values and symbols, only if it had a stylized, well-organized character. In the course of time, the former approach prevailed, because it took much difficult effort to organize complex ceremonies—the preparation of scenery, costumes, rehearsals, and the like. The stylized, formalistic ceremonies also alienated the participants from the audience, and over time became an object of parody. What remained later was mainly the repertoire of songs specially written for them.

Both the text and the staging instructions were written by a small number of writers or "stagers," but in each school there was at least one person tasked with implementing these instructions. These teachers served as the local stagers; it was their responsibility to take the guidelines and turn them into a performance. When some of these ceremonies were performed outside the schools, in the communal space, these teachers also became community stagers, and the parents' involvement in organizing the festivities made them active partners too. The common version of the ceremony and the public nature of some of the festivals made the TC, and the teachers following its guidelines, creators and stagers of culture in the center of the stage of the new Hebrew culture. The TC meetings dealt with organizational matters, assessments of previous celebrations and possible improvements. In this way, this group of entrepreneurs succeeded in making holidays a major item on the agenda of the educational system and in bringing about a large degree of centralization and uniformity. This group then played a major role in creating both formal popular culture and national feasts. In other words, they created the festive lore of the new Jewish society in Eretz-Israel.

In the literature concerning the meaning and functions of historical collective memory and of national traditions, a central role was assigned to myths and festivals distinctly historical-national in nature, such as Hanukkah (commemoration of the Maccabean revolt) and Lag Ba'Omer (commemoration of the Bar Kochba revolt). However, the key status granted to festivals like Tu BiShevat and the Feast of First Fruits, which were not linked to national heroic events, along with their elaborate staging, shows that the collective historical memory of the Jewish society in Eretz-Israel was more complex and multi-layered than the literature would have us believe. The lore of festivals and ceremonies in schools and the modes of their staging shows that the identity of the new Jewish society, and the official popular culture within it, was multifaceted.

7

The Urban Stagers and the Town as an Open-Air Stage

Tel Aviv: The First Hebrew City as a Public Stage

The use of the city as a stage for festivities, ceremonies and the activity of stagers has both advantages and disadvantages. On one hand, it has a large number of spectators, squares, and streets, and the organizations and institutions operating in it have financial resources. It also has an artistic community of writers, artists, theater people and the like—both amateurs and professional. On the other hand, the city's inhabitants are a stratified and sometimes multicultural population, whose diverse interests and values preclude the organicity and intimacy of the rural society and limit the authority over the populace. In any event, the advantages outweighed the disadvantages, and the city became a central stage for public ceremonies, processions and festivals, which fulfilled varying functions in the organization of urban life.

City processions, ceremonies, and carnivals are "statements unfurled in the streets, through which the city represents itself to itself."[1] Through them the city presents itself, and its self-image, to outsiders, trying to create (often even fabricate) a unique urban personality. The performative scene of the city is manifested in the way residents perceive their city's place within the more general (national) context, the nature of urban society, and the way its real and metaphorical boundaries are fixed. The city is perceived as having a distinct "personality," "identity," and "soul," and not merely as a place of residence in which anonymity rules. It is important, therefore, to shape this "personality" by creating an urban lifestyle and rhythm, in order to fix the boundaries of the city within the outside space, as well as to establish its inner geography. Urban festivals, ceremonies, and rituals are an integral part of the character and personality of a city.

We will deal here mainly with the city of Tel Aviv, since it was the central Jewish urban environment in modern Eretz-Israel. We will focus on the key festivities, since we can reconstruct their staging process. Since Tel Aviv had the largest number of schools and pupils, the festivities in the schools (described in the previous chapter) were an inseparable part of the city's ceremonial and holiday life and parents formed the audience at many of these events.

Almost from its first days, the city of Tel Aviv was aware of the need to shape both its urban lifestyle and its image by various means, including the designation of the city open-air (outdoor) space as a public performative site. Open-air urban culture was perceived as a means of creating the urban physical space and of enforcing and demonstrating the solidarity of urban society. While in Zionist historical writings we can find very frequently the view that it was in the rural environment that national culture, including popular culture, was created, the fact remains that the city was the center of cultural creativity in every sphere, and it was a central, even ideal, setting for experimentation with official folk culture. Whereas Jewish residents in American towns (New York, for example), conducted occasional parades,[2] in Tel Aviv, the Jewish control over the urban public sphere provided both the need and the opportunity to create a new urban lifestyle. Since Tel Aviv had no monumental buildings, historical monuments, or wide squares, it was the festivals that created a temporary ceremonial ("sacred") topography.

What Made Tel Aviv a "Hebrew City"?

Tel Aviv was named "the first Hebrew city" because it was the first urban settlement established by Jews in Eretz-Israel in the modern era, all of its residents were Jews, and the dominant language in its public and cultural life was Hebrew. The suburb, and later the city, were managed from the start by a township council, elected by general elections, and its urban-community lifestyle was democratic and modern. As a result, the city of Tel Aviv was a modern, sovereign, democratic Jewish urban community; it was almost a "Jewish state in the making." Alter Droyanov (1870–1938), Tel Aviv's first historian, wrote about this, saying that the Jewish community in Jaffa, "could not celebrate this Hebrew festival [Purim] in the Arab city (Jaffa)." Needless to say, Droyanov knew precisely what was special about the character of the urban-public space insofar as organizing and staging festivities and ceremonies in it were concerned. Only in Tel Aviv could the urban community turn the urban space into a stage for ceremonies and festivities. Only in Tel Aviv could an active group of stagers emerge, engaging in stage and set design, and in the creation of open-air collective performances. The urban festivals, particularly the Purim festival, reflected the way the stagers, as well as "the city," perceived the nature of Zionism and various historical and political events; it expressed a wide range of symbols and icons, and reflected the high esteem in which art and artistic products were held. City festivities were, in a sense, a public open-air and artistic dramatized representation of both the "real" Jewish reality in Eretz-Israel and its self-image and even its daydreams.

Founded in 1909 as a modern Jewish suburb of Arab Jaffa, in 1921, Tel Aviv became a municipality, independent of Jaffa, and later, in 1934, a township. In the eyes of its residents, however, it was a city right from the start, the ideal combination of a Jewish-Hebrew city and a modern European-style city transplanted in the East with all its major institutions (public library, art museum, theater, opera, etc.)[3] The rate of the city's demographic growth (which was entirely Jewish) was unprecedented: in 1921 it had 3,604 inhabitants, in 1933, 80,000, in 1937, 150,000, and in 1948, 220,000. In 1922, about 18 percent of the Jews in Eretz-Israel lived in it, and this percentage grew in 1946 to 30 percent. It became the metropolitan urban center of the entire Yishuv from public, economic-commercial, and cultural standpoints.

This rapid urban growth met with harsh criticism from different circles opposing urbanization, which they considered utterly antithetical to the dominant ethos and ideology of Zionism, which viewed agricultural settlement as the essential basis of Jewish society. This criticism came mainly from the spokesmen of the labor movement, many of whom were residents of the city (or of other urban communities). Despite this, they perceived the city according to their anti-urban orientation and principles, viewing this rapid growth as artificial, even dangerous, inducing most Jewish immigrants to choose city life and attracting Jewish private capital, the investors preferring the city economy. Urban lifestyle was regarded by these critics as "artificial," based on imitating "external" cultural fashions, such as "Warsaw fashions," or "Odessa fashions"—that is, the lifestyle and manners adopted by the Jewish-Russian, or Polish-Russian bourgeoisie and petit bourgeoisie.[4] Another negative image was that the new city was becoming a "Levantine-Oriental" city.[5]

In contrast to this anti-urban stance, others formulated a pro-urban position, and fostered a sense of urban patriotism, portraying the city as one of the major achievements of the Zionist endeavor in Palestine. Others even nurtured a sense of urban motherland, or *Heimat*, with which the residents had deep emotional ties. Tel Aviv was described as a Jewish metropolis and the center of modern Hebrew culture. But texts praising Tel Aviv were not sufficient, and thus urban patriotism and solidarity supplied the performative dimension and regular open-air performances were staged, aimed to demonstrate the central place of urban life in modern Eretz-Israel and to express the role of the city as a center of the public (nationwide) stage. The staging of public events and various public ceremonies played an important role in the effort to foster civic-municipal pride, and to strengthen solidarity within the different social sectors of the urban community. Urban leaders and cultural entrepreneurs saw the city as a setting in which a distinct, national, Jewish urban culture could be nurtured. In other words, they believed that the city—not only the village—was a proper setting for the creation of an authentic modern national Hebrew culture.

Just as important, the city itself was a central "hero" in these performances. These aimed to underscore the national and metropolitan character of the city and to elevate its importance and prestige. It local history, heroes, and images became an integral part of the performative repertoire.

The municipality was very conscious of the importance of open-air public culture, and was involved in organizing and staging various city-wide public ceremonies. These events included organizing the visits of high-ranking guests, inaugurating public buildings, and holding various festivities as well as mourning and memorial ceremonies. The municipality's policy was to celebrate as many events as possible by holding a ceremony or a festivity, in order to imbue them with symbolic significance. As a result, the city's streets and some of its squares became stages for festivals, processions, and parades. The fact that Tel Aviv was a large urban community was perceived as a vital prerequisite for the creation of such a culture. It could also utilize its large population of schoolchildren as performers, since most of the schools were under the municipality's administration. As a result of the city's urban development, relatively long, paved streets were available that could serve as a stage for parades and carnivals. Several large playing fields were also available, including, first and foremost, a large sports stadium—the Maccabee Stadium—in northern Tel Aviv, near the Yarkon River, which was built in 1934.

Since Tel Aviv was the economic and commercial center of Eretz-Israel, many economic and commercial organizations—private and public—contributed money to finance the production of public ceremonies. In 1929, for example, Mayor Meir Dizengoff (1861–1936) appealed to the city's merchants to contribute to the festivities, arguing that cities interested in tourism organize public festivities, which bring commercial prosperity in their wake.[6] The municipality itself did its share as well by erecting suitable scenery for the festivities, including decorated gates, flags, greenery, candelabra, and colored lighting on public buildings.

Several factors, then, combined to make Tel Aviv this center of performative culture: the nature of the municipal public space and the feasibility of choosing and preparing a suitable site, on one hand, and on the other, the city leadership's awareness of the importance of creating an urban cycle of festivals and public events. They understood that these should be held outdoors at fixed dates, and that their organization must not be spontaneous, or left to individual entrepreneurs.

In many urban societies, public festivals and carnivals are structured by the local middle class.[7] This holds true in the case of Tel Aviv. The city was one of those modern cities whose open-air culture was designed and constructed by the local middle class with the assistance of business people and elements of the professional community. However, representatives of the working class were among the organizers, workers took active part in the performances, and they were among the crowd. Moreover, a central part of the symbolic lore of the ceremonies was devoted to symbols representing the value attributed to work and to agricultural settlements. Thus Tel Aviv's festivities were both a local-urban event and a national statement.

Furthermore, in the case of Tel Aviv, the middle class did not act simply in accordance with a class ideology, commercial interests, or urban local patriotism; its actions were taken in keeping with the overall spirit of the aims, ethos, and symbolism of the national ideology, which were not urban-orientated in nature.[8]

City of Festivities

Owing to all this, Tel Aviv, almost from its inception, acquired the image of a bustling city, filled with outdoor public events and performances, both spontaneous and organized.

In her book *Ben haKramim,* Yehudith Harari (1885–1979), a teacher and one of the first residents of Tel Aviv, describes the city during its first twenty-five years (1909–34) as a young city with a vibrant outdoor life, in which Hebrew festivals took on a new form; as a place where the festivals "renew themselves through contact with nature and the natural life emanating from it [the city]."[9] This is how she describes a Tu biShevat procession held before World War I: "All boundaries, all borders have been transcended. . . . We draw upon each other, we are brethren, we are Hebrews. The procession draws closer to Ahuzat Bayit,[10] and from all sides, from all the lanes, people throng to join it . . . the festivity begins. It was just a taste of jubilation, Hebrew merry-making, life bursting forth, without any order, without any plan, people throwing flowers and festoons at one another."

According to this recollection, urban space and landscape were ideal and pure "nature," no less so than rural space and landscape. Moreover, in these ideal recollections, ceremonies are perceived as a social-collective act able to transcend the social (and cultural) boundaries between residents. Many other recollections of this period depict Tel Aviv as a "joyous city," or as a "city of theater" whose streets served as an arena for regular festivities, parades and carnivals; a city whose residents exploited their complete control over the public-urban space in order to turn it into a new performative arena. As an example, the following is a description of urban life in the twenties and thirties by Gila Oriel, who for many years was the secretary of Mayor Meir Dizengoff: "Tel Aviv of those days was a city of joyous occasions and festivities. On Purim there was a colorful carnival in which thousands of celebrants took part.... On Hanukkah, processions of schoolchildren would march through the main streets, carrying burning torches in their hands. The sight of these children in their holiday best, bearing torches, was both invigorating and thrilling."[11]

In his novel *Yemot haMaschiach* (*Days of the Messiah*, 1938), author J. D. Berkowitz (1885–1967) describes the Purim festivities in Tel Aviv in the second half of the 1920s, as seen through the eyes of a Jewish tourist from the United States. To the tourist, the Tel Aviv Purim carnival looked meager and provincial, but also was filled with real collective-public joyousness. What he found most moving was the fact that the Jewish festival was "celebrated in public," and expressed "Jewish joy ringing out in the open, *in the main streets*" (our emphasis).[12] Berkowitz stresses the fact that Tel Aviv provided the Jewish public, for the first time, a large free urban open space and gave the stagers a public stage on which to mount open-air ceremonies.

It should be noted that in Berkowitz's description, the joy of Purim is perceived as primarily spontaneous, not as an organized celebration. In fact, as we shall see, like any carnival, the Purim festivities in Tel Aviv were organized events, and their staging was meticulously planned. Many private and public entities, including commercial firms, participated in the planning, organization, and production. However, without the financial and organizational aid of the municipal authority, it would not have been possible to carry out the public performances.

The perception of Tel Aviv as a "city of festivities," or as "a city of joyousness" led some of its critics to describe the city as flooded with a "plague of festivities": "For several days each and every year, how much money and energy do we waste on these 'festivities,' on this drawn-out Purim festival? ... And how much *deception* both internal, and even more so, external, pervades all of these 'festivities.' Internally, they are a source of vanity imaging, outwardly, they are a stumbling block before the blind. . . . Why should you, the hungry and grieving, disguise yourselves as satiated bridegrooms?"[13]

After 1936, there were fewer outdoor activities. The "Arab Revolt" (1936–38 riots), followed by the years of World War II and the tense years of the Yishuv's struggle against British policy (1945–48), did not provide an appropriate background for open-air festivities, and indeed the performative public activity declined. Naturally, there is much exaggeration in the depiction of Tel Aviv as a city of joy or of festivities; however, since the time of the destruction of the Second Temple there had been no other location that embraced the cultural nature of the outdoor urban life as did Tel Aviv.

The Urban Stagers

Tel Aviv was, then, from its inception, an open-air stage awaiting its stagers. The initiative came at first from individuals, who were assisted by the municipality (as well as by public organizations such as the JNF), but very soon the organization of ad hoc committees became regular and institutionalized. The large number of teachers, artists, theater people, writers, men of letters, composers, and the like living in the city was another factor behind the emergence of a group of stagers, who regarded the city as a public cultural stage and were active throughout the period by staging various events on this stage.

The archives of the Tel Aviv Municipality contain documentation, albeit not systematically arranged, on the work of the various ad hoc committees that organized festivities and ceremonies in the city during the 1920s and 1930s. The archives mostly consist of brief minutes and summaries of the committees' meetings and decisions. They show that much attention was devoted both to the overall structure and the ordering of each festival, seeking to formulate a program characterized by "order as well as quality." These committees were made up of senior representatives of the municipal council, teachers, authors, and artists, as well as representatives of the JNF and the municipal police.

These ad hoc committees corresponded with the various concerned bodies, dealt with details (location, tickets, order of the performances, organization of the audience, preparation of the props, recruitment of performers, etc.), and publicized the programs in a special publication. Every single event of a public nature that took place in the city was preceded by thorough planning. For example, the visit of the British elder statesman Lord Arthur Balfour to Tel Aviv on March 26, 1925, at which time he was made an honorable citizen of the city, was meticulously planned. An ad hoc committee, set up to organize the visit, decided on the route he would travel, prepared flags to decorate the streets, decided who would be among those receiving the guest, designed the structure of the gates of honor, and put together the program for the ball to be held in his honor (he came to Palestine to attend the inauguration ceremony of the Hebrew University on Mt. Scopus in Jerusalem). The council also allocated a certain sum of money to members of the Maccabee sports association to enable them to purchase special uniforms for the reception (50 Egyptian pounds which was equivalent to about 50 pounds sterling).[14] Similar preparations were made for every visit by an important personality—Zionist or otherwise—whose visit to the city became a municipal event.

Over the course of time, those engaged in organizing festivals gained experience and became more proficient, and some of the festivities became logistically complicated affairs.

The main figures involved in organizing public festivities in the city during the first period of its performative life were two teachers from the Herzliya gymnasium: Dr. Chaim Harari, and Avraham Aldema (Eisenstein, 1884–1963), an art teacher at the Herzliya gymnasium. Harari, we will recall, studied in Paris and Switzerland, took a study tour through Italy, and was very impressed by the annual carnivals held in various cities. His wife, Yehudith Harari, relates that he invested enormous efforts "to endow national festivals with new content and imposing form," adding that "he devoted many hours of his time at the gymnasium to days of commemoration, mourning and celebration."[15] Aldema was sent in 1909 by the Herzliya gymnasium authorities to Switzerland to pursue higher studies in pedagogical art. Another key figure in organizing the Tel Aviv festivities was Barukh Agadati (Koschinsky, 1895–1976), a pioneer of modern dance in Eretz-Israel and creator of the first Hebrew full-length speaking movie. Inspired by the Nice carnival (whose history goes back to the middle of the nineteenth century),[16] Agadati began, in 1921, to organize Purim balls held in various halls, during which a queen of the ball was chosen and crowned as Queen Esther. In 1929, Agadati organized a parade of the participants at the ball, which was added to the municipal Purim festivities, turning them into a municipal carnival. Various artists and theater people, residents of Tel Aviv, arranged the artistic side of the performances in these festivities.[17]

At first, Aldema and Harari shaped the memorial days and festivals for the gymnasium, and later for the entire city. Aldema recalls that in 1912 he concluded that Purim should be celebrated in organized festivities, and he then organized the first Purim parade in Tel Aviv. He prepared masks that represented various scenes from the Bible or the life of the country (Mordechai on a horse, Jephthah's daughter and her female companions, David with Goliath's head, and the like). The parade left the gymnasium's yard and went through the main street of the suburb (Herzl Street). According to his memoirs, this parade made a huge impression, and Meir Dizengoff, then head of the suburb committee, invited him to thank him and promised him financial aid for the organization of the following year's carnival.[18]

In May 1913, Aldema and his colleagues asked the permission of the municipal council of the new suburb to organize a public open-air flower festival on Shavuoth. They proposed a procession of children adorned with flowers on Nahalat Benyamin St., one of the main thoroughfares. Decorated gates would be erected in the street and the procession would be accompanied by trumpet blasts. They stated: "The close link between the festival and freshness so appeal to all our hearts, for we all want to create a natural, healthy life here. And the aesthetic side of the festival too, the competition between greenery and flowers—all this introduced such an invigorating fresh quality into our poor, dull lives, at least for the moment."[19] The reaction of the council was negative; it argued that it would be difficult to maintain public order. Aldema responded by stating that although it would be difficult to arrange the participation of all the suburb's residents in the festival, it was not impossible, provided the committee would grant the required assistance.

In the second period, the post–World War I years, and up until 1936, the municipal authorities, and later the city council, became more and more involved in organizing public festivity. Before the 1926 Purim festival, the city council in conjunction with the JNF was established to organize it for the first time. Its budget was allocated by the city council, the JNF and various public and private bodies.[20] The committee was charged with the task of preparing the festivities program, planning the decoration of the city, advising those preparing pageants, and deciding on the order of the carnival procession. It convened every Friday at noon. An indication that the municipality was greatly involved in organizing the festivities is the fact that its Secretary, Yehudah Nadivi (1899–1981) was sent in the winter of 1928 to visit the annual Oktoberfest in Munich (Germany), to learn how to organize a city carnival.[21] Nadivi brought back much material from Germany about the Oktoberfest and other various local carnivals, which he provided the ad hoc committee. Upon returning from his tour, on February 9, 1929, he wrote to the committee: "Enclosed is material that will help you in your work of preparing the carnival program."[22] Influenced by this material, the committee decided to hold a three-day carnival on Purim, which would include, on the third day, the coronation ceremony of a "Queen Esther," which began as a private initiative. The members of the committee for Purim Projects believed that proper organization of the ceremony would prove the city's capability of producing and implementing popular festivities, bringing it prestige. If the festivities were a success, the members declared, this would also show the city as a controlled, organized space, and that its society developed local patriotism as an integral part of modern Jewish-Hebrew nationalism. The Committee for Purim Projects suggested that: "A group of artists and engineers should be assigned the task of finding the right artistic ways to combine all of these individual impressions, turning the thousands of pictures into one ensemble of a flourishing city, in the throes of creative endeavor, dipped in a sea of colors and electric splendor—a complete portrait of artistic enterprise."[23]

The committee also decided to expand the festivities, making it a two-day event, with an investment of 250 Palestine £ (about 259 £).[24] At the end of 1929, Dizengoff wrote to various artists in the city asking them to join in the organization of the next Purim festival:

> As you know, every year we hold a Purim carnival in Tel Aviv with various parades. This carnival attracts large numbers of people, but to our regret, we must admit that last year it had no content, neither historical nor artistic. I would be very glad if you would agree to introduce a theme into the carnival, something that would satisfy every requirement, insofar as art, beauty and history are concerned. It would be a good idea, for example, if we could arrange parades based on the Holy Scriptures, the Bible and Jewish history in general. There were some suggestions to organize parades with the theme of Miriam,[25] Deborah the prophetess, and the like. Others suggested a scene based on the motif "Sun, stand still at Gibeon and moon in the Valley of Ayalon" or "Moses on Mt. Nevo."
>
> Therefore, I would like to immediately set up a committee for this purpose. it must be composed of artists, writers, theater people as well as others who know something of aesthetics and similar matters.[26]

This letter suggests that various proposals did not satisfy Dizengoff, who had therefore decided to try and establish an organizational committee, made up of the finest artistic talents in the city. It aimed to "improve the Purim carnival in Tel Aviv, making it more beautiful, artistic and to see that it was run better." The committee received various suggestions from the city's residents about the carnival's organization. The mayor's intensive involvement in the festive activity reflects his awareness of the significant functions that this festivity plays in the life of the city. There was also close cooperation between the municipality and the JNF and the TC. The latter made its contribution to the quality of the festivities when the teachers extended their activity inside the schools to the entire public urban space. In accordance with the committee guidelines, colored lights were installed in the main streets, and all the parks, and stores and public institutions were decorated. In addition, gates painted by important Tel Aviv artists using themes from the Book of Esther were placed at central locations.[27]

A committee was also appointed to prepare and organize the 1931 Purim festivities. It published a pamphlet titled *A Guide for the Festivities and the Carnival*, containing the program of the festivities, rules for the spectators' behavior, and a list of prizes.[28] Here, for the first time, we have a detailed list of the members of this committee. These were A. Aldema and J. Nadivi, whom we have already mentioned; Nahum Guttman (1898–1980), an artist and author, whose stories and paintings of Tel Aviv history created the "mythology" of the city from its beginnings; Moshe Halevi (1895–1974), a theatre director and founder (in 1925) of the Ohel workers theatre; Mordechai Namirovsky (Namir, 1897–1975) representative of the workers faction in the municipal council; David Zvi Pinkas (1895–1952), a member of the HaMizrachi party (the national religious party); and D. Gefen, A. Gerchlis, A. Kamini, J. Shihman and J. Shatzov. Moshe Halevi was in charge of the artistic organization, the artistic aspect was supervised by Nahum Guttman, and the scenery by Schifman (the city engineer). Another man who was active in organizing festivities from 1931 was the writer A. Z. Ben-Yishai (1902–77), the editor of the municipality's official newspaper, *Yedioth Tel Aviv* (*Tel Aviv News*).

Bialik, "the national poet," and the central figure of Tel Aviv's cultural life, was also very involved in the committee organizing the festivities and was an active member of the panel of judges for the competitions. Bialik ascribed much importance to popular festivities and their performative aspect.

From 1931 to 1935, the committee published a special "official newsletter" about the festivities which included poems and songs (music and lyrics) connected with the festival (the newsletter was briefly published again in the 1940s).[29] The songs emphasized the importance of Tel Aviv as the setting of the carnival. Here are two of the songs praising the city:

> Rejoice with a cheerful heart
> Tel Aviv and all its folk.
> Every plot in it, every part
> Into a blooming garden we will make.
> Blessed is he who strains and toils
> He who invests in the beloved city.
> Together we will make a twosome
> Of capital and labor
>   (Yehudah Karni, "Rejoice")

> In white, green and blue fine linen
> Clothe yourself, Tel Aviv.
> Riding on his father's shoulders
> Every child will call out hurray!
> (Y. Karni, "A Song for Purim")

Later testimonies by some of the stagers reveal the sources they emulated and the ideas that influenced the staging principles they proposed. Moshe Halevy, for example, regarded the parade as the heart of the carnival. He believed that a Jewish audience had no tradition of spontaneous joy (like the French or the Italians), and that therefore the carnival had to be an organized event.[30] The committee also underscored the need for order and discipline among the spectators who were asked to participate passively during the carnival parade, while the public at large could revel and express its joy in other activities, particularly dancing in the streets.

From the content of the Purim festivities, which we will describe later in this chapter, and the manner in which the parade was staged, it is obvious that the designers and stagers copied elements from other carnivals (the parade itself with the masked participants, the use of fireworks, confetti, flowers and the like), but they were also creative and original, and tried to combine traditional Jewish and modern national elements. In any event, despite the introduction of biblical motifs, or motifs from Jewish history, the Purim carnival was clearly a new, innovative element in the history of Jewish festival culture.

The Lore of Urban Ceremonies: Occasional Ceremonies

The municipality planned and held receptions, funerals, and memorial ceremonies in an attempt to present the city as an organized urban community. Gila Oriel writes that, "special celebrations were held in Tel Aviv on the occasion of visits by such important personages as Balfour and Rothschild; colored lights were strung along the streets and school children waved flags as well as flowers from the baskets they held."[31] We have seen that the visits of distinguished people to the suburb—and later, to the city—were indeed scrupulously planned, and great attention was paid to the "small," symbolic details.

An example of a festive ceremony that took place during the city's early years is the one held in honor of the first graduating class of the Herzliya gymnasium in 1913. The newspaper *HaHerut* described it as follows: "The ceremony began at eleven o'clock in the morning. Two large, beautiful flags flew at the main entrance: the blue and white national flag on the right, and the red

Ottoman flag on the left. At the door to the auditorium, on the top floor, a model of the gate of Jaffa,[32] made of green vine leaves, had been erected, with a picture of Herzl framed by a Star of David, also made of fresh grape leaves, adorning the top."[33]

The decorations and the organization of the ceremony were undoubtedly the work of the teachers of the gymnasium, headed by the previously mentioned Avraham Aldema. Reception ceremonies held for visiting dignitaries were also apparently organized by the same stagers.

The organization of mourning and memorial days, as well as the staging of the funerals of important people, provide additional examples of staged public events. Public funerals, organized by the city council, combined traditional content with a national message. All the funerals included a procession that passed through the streets of the city to the cemetery on Trumpeldor Street.

Another example of an organized urban festivity was the celebration of the twentieth anniversary of the founding of Tel Aviv on May 2, 1929. The order of the festivities, as it was established by the arrangements committee, was as follows: At 2:30 P.M. festivities were held in an open area in the center of Tel Aviv, during which a procession of schoolchildren, the city founders, and members of the city council walked onto the field, carrying torches. The procession made its way from the Herzliya gymnasium schoolyard through the main streets, surrounded by a chain of torches, and marched toward the illuminated municipality building. Residents were asked to decorate their homes with national flags, carpets, and the like, The city founders went up to the balcony where they were received by the orchestra playing Bialik's poem "Vatechazeknah," and fireworks were set off from the building's roof. At the end of the procession, a jubilee party was held, attended by schoolchildren and guest artists.[34]

We have records of a meeting called by the mayor to discuss the nature of the festivities marking Tel Aviv's twenty-fifth anniversary in April 1934. Among those invited to the meeting were Bialik, who suggested there be three days of carefully planned festivities that would present the city's accomplishments. Bialik also proposed declaring a national costume competition for men, women, and children that would also comprised of a combination of national and modern European elements. The outfits would be worn, if not throughout the entire year, then at least during the days of the festival, in the parades, and so on.[35]

Public sports events also became national-urban events, which were intended to underscore the importance of sports and physical education in the new culture, and to emphasize the fact that Tel Aviv was the center of Jewish sports. The major event was the Maccabiah—an international competition of Jewish athletes in all professional sports. The first Maccabiah was held in Tel

Aviv in March–April 1932, in a stadium built especially for this purpose in north Tel Aviv. The Tel Aviv municipality, organizer of the Maccabiah, staged an impressive opening ceremony that included a procession of the delegations (in which some four thousand athletes participated), carrying their flags through the streets of Tel Aviv, led by the mayor on horseback.

These various events all amounted to a demonstration of urbanity, an expression of the city's status and of autonomous Jewish rule over it, and of its status as a well-organized community with a unique urban culture.

Planning the Purim Carnival as a Street Theater and a Nationalfest

Tel Aviv was apparently the first space in which Jewish traditional festivals left the closed space of the home, the synagogue, or the assembly hall and went out into the urban open air.[36] As noted, parades along the city streets were organized for most festivals, each one designed to suit the spirit of the festival. At Hanukkah, for example, a procession of schoolchildren holding lit candles or torches was held along the city streets. The municipality added to the decorations by adorning the city's public buildings with menorahs (candelabras). Large crowds took part in the Hanukkah parades through the streets of Tel Aviv. In 1928, for example, some six thousand school children participated in the festival parade accompanied by the city police orchestra.[37]

On Tu biShevat, and on the Festival of the First Fruits, ceremonies based on the plan outlined by the TC were held, but they were city-wide events, not events held separately in each school. The planting on Tu biShevat took place in city gardens and groves, and the parade of planters proceeded along the streets on the their way to the planting site, with the children attired in festive clothing and wearing wreaths on their heads. Gates topped with palm fronds were sometimes erected in the open space, as in the festivals held in the schools. The planting itself was accompanied by a ceremony that included trumpet blasts, choral singing, dancing, and a display of masks connected to the festival. Although one might see in these plantings, which took place in the city, an expression of the ethos of planting as part of the ideology of the redemption of the land, we must remember that, from its inception, Tel Aviv wanted to be a city of gardens, and not a garden city. In other words, it wanted to be a city that had green spaces, and so we may consider these planting ceremonies an inseparable part of the "homeland" consciousness, urban style. In Tel Aviv, the Festival of First Fruits took on the character of a "festival of flowers," inspired by the tradition of flower festivals held in various European countries. Parades of kindergarten and schoolchildren bedecked with flowers were held. Over the years, the festival parade became more sophisticated, and included wagons and other vehicles decorated with greenery, flowers, and flags. The closing ceremony was held in a large public area and was similar to the ceremony of the presenting of first fruits.

In effect, these two festivals were celebrated according to patterns resembling those in the schools—but before a larger audience, and in public spaces. In any case, staging in both these festivals—Tu biShevat and Shavuot (the Festival of the First Fruits)—was limited, the participants were mainly schoolchildren, and most of the stagers were apparently school teachers. This was not the case with the Purim festivities.

The largest and most highly organized festival in the city was the Purim carnival, which became the festival that characterized Tel Aviv, and was even called "the Festival of Tel Aviv" and the city was named "the city of Shushan." It attracted many visitors from outside the city, so many that in the comic play titled "To the *Adloyada* in Tel Aviv," the flocking of guests to the city is described as follows: "Everything was canceled, gone from the world, and only Tel Aviv remained. We were in the plowing and sowing season, the planting season. There was much work to be done, there had been little rain, we were preoccupied with worry, and for them—Tel Aviv, the carnival, Purim parties! Babies in cradles and old men leaning on their canes—their hearts are all in Tel Aviv. I'm telling you, they've all gone mad."

As we have seen, the Purim carnival became an urban tradition which was sponsored by the municipality from 1929. In 1932, a special committee chose the name for the Purim carnival proposed by the writer, Shmuel Yosef Agnon: *Adloyada* (based on words from the Talmudic tractate, *Megillah* VII (*Ad de-lo yada*—"until one can no longer tell the difference"). Commissioned poets, composers, and choreographers were urged to create new works especially for the festival.

Purim was the most exile-oriented holiday of the Jewish festivals, commemorating a case of Jewish dependence upon the will of a Gentile ruler, but at the same time it expressed a restricted permissive spirit, far from becoming a Dionysian event. It was perceived as a holiday of joy, and in the course of the years, under the influence of Christian carnivals, Jews adopted the habit of wearing disguises and masks, and performing Purim theatrical shows (*Purim Schpiel*) and parodies. Actors used to parade from house to house ready to perform their plays.[38] That said, it was not these traditional parades that served as a historical precedent, and the Purim carnivals in Tel Aviv were a new innovation, based on the model of the European carnivals, but trying to give a distinctive modern Jewish-Hebrew character. In other words, both traditional costumes and modern costumes were borrowed. In Tel Aviv it became a mixture of folk ceremony and a city festival. "Carnivals," writes Abner Cohen, "are irreducible culture, but, like all other cultural forms, are seldom free of political significance. They range in their political functions from the maintenance of the established order, to serve as 'rituals of rebellion,' and the articulation of protest, resistance and violence against that order."[39] In Tel Aviv, the Purim carnival was used as a public opportunity for protest against the politics of the British government in Palestine, and also to lampoon the Yishuv institutions and the municipality. The atmosphere of the carnival was a combination of "Dionysian" elements and national symbols (some of which were mobilized for current political aims). In no case was there any fear that the carnival might diverge from the organized framework and turn into a wild, unrestrained event. Nor did it reflect in any way class distinctions, as often happened in other carnivals, both because of the national and local-urban nature of the Purim carnival and because unlike other modern cities, Tel Aviv did not have a poor proletariat on a large scale.

Purim festivals were large municipal productions that became increasingly more sophisticated over time. The municipality paid artists to decorate the city and build scenery (including painted gates inspired by the Book of Esther). The route of the carnival parade was lengthened, owing to the fact that Tel Aviv had spread northward during the 1930s, and the number of spectators reached tens of thousands. During the 1930s, the parade included displays with historical and current-satiric content. The municipality set up decorative lights and the organizing committee changed street names to names associated with Purim. The carnival temporarily transformed Tel Aviv into a street theater. After the parade, there was folk dancing in the street and a folk dance for the entire populace called the "Tel Aviviya," created especially for the occasion.

There were four stages in the development of the staging of the carnival in Tel Aviv. In 1923 the parade began with the reading of the Book of Esther in the Great Synagogue on Allenby Street. Members of the sports associations walked along the streets with torches and announced, to the blasts of a trumpet, the parade of "Queen Esther," who came to the city hall square on Bialik Street wearing royal garb and her crown. The municipal police orchestra welcomed her by playing a Purim song, and the mayor escorted her to the balcony overlooking the square, where he proclaimed her queen of the city.

The next day, the mayor, wearing a top hat and carrying a cane, led the parade on horseback, attended by mounted escorts. "Queen Esther" followed him in a decorated carriage driven by a man in blackface, and behind them came the rest of the characters of the Book of Esther, figures representing the tribes of Israel, and wagons carrying floats on relevant subjects. The costumes, decorations, and masks made the parade a very colorful one. This particular order was preserved throughout the period of the carnival's existence.

The program of the 1929 festivities and carnival, set up by the Organizing Committee for the Purim festivities and carnival, was far more ordered:

THE PROGRAM

Monday

7 PM—Bonfires at various points in the city to announce the opening of the festivities.

7 PM—HaPoel[40] in a comic parade with torches—public dancing in the streets.

7:30 PM—HaMaccabee[41] in a comic parade, with torches

7:30 PM—Tel Aviv mayor's official reception of 'Queen Esther' at city hall. . . . After being received, the 'Queen,' escorted by her honor guard, will leave city hall and return to her home

The police orchestra will play during the Queen's reception at city hall.

Tuesday

10 AM—A procession of kindergarten children, accompanied by the police orchestra and Brit-Trumpeldor.[42]

1 PM—HaMaccabee parade . . . mock-athletic parades will be held.

1:30 PM—Comic gymnastics by HaPoel.

2:30 PM—HaPoel in a comic parade . . . games, comic gymnastics and soccer matches.

3 PM—A parade of mothers with decorated baby carriages—the orchestra will play during the parade.

6 PM—Organized parades from the Maccabee and HaPoel fields.

Wednesday

9 AM—Foot race.

2 PM—The carnival.

2 PM—'Queen Esther' will appear with her entourage and honor guard. The parade, led by the Queen, will then pass through the streets. . . . At 48 Allenby Street, there will be public dancing to the music of an orchestra.

The organizing committee called on the public to maintain order and asked the city's residents to decorate their houses and places of business. It announced that prizes would be given to the most beautifully decorated building and to the participants in the carnival parade. Bialik and Dizengoff were among the judges.

The Adloyada, the Purim parade, of 1930 was canceled because of the August 1929 riots, in which scores of Jews were murdered by Arab rioters (particularly in Hebron). In subsequent years (1931–35), the carnivals became more organized and in effect developed into national festivities. During those years, the urban stagers had more means at their disposal than in previous years which they employed to organize rich, artistic, and colorful outdoor processions, attended by the masses, which also functioned to impart both national and local-urban messages.

In 1932 the committee scheduled a program that called for the festival to be opened by a group of trumpeters on the roofs of the houses lining the main streets. An "electric flame" lasting for five minutes would mark the opening of the festival. Two groups of criers, each led by an orchestra, would walk through the streets of the city, calling the public to the field where the opening would take place. The heralds would carry humorously decorated torches and signs with verses from the Book of Esther. The flag of the *Adloyada* would be carried at the head of the parade. Actors, a choir, and an orchestra would take part in the festive opening. The second day of the festivities would be a day of entertainment that would include a parade of babies (representing the future dimension of the Yishuv), a street concert, a strolling choir, mock boxing matches in the street, and folk dancing. Scheduled for the third day were a foot race, a bicycle procession, and the *Adloyada*.

In accordance with the committee's guidelines, electric lights were strung at various places, flags were hung from lampposts, and a gate of honor was erected. We also learn from the text of the program that the committee had reviewed a number of proposals regarding the nature of the costumes appearing in the carnival parade, and had chosen the ones it thought were the best.[43]

On January 29, 1934, the committee unanimously decided to take the position that no attempt should be made to arrange the festival, since, in its view "Either the festivities will be held or they won't be held. If they are held, they must be appropriate for a city in their form and their planning. The committee felt there was no need to discuss not holding the festivities, not only from the standpoint of the residents of the city and the country but also taking into account the fact that these festivities had already been widely publicized abroad."[44] As a result, a handbill was published titled "In Preparation for Purim," which stated that the Purim carnival in the city was intended to give the Jewish residents of the city—and the country—three days of entertainment and holiday joy that would infuse them with high spirits, faith, and hope:

> It has already become a tradition: for the days of Purim, Tel Aviv is organizing public festivities, games for the young and old, plays, parades, concerts, dances—our entire city will rejoice. We hereby invite all the citizens of the city, each and every one of its residents, to take part in this all-inclusive popular demonstration. We all welcome our guests, we must all make them happy and we will all participate in the parades and artistic gatherings and this festival will be a grandiose symphony presented by the entire populace happy to come together after completing their hard work, and after fulfilling their sacred duties, and when the days of joy are ended, we shall return, every one of us to our daily lives.[45]

The following detailed program for the three days of the festival was determined:

The opening night began with a reading of the Book of Esther in the Great Synagogue on Allenby Street, transmitted to the surrounding streets through loudspeakers. The opening ceremony of the "secular" festival, directed by Moshe Halevi, began at seven o'clock in the evening with trumpet blasts, the performance of two scenes from *Megillat Esther* (the Scroll of Esther) by poet and teacher Kadish Yehudah Sillman (1880–1937), a dance titled *Hatzer ha-Melech* (The King's Court), the crowning of "Queen Esther," fireworks, and a performance of the song, *Shoshanat Yaacov* by the opera choir and the public. Then there was folk dancing until midnight. On the second day, there was entertainment for children, and starting at noon, a series of performing artists appeared. At two-thirty in the afternoon on the third day, the *Adloyada* parade passed through the streets of the city, a parade of artistic floats planned by the organizing committee. It included masks on biblical subjects, topics taken from daily life, and products made in Eretz-Israel, as well as floats representing the various centers of Jewish population. Bialik and Moshe Halevi decided upon the content of these floats. When the parade ended, there was once again folk dancing in the streets.

Some considered the carnivals and balls a blatant demonstration of ostentatiousness, an unnecessary extravagance, and a waste of public funds. This criticism did not keep the workers from taking an active part in the festivities. The objection voiced by observant Jews in the city was that the festivities expressed a spirit of unconstrained permissiveness and lewdness; imitations of "Greek and Roman ways, and ancient pagan ways . . . steeped in drunkenness and abject debauchery." The pressure from the religious sector resulted in the cancellation of the ceremony to select "Queen Esther" that had been held from 1926 to 1931.[46]

In any event, during the years the public Purim carnival was held, the criticism neither damaged the festivities and the festive feeling, nor did it prevent Purim from becoming the central festival in the system of festivals developed by the city. The February 1936 decision to cancel the *Adloyada* due to the violent events of the so-called Arab Revolt was met with frustration in some circles. Businessmen saw the cancellation as an economic blow, and the poet, Nathan Alterman wrote: "Well—you have seen that we created a bit of tradition / And now it is over. Enough for the time being."[47] Various organizations objected to the decision. For example, the industrialists' association wrote to the municipality on March 2, 1936, saying that the custom of holding the carnival had become a mainstay of the city, and it must therefore be continued. Clearly, the industrialists were not motivated only by the joy of the holiday, but by economic interests as well, but their opinion was shared by many others.[48]

The "Dionysian" character of the Purim carnival in Tel Aviv should not be exaggerated. The carnival atmosphere is much more intense in memory than it was in reality in the 1920s and 30s, and the fact that the city "masqueraded" by having street names changed and the like, did not turn it into some "imaginary, uninhibited" city diametrically opposed to everyday reality, just as a counter-culture, however brief, was not created. The "Dionysian" atmosphere, if any, permeated the private Purim balls. Purim, nonetheless, was an official-folk, open-air festival in which the social and political differences that divided the city's population were blurred, creating a reality divested of certain social values. It is even likely that the city of Tel Aviv was well aware of the fact that this brief masquerading enabled it to fulfill a particular social-cultural function. Although some traditional elements were integrated, the three days of festivities centered around the urban carnival, were an emulation of the folk-urban festivities held in European cities. Just as the desire to establish the sort of cultural institutions found in these cities had led Tel Aviv of the 1920s and 1930s to establish an opera, theater, various musical groups (the Philharmonic was founded in 1936), an art museum and the like, so too, the Purim carnival was organized to reflect the European, secular character of the city.

In addition to the carnival parade, there were Purim balls open to ticket holders only. Those held in Tel Aviv were private parties, or balls organized by various public bodies, and they were a combination of masquerade ball and popular party. For them, too, a repertoire of songs and dances was created and widely adapted. The costumes worn at the balls reflected various orientations—ranging from fashions based on movies up to costumes relating to current events. These balls were staged by entrepreneur-impresarios who wrote the programs. In some balls the artistic program included popular theater plays, reading from Hebrew and European literature, and the like.[49]

Festivities in "Red Haifa"

Ceremonies and festivities were held in other cities as well, although on a much smaller scale. In Haifa, also known as "red Haifa," due to the strong presence and political power of the General Labor Federation in the city, the main stagers were the community committee (a voluntary organization) and the organized labor movement, in conjunction with the JNF, rather than the municipality (which was a mixed, Jewish-Arab municipality).[50]

We have no documentation about the stagers and how they organized the various festivities in Haifa. In general, on holidays, the festivals were celebrated in very much the same way as in other parts of the country, due to the involvement of the TC. But since the Labor Federation was active in organizing the festivities, they often took on a different quality, one that underscored the values and ethos of the Eretz-Israel labor movement, and reflected Haifa's character as an industrial city and a city of workers, in contrast to the "middle-class" character of the festivals in Tel Aviv.

For example, the Festival of the First Fruits celebration in June 1932 was organized by a special committee, appointed by the community committee and the JNF. We have no information regarding the identity of the committee members, but we can assume they included cultural activists and local artists. The festivities lasted three days and included an elaborate artistic program, arranged and performed by the artistic departments of the kibbutz movement and the Labor Federation. The second day of the festivities featured a parade of schoolchildren and members of sports associations bearing first fruits. The high point of the festivity was the "coronation of the first fruits," which concluded the parade. This ceremony was accompanied by an orchestra and a choir, and ended with folk dancing. On the third day, end-of-festivity parties were held.

The striking fact is that the Festival of First Fruits celebration lasted three days. The "labor" character of the festivities was expressed in the artistic repertoire, which included ceremonies that stressed—in addition to traditional texts—the value of work and of tilling the soil. However the most remarkable aspect was the central role assigned to performances by artists, both professional and amateur. The aim of the organizing committee apparently was to turn Haifa, on the day of the festival, into a sort of public stage for artistic performances.[51]

Festivities and ceremonies were held not only in Tel Aviv or Haifa, but in nearly every Jewish rural settlement. Tel Aviv was unique due to the size and scope of the festivities, the participants, and the spectators. After 1936 the security situation and the national mood precluded the continuation of large open-space festivities. For more than ten years festivities were held mainly indoors, in kindergartens, schools, and halls. But the patterns and repertoire they produced became the distinctive feature of the Hebrew culture. When the outdoors became safe again, after the War of Independence, festivities and ceremonies were once again held outside, on a larger scale and with much more organization. Their focus shifted from Purim to the Independence Day celebration held in the month of Iyar (May).

8

Festivals in the Kibbutz: Stagers and Staging in a Communal Society

Between "Nature" and "Culture": The Kibbutz as a Stage

"The Israeli city has no festivals"—this comment was made in December 1964 by Arieh Ben-Gurion (1916–98), founder of the festival archives in Kibbutz Beit HaShita,[1] and reflects the view that a "real" festival and ceremony can be performed only in a rural-agricultural community in a "natural" landscape, where all the members of the community take an active part, fully expressing the sense of *Gemeinschaft*, which can exist only in a tightly bound society like the kibbutz. The kibbutz was thought to be the form of settlement and society that represented the new essence of Jewish life in Eretz-Israel, and a consummate expression of the national revival and its link to soil and homeland. This position produced the expectation that in the kibbutz the initiative of organizing ceremonies and festivals would originate from below, as in "primitive societies" perhaps, instead of being the product of bureaucratization as in the urban society and the educational system. This was not destined to become reality, despite the fact that cultural entrepreneurs and stagers in the kibbutz society acted on a voluntary basis only. The respective bureaucratization processes in the urban society and the kibbutz had little in common; even so, the performative element in the kibbutz could not have come into being as a spontaneous contribution from below, without the stagers' function as a unique, organized group.

More than that: we have already seen that while the Israeli city had its festivals, the early years of the existence of the kibbutz community passed without the celebration of festivals, and without the development of patterns for new festivals. At the same time, the kibbutz society was aware of the need for institutionalization of an "authentic festive culture," because it realized that festivals and ceremonies had an important societal and cultural function. It also formulated ideology to rationalize and justify the organized act of creating these festivals and ceremonies. The need for ideological legitimacy in this regard was due to the fact that institutionalization of festivals was perceived as a "bourgeois manifestation," on the one hand, and as an expression of allegiance to the religious tradition, on the other. Thus a seemingly conservative and traditional socio-cultural institution was in need of legitimacy in a society that saw itself as utterly new.

The rural kibbutz community[2] regarded itself as the social unit in which this new culture would receive maximum expression in the search for a unique festive and performative dimension in the kibbutz movement.[3] This society perceived itself as revolutionary in essence and as an alternative—and opposition—both to the traditional-religious Jewish society and to the urban bourgeoisie Jewish society. It aspired to reshape its lifestyle and way of life in a way which would, inter alia, create clear boundaries between the kibbutz lifestyle and that of the "outside world." New festivals were perceived as an integral and vital part of this new life. Thus the Hebrew rural settlements, particularly the kibbutzim, were regarded as the "natural" place in which the new Hebrew Eretz-Israeli cycle of festivals would be created, one that would be accepted by the entire Jewish society. Kibbutz members also felt the need to express, through festivals and festivities, the agricultural character of the kibbutz, the ethos of working the soil, the ideology of a "return to nature" and the link to the land as a consummate expression of the new Jewish territorial nationalism. According to this ideology, the kibbutz festivals and ceremonies were intended to replace religious festivals and ceremonies and to provide the rural-agricultural society with the "organic" and "folk" dimension it lacked.

The kibbutz's festivals were intended to replace the traditional patterns of festival celebration and to express the following elements:

1. The nature of the new Hebrew culture;
2. The nature of the communal kibbutz society; the kibbutz society believed that its festivals are authentic, not "organized and alienated," as in the urban society (or, for other reasons, as in the Diaspora).
3. The fact that this society is a rural-agricultural society (specifically, the ideology and ethos of a "return to the land" and of tilling the soil).

From its inception, then, the communal rural society was aware of the need for festivals and ceremonies, but the lack of an orderly cycle of festivals was felt more keenly when these communities grew larger and became institutionalized. Mattityahu Shalem (Weiner, 1904–75) a poet and composer from Kibbutz Beit Alpha,[4] who was one of the main contributors to the repertoire of Hebrew popular songs and the key stager of festivals in the kibbutz movement, wrote that "there was a need to weave the fabric of the group from its inception in all areas," and that permanent patterns of festival celebration were an integral part of this fabric. Moreover, kibbutz members were occupied with philosophical and ideological discussions of such topics as the relationship between "nature" and "culture," between "religion" and "culture," and between "spontaneity" and "organization." They also addressed the origins of the festivals in the Jewish tradition in order to prove the holidays were always a product of initiative and always underwent variation, adaptation, and even renewal. In September 1928, in a series of talks held in Kibbutz Ein Harod, founded in 1921, the nature and role of festivals was discussed against the background of these themes.[5] The recurrent motif in these deliberations and others was that the traditional holidays and festivals ("the festivals of our forefathers") held no meaning for members of the secular-revolutionary generation, but that no social unit could exist without festivals. The re-creation of festivals was perceived as an inseparable part of the creativity and vitality of kibbutz life. This, of course, gave rise to the dilemma of whether to integrate new components into the traditional festivals by changing their meaning, or to invent new festivals. The answer was that the kibbutz should preserve both courses of action.

The creation of festivals in the kibbutz was a gradual process, underpinned by an awareness of the need for them, attended by numerous discussions about the significance of each festival, about the values and symbols it should express, and about how it should be staged. The system of festivals and the ritual of the Catholic Church often served as a model for the theatrical-dramatic aspect of the festival and its permanent and structured character.[6] Yitzhak Tabenkin (1887–1971), one of the leaders and ideologues of the kibbutz movement, cited the fact that even in an age of secularism, Christian society continued to preserve festivals that were religious in nature. Catholicism knew how to elevate festivals to a level of artistic genius and to employ any materials or means to achieve the festival's goals. He concluded that the kibbutz movement ought likewise not to abandon festivals, even if they were anchored in religious tradition and values, but rather should infuse new meaning into them. Without festivals kibbutz life would be dull and bare, divested of a vital experiential dimension which maintains a link of continuity to the historical-cultural past, fixes set times for celebration and collective joyousness, and deepens intra-kibbutz solidarity. Since the key element in the kibbutz way of life is the land and work on the land, the kibbutz festivals had to be based on the renewal and re-creation of the traditional-religious festivals connected, in one way or another, with work on the land and with nature. Tabenkin was therefore convinced that a major test of the kibbutz movement's creative genius was its ability to create a new system of festivals with a quasi-ritual character.[7] Festivals in the kibbutz had to provide a concrete expression of the ethos of working the land. This led to the conclusion that a modest, Spartan festival would not do; on the contrary, it had to be truly artistic and festive. Its purpose was to serve as an essential complement to the ideological-verbal dimension (texts and lectures). In M. Shalem's view, the means of dramatizing, performing and celebrating the festival had to include: "Singing, playing musical instruments, recitation, decoration, dancing, acting, symbols, and the like. Without these elements, there cannot be a festive experience. These are the raw materials which have the power to build, shape, and give form to character." Since new tools must be created in the absence of tradition, "the implementers are the ones who determine the fate of the innovation, for better or worse."[8]

The creators of the festival repertoire in the kibbutz society were faced with a dilemma: how to combine the revolutionary-radical and secular ideology of the kibbutz with the creation of a new tradition, based on the old tradition and deeply rooted in the Jewish religion. And how to create—within a very short time—a cohesive tradition. The basic assumption was that it was impossible to constantly keep renewing the festivals. For the new tradition to be accepted, internalized, and institutionalized, it was necessary to create a permanent cycle, a set pattern following the same rules.

For the social group, festivals and festivities not only provide a sense of solidarity and public expression and serve as an important means of imparting values and symbols; they also designate a defined space of time within secular time, a time of spirituality ("a festive feeling") and of religiosity. For example, David Shmeterling (Gilad), a member of Kibbutz Degania A in the Jordan Valley, who had a university education, wrote in 1924 in an article titled "Festivals," that the festival is the connecting thread between the sacred and the secular, and hence the kibbutz movement ought to create authentic festivals. But, he added, it should create them not "in a helter-skelter" manner, but should plan them with forethought. He called on the movement to collect aesthetic and decorative material suitable for the specific festival. To counter the claim that an institutionalized festival has a formalistic nature, Shmeterling stated that only an institutionalized festival can fulfill its designated role.[9] Therefore, every festival was celebrated collectively. Festivities held in public require more complex staging. As a result, the major combined effort of writing texts (as well as the musical aspect) and staging was conducted for those festivities with the active participation of the entire local society.

The awareness of the need for festivals grew as the kibbutz society matured and a children's society began to develop, mainly during the 1920s. This was a significant development, since festivals were thought to hold a special meaning for children, and were seen as a means of imparting the cultural legacy to the younger generation.

Planning in a Spontaneous Society

Generally speaking, the kibbutz society faced two problems: how to create the texts for the ceremony and the festival, and how to give these texts their performative dimension. In discussions of the time the complaint was often voiced that ideological debates over the essence and content of the festival would not suffice, nor would the texts in themselves be ample. A festival also reflects the beliefs and worldview of the community by means of its *form*, namely through staging, movement, and performance. Only texts and performances mutually well adapted can create a whole cultural system. These ideological discussions and the project of creating literary texts reflecting two new pictures—that of the Jewish past and future—now urgently required the creation of the performative dimension. In response to this need, the group of stagers emerged and consciously undertook to fulfill this role.

The main arguments indicate that the kibbutz community believed that traditional festivals and festivities could be revitalized in the kibbutz, in its capacity as a rural-agricultural entity and social-intimate society. It believed that by celebrating festivals that reflect the agricultural cycle and the cycle of nature, the kibbutz society would return to the ideal of direct bonding with land, soil and territory. The paradox here is that a modern revolutionary society regarded a return to the agricultural festival as a return to the ideal, harmonious natural state. In other words, the debate over the essence and content of the kibbutz cycle of festivals was an immanent part of the more general debate surrounding the relationship between Hebrew culture and Jewish religion, which also reflected the debate about the kibbutz as an alternative to the "other" world outside it. The debate was also marked by longings for the world of tradition that the kibbutz community had abandoned, as well as by a desire to replace it with a complete alternative world.

At first the argument was that the kibbutz needed a completely new version of the traditional festival, which ought to be the outcome of a spontaneous, authentic process, from "within" the social group, not an "artificial" one dictated by an institutionalized entity. However, it soon became clear that the kibbutz society could not rely on spontaneous development and creativity, but had to plan and initiate a system of festivals. In other words, even within the framework of the intimate group, cultural entrepreneurs and stagers were needed to construct and institutionalize a system of festivals. There was a sense that a spontaneous creation might lack the most important elements of ceremony and festival—uniformity and regularity. This led to the conclusion that the organization and staging of the festival had to be well planned and regulated.

M. Shalem wrote the following in this regard: "The question is how we can revive the beneficial and direct spontaneity, how we can free the community, and the individual within it, of their inhibitions, so as to express values and the joy of life. Nor can we be endlessly introducing new patterns each year. We will never achieve any coalescence if everything is transient and fleeting."[10]

Planning, then, was not necessarily understood as a contradiction with authenticity. Author David Meletz (1899–1981), a member of Ein Harod, noted this paradox in an article titled "On Our Cultural Work," in which he wrote that a modern social unit cannot spontaneously and gradually develop festivals from within itself, as "naive" primal societies did, because modern man creates festivals not spontaneously, but as a result of his awareness of their significance. This awareness, Meletz asserted, reinforces the "artificial" or "false" dimension of the creative product, which actually ought to be "natural" and primal in nature. Therefore, he added, there is a difference between community singing, which is a kind of "spontaneous" prayer in modern society, giving expression to an "inner truth," and festivals, which call for organization.[11] It soon transpired that the putatively spontaneous element of song and dance had to be created in a deliberate and organized fashion. Although the kibbutz members looked to the model of a primal rural society, in which song and dance are supposedly a product of spontaneous creation, they were at the same time consumers of high culture, and hence of song and dance as artistic creations. This led them to demand that song and dance be elevated to the "level of art," and that "spontaneous dance" be imbued with cultural meaning.[12] Thus in the very place where it was "natural" to expect that the form of the festivals should have reflected simplicity, even Spartanism, much emphasis was placed on the form and aesthetic aspect of the festival.

In any event, since song and dance in the framework of a structured festivity could not be "spontaneous," there was a need for writers of lyrics, composers, and choreographers to create songs and dances consistent with the worldview of the kibbutz movement, and their performance had to be staged as part of the ceremony and festival. Within a short time, then, the realization began to take hold that the "inner truth" could not be given expression and form in a spontaneous manner, but only by creators—literary and theater personalities, painters and composers.

It was, then, in the kibbutz setting that the tension between the desire for spontaneous emergence of the festival and the desire to plan and organize it was most strongly felt.

The Kibbutz Stagers and Their Principles of Staging

As we have noted, this new tradition and its accompanying folklore were not supposed to be the product of a spontaneous creative development, but rather the result of organized activity. The festivals were planned and staged by a committee—a local culture committee—which was assigned the task of reshaping the calendar. In other words, this example shows that even in the kibbutz—an organic-intimate group—performative creativity did not come from below, from all the members, but rather from a committee.

It is usually assumed that festival ceremonies in the kibbutz were a collective creation by nearly anonymous artists, each of whom made a modest contribution to the production of the texts and the music as well as to the staging process. In actual fact, everyone in the kibbutz would have known which members actively participated in creating these ceremonies. The fact that their names did not appear in the records, if any were kept, renders them anonymous only as far as the historian (or anthropologist) is concerned, but not for the society in which they lived and worked, certainly not during the specific period in which they were active. In this regard, the case of the kibbutz society may teach us something about other intimate societies—they were aware of the identity of the stagers, but did not take the trouble to document their contribution, as this was regarded part of a collective project.

In every kibbutz this committee was made up of a small group of members, and usually included teachers and artists. Kibbutzim that had members with an artistic bent or artistic training (composers, poets, theater people) succeeded in constructing and staging festivals that were more sophisticated than those in other kibbutzim. The artists, who were kibbutz members, believed their activity made an important contribution to kibbutz life, and a considerable portion of their work was geared toward festival ceremonies. Over time, this creative activity lessened, and the focus moved to the field of staging itself.[13] These communal (local) stagers and dramatists were usually organized in a culture committee. Such committees included local teachers, writers and artists, and those actively engaged in cultural affairs, who were known as *tarbutnikim* (people responsible for cultural activities). The job of the committee and its members was to shape the ceremony, its texts and the manner in which it would be staged. Not all the members of the kibbutz took an active part in the ceremony and, in any event, roles were clearly assigned.[14] In the kibbutz movement, a few of these stagers were better known, since their activity had an impact beyond the confines of their own kibbutzim: Mattityahu Shalem; his wife, Leah Bernstein, a professional dancer who created dances for various festivals; Yehuda Sharett (Shertok, 1901–75), a composer and member of Kibbutz Ein Harod from 1926, who wrote musical works for pageants stressing the interaction between the performers and the audience, and Nahum Benari (Bronsky), a teacher, also a member of Kibbutz Ein Harod from 1924, who was the most active kibbutz stager during the period in question. All four were well aware of the role they had undertaken and wrote about the principles underlying their work.

M. Shalem writes in his memoirs that the time he spent in a Ruthenian village in Bukovina, on his way to Eretz-Israel in 1922, was a profound experience. It provided him with a close acquaintance with life in a community "unchanged in its lack of progress, with much good nature and a rich folklore that enchanted me. I took an active part in the village celebrations, harvesting, corn picking, weddings and other events accompanied by singing and dancing." After he immigrated to Eretz-Israel, Shalem spent some time among village Arabs and Bedouins, which also left a deep impression on him, evoking memories of "that same Ruthenian village." These two experiences enhanced his interest in folklore, and made him aware of its importance in rural life.[15] He also claimed that he borrowed his staging principles from the religious tradition of the First and Second Temple periods—mass gatherings on festival days, processions and the like.

Nahum Benari wrote that the festival ought to authentically express an inner experience and be part of the culture of the generation, not an imitation of traditional ceremonies, and that this task had been given to people from the field of literature and theater, artists, and composers. In his view, these people were not merely creators of culture, but also cultural leaders and pioneers. He wrote: "It is true that a perfect form for the festivals won't be created in one generation, certainly not in a generation like ours. The upheavals in the life of our nation in these times are profound, and the change that has occurred in the life of the Hebrew community in the Land (of Israel) has also left a profound imprint—and all these call for a sincere, profound expression of what the festival symbolized in our lives."[16]

Another personality active in this area was the choreographer, Rivka Shturman (1903–2001), also a member of Kibbutz Ein Harod from 1937.[17] In an interview in August 1985, she defined herself—and the other creators of festivals—as "folk artists," who were motivated by the desire to create a *folk festival in an artistic format,* driven by a "spiritual soul," and not by an ideology or a doctrine (a claim that is inconsistent with what was stated above regarding the other festival creators, who were guided by a clear-cut cultural conception). Shturman also described the stagers' method of work as not being part of an organized effort (by a culture committee), but as a personal-spontaneous creative effort by a small group of entrepreneurs and creators.[18] However, according to her own testimony, she borrowed the hand and arm movements for her Omer festival dance from ancient Egyptian frescoes, and searched in various sources for appropriate dance movements. This is another indication that the ostensibly personal-spontaneous creations were based on specific models and intended to fulfill a pre-defined function in the celebration of the festival. In any event, the artistic sphere in which the highest degree of staging creativity was displayed was that of folk dancing.

In addition to those mentioned above, a long list of cultural activists and local artists were active in the kibbutz movement, some of them in charge of organizing the festivities, some engaged in creating the repertoire and staging the festivals. Most of them were well known in their kibbutzim, but remained anonymous to the public at large—simply a few more figures in the gallery of anonymous creators of culture who worked behind the scenes.[19] They were all part of the collective.

At some kibbutzim, the culture committee called a meeting of members interested in an "informal talk" to discuss how to organize the festival and to make various suggestions. From the partial documentation that still exists, it turns out that in nearly every kibbutz there were disagreements on this subject. The discussions about how to celebrate the festival indicate that members were constantly dissatisfied with the patterns of the festival and the way it was performed. The main complaints centered on the way it was staged, the insufficient means that were available (the lack of an orchestra, for example), the fact that the tasks assigned to the participating children were too difficult, and the audience's passivity. We see, then, that the stagers were constantly at the receiving end of harsh criticism, and they themselves were aware of their failure to stage a festival that would be well received by the public. In other words, the main point of criticism was that a fitting pattern had not been created for the festival, and that the stagers had not succeeded in creating and performing a spontaneous festivity! The lack of success and the disappointment were all the more marked due to the assumption that the intimate kibbutz society was the most suitable setting in which to organize a spontaneous festivity.

The kibbutz stagers' point of departure was the notion that the festival ought to express the common intimate experience of the individual and the collective. It should reflect the "depth" of this experience by depicting it through a variety of non-verbal means, which are more important than the spoken word. The musical dimension, the stage (the kibbutz yard, the field), the scenery, acting, folk dancing, were all placed at the center of the festival.[20] In many cases, special folk costumes, suitable for the festival were designed.

The major innovation in the patterns of festival staging in the kibbutz was the pageant: a quasi-theatrical play for a festival, it was performed by amateurs reading texts and dancing, with the active participation of the audience, to avoid creating a barrier between it and the performers. Since the pageant was a central feature of the festival, it called for advance preparations, and hence it inevitably involved the activity of a group that decided upon the texts to be used and the staging.

We do not have the minutes of most meetings held by local culture committees. The few that remained provide only the final decisions, omitting the discussions or the different suggestions raised in the course of the meetings.[21] Therefore, a description of the plans and the festivities as they were actually carried out will have to suffice. We will give only a few examples here, since the staging principles were basically the same in all the kibbutzim.

THE KIBBUTZ CYCLE OF FESTIVALS

Festival of Tabernacles (Succoth; the Harvest Festival)

The traditional structure of the Festival of Tabernacles, celebrated in a *succah* (a hut roofed with branches), did not offer many opportunities for staging. Consequently, only a few attempts to stage a new version of the festival were made. Such an attempt was made at Ein Harod (in the Jezreel Valley near the Ein Harod spring) during the 1920s, initiated and staged by Nahum Benari, one of the kibbutz founders, who was a very active participant in the discussions held on the essence and role of festivals.

Here is a description of the Festival of Tabernacles as celebrated in the kibbutz in 1924 in accordance with Benari's guidelines:

> A guardhouse was set up on the threshing floor and decorated with palm branches. The festivity took place on the last day of the harvest festival. Pieces of the fruit of the land were placed in the *succah* . . . in the afternoon, the children went to the threshing-floor and burst into song. Above the *succah*, the *Ushpizin*[22] made their appearance . . . actually children in disguise, and blessed the new year. After they had tasted of the fruit, this part of the festival was over. The major part began in the evening. The Ein

Harod bell rang and everyone gathered near the children's house. The boys came out carrying colored lanterns and palm branches, and the girls carried pitchers. The procession passed by, singing, until it reached the cave from which the Ein Harod spring flows. The children entered the cave and lit candles, which were attached to protrusions in the rock at every corner of the cave . . . singing "With joy you will draw water from the springs of salvation" (*Isaiah* 12:3), they filled the pitchers. From there they went to the square and lit a bonfire. They encircled the bonfire, singing . . . they poured water on the fire, danced and sang "Rain, Rain" and other songs. Throngs of dancers danced in rows. Everyone crowded into the rows of dancers, and the dances went on and on.[23]

This is an example of an attempt to stage a ceremony both ritual and esthetic in nature, combining historical symbols (eating the fruit of the land, going to the water source, waving palm branches) with universal elements (water, fire).

Hanukkah and Purim

The Hanukkah festival was celebrated in the agricultural settlements indoors, in halls, rather than in an open space. Although the festival was assigned a national meaning in Hebrew culture, and became, as we mentioned, a central festival in modern Jewish nationalism, pageants—combining text and performance—were written for it only later, and it was celebrated mainly in the children's society. Hanukkah was celebrated indoors, in the form of parties, and was not staged.

The Purim festival as well was usually an occasion for a comic play about life on the kibbutz and was an indoor ceremony.

Passover

The Passover seder at the kibbutz was celebrated from the beginning of the development of kibbutz society in the 1920s, since it symbolized both the longing for family life and national-social redemption. As a result, Passover was the focus of most of the kibbutz movement's attention and creative activity in the literary domain—that is, in the text. This creative activity took the form mainly of writing new versions of the Haggadah (the first such new version was written in 1935), and of reshaping the collective Passover seder.[24] We are not going to discuss the structure and textual nature of the kibbutz Haggadoth, but will simply note that since the seder was held indoors in the main dining room, with the participants sitting round tables, the main innovation was everyone's active participation in reading the Haggadah, in a pre-arranged order, with a group of "actors" (reciters, singers and a choir) playing the main roles. The connection made in the text between Passover as a festival of spring, an agricultural festival and a festival of freedom, was often expressed in a ceremony, at which sheaves of wheat were brought into the hall, in a procession with dancing.

A great deal of thought was devoted to the Passover festival, particularly the textual aspect. A new version of the Haggadah was written and the patterns of jointly celebrating the Passover seder by all the members were reorganized. Of all the traditional festivals, Passover was given the most attention insofar as the textual aspect was concerned. The first Passover haggadoth for the kibbutzim were amusing, reflecting the desire to break away from the traditional content. Only in 1935 did the kibbutzim begin writing more serious haggadoth, and in 1944 a special discussion was held by cultural entrepreneurs from the kibbutzim on the issue of a new, uniform text for a kibbutz Haggadah.[25]

One way of overcoming the fact that Passover was an indoor festivity was by attaching an agricultural festival to it. This was the festival of the Omer (harvest of barley), celebrated after Passover.

Shavuot (Chag Ha'Omer)

The two major festivals reshaped by the kibbutz movement were Tu biShevat (the New Year of Trees) and Shavuot (the Festival of First Fruits, or Chag ha'Omer—the Harvest Festival).[26] The reason is clear: these were essentially agricultural festivals linked to nature and the land, and they could be celebrated in an open space, in the yard or field. As a result, the festivals of Shavuot and Tu biShevat were the two holidays in which most of the creative activity was invested in the staging.

The first newly shaped festival on the kibbutz was Shavuot, whose religious significance (the handing down of the Torah) was nullified, and it was transformed into a festival of an agricultural nature—*hag Ha-Bikurim* or the Festival of First Fruits. (The first attempt at this was made at the agricultural school, Mikveh Israel, in 1914). It was celebrated for the first time in 1924 on Kibbutz Ein Harod, near the biblical spring of Harod, in the Jezreel Valley. Hag ha-Gez (the sheep-shearing festival) was an entirely new festival celebrated for the first time at Kibbutz Beit Alpha in 1924. This festival was intended to be a nature festival, expressing and illustrating the experiential and symbolic bond between the kibbutz and the land and work on the land. Shalem wrote that the festival's organization was not only a product of the spiritual encounter with the land in the Jezreel Valley but was also inspired by the pilgrimages to Jerusalem during the Second Temple period, and the earlier regional assemblies. Over the course of time, various artists, kibbutz members, began participating in the creation of a ceremonial pageant focusing on the corn harvest and the Festival of First Fruits. Very few changes were made in the format of the festival over the years and the scope of the stagers' inventiveness was limited. Vehicles (tractors), their platforms adorned with greenery and fruit were introduced into the procession, and the festival pageants were improved and dramatic pieces were added to them.

Here, for example, is one impression of this festival in Ein Harod, which is described as a "real revolution":

> Most of the young men wear white shirts, the more fastidious among them wear a corded belt with tassels around their waist, and breeches and leather boots, as is fitting for a watchman on horseback. The girls wear black pinafores or the typical long blue cotton dresses of the pioneer women. The children are all dressed up, in yellow Russian-style blouses with embroidery at the neck, sitting crowded together in the wagon like lambs—and now the announcer proclaims the start of the procession, and it begins moving toward its final destination at the threshing floor.
>
> The bearers of the first fruits walk at the head, followed by the group carrying field crops with their tools: a tractor and plow, a team with a disk-harrow, a team with a seed drill, a roller, a binder, a hay turner, a wagon filled with hay, a threshing machine with a tractor, a wagon loaded with bread and flour, followed by a planting wagon full of trees, the first vegetables from the vegetable garden, a wagon filled with the first attempts at growing tobacco ... and last but not least, bringing up the rear, a wagon of children, followed by the whole throng, some on vehicles, others on foot. First, on a red horse—a knight—after the horseman, boys and girls in colorful costumes walk in step, the girls carrying pitchers on their shoulders and wreaths of flowers on their heads. The boys carry a huge bunch of grapes on a pole. The head of the procession is already at the gate of honor and entering the threshing floor, where he proclaims the commencement of the ceremony of the bringing of first fruits.
>
> It opens with a children's choir accompanied by violins. Immediately afterwards, delegations from the settlements mount the stage. And then someone calls out and describes all the gifts of first fruits and who has sent them.

And the writer concludes:

Yes, we have done something really revolutionary and celebrate the festival differently than our fathers did in the Diaspora, for they were forced to make do with less ... closed in between the four walls of synagogues and family homes. Now we have returned to the field and to the picturesque masses of our people. In the Diaspora this was a household festival, filled only with spiritual content, with hymns and prayers and symbols of the festival, vestiges of the physical glory that existed in the past. Yet the meaning of the greenery is in the Festival of First Fruits and citrus fruits and palm branches in the Feast of Tabernacles. And just as in our agricultural work today, when we drill wells and cut through rock to get to the clear ground water, thus we are commanded to exert an effort to get to the very source of our festivals and to raise from the depths of the past life of the Jewish people the fresh "ground water" of our ancient culture, so that it may once again flow in the channels of influence that had been clogged throughout all the years of life in the Diaspora.[27]

In May 1937 a seminar was held at Kibbutz Ein Harod to discuss the organization of the festival. A detailed program was formulated, as follows:

The festival opens with a first fruits procession of children from the schools and the kindergartens. At its head is a group of girls playing flutes followed by those bearing the first fruits. Leading the procession is a girl dressed in white, holding a palm branch, and riding on a mare adorned in blue.

The participants join in the procession, and from it groups of four emerge, and separate into bearers of different first fruits, according to the different branches in the kibbutz, singing the song "Anu banu artzah, livnot ulehibanot bah" ("We have come to this land, to build it and be built in it").

The main ceremony is held outside, in front of the dining hall. The bearers of the first fruits mount the stage, as the announcer calls them, bringing their produce. The ceremony is accompanied by the reading of verses, which are appropriate to the various agricultural branches of the kibbutz, and ends with the flutists singing and dancing.[28]

After the festival, a meeting was held to review how the festival had been celebrated and any shortcomings that had been noted in it, and aiming also to "perfect the form of the festival." Although there were some who were very enthusiastic about the performance of the festival, most of them were highly critical.

A uniform version of celebrating this festival was not adopted, but it centered on the ceremony of harvesting the grain in the field, accompanied by a pageant and dancing. Over the years, a rich folklore of songs and dances was created for this festival.

Here, for example, is a description of the pageant for the bringing in of the grain. It was proposed by Mattityahu Shalem in 1947 and published by the Culture Center of the General Labor Federation:[29]

> The festival begins towards the evening with a trumpet blast from the water tower. The kibbutz members throng to the decorated gate of the yard, and pass through it to the field. In front of them, a group of riders ride on decorated horses, followed by the kibbutz old-timers and a procession of schoolchildren and kindergartners dressed in blue and white with wreaths of flowers on their heads. After them come the harvesters with their scythes, wearing blue trousers and white shirts, and the girls, in traditional dress, gather the cut wheat stalks into sheaves. A decorated flatbed wagon harnessed to a team of white horses follows the procession, along with singers and an ensemble of flutes and percussion instruments.
>
> The ceremony opens with the crier's proclamation and singing. Then the procession turns and walks to the field of grain. The procession and the audience form a circle around the field, the flute ensemble plays and a short pageant is performed, including festival songs and the reading of verses, with the participation of the criers and audience. The harvest begins in the midst of this ceremony, as the crier and the audience accompany it, reading appropriate verses and singing. The sheaves are brought to the stage and torches are lit. On the stage, the ceremony of waving the sheaves is held. The harvesters and the audience then dance.

It is not difficult to understand why the patterns of this ceremony were not permanently adopted. It was too theatrical to suit the society in which it was meant to be performed.

It is interesting to note that the religious circles opposed the appropriation of the Festival of First Fruits by the kibbutz movement. In 1924 they brought strong pressure to bear on the General Labor Federation to take steps to cancel the regional celebration of the festival. The argument was that the festivity led to the desecration of the religious holiday, but mainly because it "secularized" a festival that marks the central place of the Temple in Jewish life. As a result, the regional festival was canceled, and it is now celebrated in each kibbutz separately. Its name has also been changed to Chagigat Zikhron haBikurim ("Festival of the Remembrance of the First Fruits"). The kibbutz was forced to accept this compromise (mainly due to the fear of an boycott), and a short pageant was added to the ceremony, describing how the festival was celebrated during Temple times. The national motif was expressed when the children, after waving the first fruits to dedicate them to the JNF, proclaimed: "Here we have brought from the first fruits of our land an offering for the redemption of the Land of Israel."

The submission of the kibbutzim to religious pressure met with severe criticism. Eliezer Libenstein (Livne, 1902–75), later one of the kibbutz movement's most important ideologues, wrote that the new festivals were created because of a recognized need for self-expression on holidays, and that self-expression cannot take the form of a return to past customs. Accordingly the religious circles were opposed not merely to the festival itself, but to what the new festival symbolized: the creation of a new folk tradition.[30] Especially alarming to the Orthodox was the celebration of Shavuot by the people en masse using symbols from Jewish tradition. It should be noted that the Orthodox objection was aimed specifically against this holiday, and not Tu biShavet, since in Shavuot they saw, in their view, a most dangerous expression of the process of secularization of a major religious holiday and its symbols, as an acquisition of the national-secular idea, while Tu biShevat did not have such an important status in Jewish tradition.

However, it was not the Orthodox objection that caused the demise of the large-scale celebration of Shavuot. Arye Ben-Gurion offers several explanations for the decline of the Festival of First Fruits in the kibbutz: the festival is celebrated at the height of the busy agricultural season and hence it is hard to find time for it; industry became one of the most important economic branches in the kibbutz and agriculture became mechanized; the ceremony became "artificial" and lost its authenticity; the children did not agree to take an active part, which meant holding baskets of fruit while sitting on tractor platforms, which are decorated with bunches of asparagus.[31] Ben-Gurion probably overlooked one other aspect: the Festival of First Fruits was created at the initiative of a group of kibbutz members who were aware of the importance of festivals in kibbutz life. This group was the initiator, the driving force, and the stager of the ceremonies and festivals, which was not always to the liking of all the members. Over time, the social pressure they were able to exert over the other members diminished, and the latter responded less and less to the initiatives of the smaller group. As the kibbutz became increasingly exposed to the "outside culture," there was less motivation to organize and stage festival ceremonies based on local talent and energy. Hence the kibbutz festival experience, intended to give organized-popular expression to the special socio-cultural identity of the kibbutz, lost its vitality and became less central to kibbutz life.

Tu biShevat

As we have already pointed out, the character of the Tu beShevat festival altered in 1890. No longer the festival of fruits, it became the festival of planting, as a result of the initiative of the historian and teacher, Zeev Yavetz, from the moshava of Zichron Yaakov. The other moshavot followed the pattern set by Zichron Yaakov, and in 1908, it was adopted by the TC, becoming one of the central festival ceremonies in the schools.

The kibbutz introduced very few innovations in the way this festival was celebrated, and the main components were the procession and the planting ceremony. The fact that Tu biShevat did not become a local folk festival is clear from a discussion held at Ein Harod in February 1936. The committee arranging the festival in the Kibbutz HaMe'uchad movement had convened to discuss why the festival—despite its agricultural character—had become a success, and how it could be turned into a kibbutz festival.[32] We do not know what conclusions were reached. The likely answer is that, in contrast to the school setting in the urban society, the kibbutz society did not need a symbolic planting ceremony, since the planting of trees was not an unusual event in kibbutzim.

The kibbutz was a distinctly secular, revolutionary society. However, at least insofar as the calendar of festivals is concerned, the kibbutz was a traditionalist society. It kept the traditional calendar, and its revolutionary nature was expressed through changing the content of the festivals, divesting them of religious content and assigning greater status to festivals embodying an agricultural character. The traditionalist nature of the kibbutz was also expressed by statements such as "the kibbutz saved the festival," which would have dwindled in the secular urban society, and because the kibbutz is a "society of believers," and as such the festival is important to them as an expression of the principles of faith, as the basis for a religious collective experience, and as an element designating sacral time within everyday life. It may be claimed that the traditionalist stand was alienated from the religious content of the festivals: The kibbutz members argued that they celebrated the ancient Jewish festivals in the "original" way; expressing authentic experience.[33]

Thus the ideology of "the renewal of life" in its totality made the kibbutz members very much aware of the need to organize festivals. This is the reason why in texts from the 1920s, the sense of void and emptiness in the absence of public festivals is keenly felt.

After the establishment of the state, the kibbutz movement intensified its efforts to create a crystallized cycle of festivals. This attempt was an inseparable part of the movement's trend of creating a national-secular culture that would endow it with a unique identity. A description of these attempts and the changes in texts and patterns of staging is outside the chronological scope of this book. In any event, it is important to note that some of the festivals—in particular the kibbutz Festival of First Fruits and the Harvest Festival—all but disappeared and were preserved in only a few kibbutzim, and even then, only in the framework of the schools and kindergartens.

Our comparison of festival ceremonies in the kibbutzim, in the urban community and in the educational system has shown that there were not a great number of differences between the two. The disparity was mainly in the manner of performance, the site, the participation, and sometimes in the repertoire. But the cycle of festivals and their content were quite similar. It may be truthfully said, then, that this new cycle of festivals, created by a group of stagers sharing similar characteristics and a similar perception of culture, and with public support, succeeded in creating a common—albeit partial—foundation of official folk culture in Jewish society in Yishuv-era Eretz-Israel.

Conclusion

In this book, we dealt first with a case study of the process of staging a new culture and with its stagers. More specifically, we focused on the creation and crystallization of ceremonies and festivals as a central aspect of the newly official (or formal) folk culture (and national festivals) in Jewish society in Eretz-Israel during the Mandatory period, and on the role of the stagers who were the inventors and organizers of these festivals and ceremonies.

We have maintained that the creation of the official popular culture was an inseparable part of the creation of the overall system of the new Hebrew culture in Eretz-Israel between 1882 and 1948, an expression of this culture, and concurrently a process that determined its identity. This overall system was constructed on the basis of a defined national-cultural worldview and the values and symbols that were part of it. Based on this worldview, belles lettres, theater, plastic arts and the like were created. However, the new Hebrew culture was not only a conglomerate of creative works but was also intended to advance new patterns of interpersonal relations, new rules of behavior, a new concept of childhood and youth, a new attitude toward the body, nature, landscape (both rural and urban), a new conception of the aesthetic facet of life, and the like.

With this in mind, the new Hebrew cultural system tried—with partial success—to create not only a new verbal dimension (represented by texts), or a figurative dimension (represented by symbols and icons), but also a performative dimension, represented and given expression by gestures, movements, and rules of behavior.[1] In other words, the new Hebrew culture—as an ideal, a utopia and a reality—was meant to create a new, all-inclusive way of life, dictated and guided by an overall ideology. The new cultural system was also meant to be all-embracing (namely, containing all traits of culture) and to give an expression to the new worldview.

There were at least three reasons for this expansive approach:

1. The ideology of cultural revival (in the sense that cultural elements from the past were revived, first and foremost—the "national language"), was

connected to cultural modernity. Revival or rejuvenation meant that Jewish culture, particularly the national Jewish culture, would contain all those cultural components regarded as part of national culture, and that these components would bear the stamp of the "authentic Hebrew spirit." The project of socio-cultural planning therefore included an attempt to plan and control as many parts of the cultural arena as possible.
2. The "secular" nature of modern Jewish nationalism, namely its detachment from the religious tradition and traditional religious life, and the desire to create an all-inclusive cultural system, made it necessary to propose an overall alternative to the religious system, one with a rich system of festivals and ceremonies. This alternative system would be constructed on the foundations of the existing religious system, but profound changes would be introduced.
3. The new social organization and the various forms of settlements created in Jewish Palestine, the desire to produce social solidarity and impart values and symbols, and to forge connections with history and the landscape, were also expressed through an effort to devise a new calendar of festivals and to reshape its content in the way in which it is dramatized. This not only called for a new corpus of texts but also for suitable new patterns of staging these festivals.

The all-inclusive (and utopian) approach to culture brought the lack of festivals and ceremonies, or in a broader sense, the lack of a folk culture, into sharp relief. We have seen that the major ideologues of Hebrew culture were not those who felt this void most keenly, but rather the group, which we have called secondary agents of culture. These were the individuals who felt the lack of a popular culture, particularly with regard to festivals, festivities, and the ceremonies and rituals which they comprise. They were the ones who endeavored to fill this void, both as writers of texts (and music) and as stagers.

Generally, the members of this group were teachers, artists, theater people, and personalities active in cultural affairs on the local scene, who were encouraged by the local leadership or by the community. However, they could never have taken their initiative any further without organized public support or the resources placed at their disposal. Since this folk culture was created by cultural entrepreneurs, guided by an explicit cultural ideology, we have called it, somewhat paradoxically, an official folk culture.

These secondary cultural entrepreneurs were aware of the functions that festivity, as an integral part of folk culture, fulfills. They had a broad notion of *culture* and hence viewed it not only as a system of laws, commandments, and canonical texts but also as having a broad "popular" layer, expressing itself through songs, dances, rituals, and ceremonies. Hence they regarded the absence of folk culture in the new Jewish society as a grievous lacuna rendering it less complete and less organic, and reducing its ability to express a whole world of experiences and needs. Awareness of this need developed not only in the rural society and the educational network but in the urban community as well.

In fact, then, a small group of planners and agents of culture were the ones who planned and institutionalized patterns of behavior, namely the performative dimension of the culture, and in particular, the system of festivities, festivals, and ceremonies. They wrote the texts and formulated the rules of staging; hence we have defined them as stagers. Some of them had a broad view of culture, but in reality, they shaped separate segments of it. Their collective activity created the staging patterns of an important part of Hebrew culture in Eretz-Israel. It is impossible to depict Hebrew society and culture in Eretz-Israel without taking account of the patterns of staging in its different layers. It is also impossible to describe the development of the society and the culture without giving the stagers' activity—the initiative, the organization, the sources of inspiration, the manner of production and the results of all these—the place it deserves.

The creators of the formal popular culture did not intend to create folklore composed of content different than that of the "high" culture; rather they wished to produce a folklore that would translate the values and symbols of the "high culture" into texts that were "simple," more easily absorbed, and also more dramatic.

The new system of holidays and ceremonies which was created and staged until 1948 fulfilled several functions simultaneously: it was part of the socialization mechanism of the various sub-societies; it was a metaphor of their perception of reality, and it attempted to act as the tool shaping the culture according to these perceptions. The control over the public (open-air) space and the way it was shaped, *inter alia* by festivities, was perceived as an important expression of the national-territorial revival and the transformation of Palestine into Hebrew territory.

The implementation of the performative dimension in the public space—streets, squares, groves, and the like—was intended to demonstrate the Jewish society's control—and ownership—of the space. The process of creating the new popular culture was, therefore, a conscious, planned, and organized process, with a group of stagers that implemented it, based on a clear concept of the desirable nature of the ceremonial system, with respect both to content and aesthetics. In other words, this was a process guided by a national ideology, which determined both the need for festivals and ceremonies and their verbal, symbolic and performative content. The stagers were able to create a new system of festivals and ceremonies due not only to the backing of a supportive bureaucracy but also due to the urgent need felt by the various social frameworks to fill this void by creating a new festive culture; therefore, the initiative was a welcome one and was met with support.

The process of creating festivals and ceremonies produced two other results: First, ceremonies and festivals transformed myths and symbols into figurative icons: land, light, gates, fruits, trees, doves.[2] Second, these were also a driving force behind the creation of folk songs, children's songs, dances, and costumes. Parts of this repertoire continued to function in Hebrew culture even after the ceremonies for which they were written were no longer performed.

We have seen that the newly created festivity and performative repertoire was broad and diverse. The patterns of the performative acts were borrowed from various sources: from the Jewish tradition and all branches of the European tradition. The practices in courts of law, as well as the organization of political parades and sports events—to name only three random examples—were borrowed directly from the European model. In these cases, no attempt was made to present them or disguise them as original creations. On the other hand, in those events thought to express and embody Hebrew culture, a conscious attempt was made to create and stage performances that were original in nature, or at least to represent them as original. In reality, these events were a combination of European models and of models taken from the Jewish tradition of various time periods, which were adapted and assembled into a new structure. The components themselves did not have to be new; the innovative aspects were the structure created from these components, their context and text, the significance attributed to them, and the way in which they were staged in the public space.

It is important to note that the festival system in all the social settings described above adhered to the traditional Hebrew calendar of festivals (with several additions), even when they were given a different content and emphasis. In this way, a common national calendar of holidays was created, one that incorporated the continuation of an old tradition, the revival of ancient traditions, and the invention of new traditions. It seems correct to say that this festive culture was internalized, and was an inseparable part of the worldview and life of the Jewish society. Most of those who created the new festive culture were immigrants from Europe, and the festivals and ceremonies reflected their worldview and the models that were familiar to them; in any case, the greater part of the Jewish population in Eretz-Israel at that time consisted of immigrants from various European countries. As for participants and spectators, immigrants from Asian and African Muslim countries (school pupils or city residents) apparently did not feel estranged from the new festivals, in which an attempt was made to introduce elements of (a revised) tradition along European lines.

The aim of the new set of rituals, festivals, and ceremonies was not only to serve as a tool for the creation and disseminating of national historical myths, symbols, and ethos, nor only to strengthen the social-national ties and inner solidarity. Thus, for example, the Festival of First Fruits and Tu biShevat, which had an important status in the new system of festivals and for which a rich repertoire, symbolic in nature, was written, were not associated with historical myth. They were intended to add a theatrical-performative dimension, with its artistic-aesthetic character, to the day-to-day life of the Jewish society. Indeed, many ceremonies aimed at serving national ideology, and its artistic components were considered a means of indoctrination. However, since much effort was devoted to the enhancement of the ceremonies' artistic value, art was able to become a part of public life. Certain parts of the performative dimension served not only as creators of stations of "sacred time" but also as creators of "pockets" of informality and joy within daily life.

The Hebrew stagers met with a great measure of success. The fact that, in later years, many of the festivals were divested of their meaning, or their message was weakened or disappeared, and thus failed to imprint this vital dimension of mystery on every rite and symbol, cannot dim the great success they enjoyed for a brief period. After 1948, the sovereign state and its various agencies took over the role of shaping the society's performative sphere. The organization of the Independence Day and Holocaust Day ceremonies was the consummate expression of this role and its fulfillment.[3] The state and its agencies succeeded in creating official rules of ceremony in the political sphere, in shaping the performative aspect of the army, in preserving patterns of festivals in the kindergartens and the lower grades of elementary school, while the state's efforts to shape ceremonial rules and lifestyles in other areas met with total failure. The attempt to create an official folk culture, insofar as the performative dimension is concerned, was successful during the time of the Yishuv, but failed in later years. This, however, in no way detracts from the importance and the value of the repertoire this attempt produced, one that continues to function until the present day. On the other hand, Israeli society in the sovereign state was much more successful than the Yishuv society in institutionalizing an official ceremonial culture and ceremoniousness.

From the historical perspective, however, seldom can we find a group of cultural entrepreneurs-stagers who were able to write (and compose) in so short a period such a large corpus of texts, designed to become a national holy scripture, to invent traditions, myths, ritual attributes, saints, and martyrs, and to stage a set of life-cycle holidays, ceremonies, and festivals which created both a new public culture and a new official folk culture, as an integral part of a new national culture. And they succeeded in creating and disseminating all of this without the aid of a coercive state authority.

The State of Israel, whose various authorities had a greater control over society (in particular the school system and the army) "from above," was very interested in bureaucratically shaping the public space and public culture, and thus its official stagers had more tools and means at their disposal. Moreover, starting from the 1970s, new inventors of tradition emerged "from below," this time in the traditional and Orthodox society. They invented inter alia a new lore of popular-religious rituals.

In this study, then, we attempt to add another chapter to the history of the new Hebrew culture. It was not the only modern culture to invent a folklore, traditions, or urban-civic festivals. However, it does seem a unique case, in which all these elements were invented and introduced almost simultaneously and within a short amount of time.

As we noted in the introduction, it seems that the history of the Hebrew culture in Eretz-Israel can serve as a case study shedding some light on the patterns of creating, constructing and institutionalizing a performative lore in other societies, where one can assume that the same mechanisms functioned even if they cannot be precisely reconstructed, as they can be in the case of the Hebrew culture.

The case of Hebrew culture in Jewish Palestine shows that one knows that a group of creators and stagers has succeeded if and when it becomes an anonymous group, whose work is regarded as a collective creation. In other words, so that the tradition may really be a "tradition," its "invented" character needs to be blurred, or even expunged.

Appendix 1

First Program for a Commemoration of the First Fruits Festivity, 1929

1. Principles

The program is based on the following principles:
1st. Avoid adopting the routine pattern of celebration, such as pupils' processions in the streets, speeches, and the like. Consequently, no speeches, not even opening and closing speeches, have been included in the program.
2nd. Have the pupils themselves conduct the ceremony.
3rd. Hold the ceremony out in nature. In those towns and moshavoth where the first fruits are collected, it should be held near the city or moshavah at a suitable location. In any event, the venue of the ceremony should never be in a hall or any building.

2. Details of the Program

1st. The pupils from grades six and seven in elementary schools and the parallel grades in high school will participate.
Note: In those schools that do not have grades six and seven, the pupils in the last two grades will participate.
2nd. The pupils from the other classes bring the first fruits into the school the day before, and the participating classes also bring their first fruits. The children in kindergartens also bring their first fruits to the kindergarten which hands them into the central location where they are to be brought.

3rd. The day the first fruits are brought throughout the country—the 7th day of Sivan—at 5 P.M.

4th. Until this hour, the bearers of the first fruits from the schools in the vicinity assemble at a pre-determined center and stand with their flags in the places marked for each school. The pupils must be adorned with greenery, and most important of all, wear wreaths of greenery on their heads.

Note: Wherever conditions permit, the entire locale will be decorated with olive leaves.

5th. No general procession is held in the streets; each school goes directly to the field allocated for the first fruits.

6th. The field is divided in two parts: one serves as a place where the participants in the festivity take up their places and the other is intended for the ceremony of receiving the first fruits.

7th. In the latter part, a first-fruits gate is put, suitably decorated (no paper decorations are to be used). In the middle of the field, there will be a wide stage.

8th. For 20 minutes, while the participants take up their places, an orchestra plays holiday melodies.

9th. Drummers and flutists should be recruited from among the schoolchildren.

10th. After the 20 minutes are up, an order is given by the chief usher to the captains of each school, and then the first fruit bearers, carrying the first fruits in baskets or in their hands, come forth and stand before their school.

Note 1: It is preferable to have the first fruits in baskets, so the bearers can carry them on their shoulders.

Note 2: The first fruits can be brought to the city or the moshava by wagon, automobile, donkeys, camels, etc. But before they arrive at the field, they should be unloaded so that each one can take his bundle or basket.

1st. After all the pupils have taken their places, there is a bugle blast, the sign for the procession of first fruit bearers to leave their assembly point and move in a procession through the gate into the first-fruits field. There they take up their places around the stage. They are followed by all the other participants who arrange themselves around the first fruit bearers.

2nd. During this procession, a choir made up of pupils from all or some of the schools sings a song, whose words are taken from verses of Psalms.

3rd. After the singing, the first fruits are waved in the air and the joint choir recites, with the proper rhythm, a proclamation of the bringing of first fruits.

4th. The first fruits are lowered and placed at the edge of the stage or on the ground next to it.
5th. The orchestra plays a song "Bringing the First Fruits."
6th. A large trumpet blast to signal the end of the ceremony.
7th. Everyone disperses and goes back to their places, accompanied by the orchestra and the singing of a special song.
8th. At the end of the festivity, it is a good idea for the schoolchildren to play games and dance to the accompaniment of the orchestra.
9th. The vital conditions for the success of the ceremony are accuracy and order.

(Prepared by the Art Committee)

Appendix 2

Commemoration of the First Fruits: Proposal for a Ceremony, 1934

Location and Arrangement of Ceremony

A. **Ceremony Enclosure**—a large flat courtyard surrounded by a fence. A path or track marked in chalk all around the enclosure (elliptical).

B. **Stage**—made of several platforms with steps. Ramps on the sides for the chorus, and in the center a watchtower and flagpole with the national flag. Signs painted with national symbols and symbols of the seven species hang from the tower.
In the center of the stage—a "pedestal" above several narrow stairs on which to place the "cornucopia of the seven species."
The stage is located at the edge of the enclosure opposite the audience.

C. **Outer gate**—serves as the entrance to the enclosure.

The gate is festooned with flags and wreaths of greenery with inscriptions relating to the holiday.

D. **First fruit gates**—seven gates for the seven columns passing through.
The gates are placed parallel to the path and a few steps from it, at equal distances from each other.
Each gate is made of two columns or arches (not too high), and are festooned with garlands of cypress leaves and the symbols of the seven species. Each gate is about 1.20m wide. Seven paths marked in chalk lead

from the gates to the stage. A semicircle about seven steps from the stage forms a border.

E. **Ramps for the first fruit garlands** are placed at each of the first fruit gates. The ramp—a light box 60 × 100 cm with a step, can be moved and has two poles with which to carry it

Cross-section of ramp.

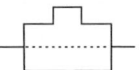

Participants

Whole classes participate in offering the first fruits. At each school's internal ceremony, most of the classes offer first fruits.

At a central regional or district ceremony, several classes are chosen from each school, generally sixth grade, and sometimes also seventh.

A. **The First Fruit Bearers** march two abreast in seven columns.

The first fruit bearers are dressed in white with white caps and a garland of leaves and flowers on their heads. Each of the bearers carries a basket filled with first fruits. **The lead pair** in each column carries a single basket of first fruits which will be used to decorate the first fruit gates.

The baskets of all the lead pairs are identical in size and appearance.

The costumes are stylistic. If possible, the garlands are of olive leaves entwined with flowers

B. **Column Leaders** march at the head of the columns and will conduct the ceremony.

They are dressed like the first fruit bearers with striped cloaks over their costumes. They carry long shepherds' staffs.

C. **The Artisans**—They receive the first fruit bearers. They are students in available [invited?] classes and are divided into three groups. They wear colorful stylistic robes. The girls among them carry drums and cymbals.

The name comes from the Mishnah, a tradition of the ancient holiday

D. **Chief Artisans** are the largest group of Artisans. Their job is to escort the procession of first fruits:

When the procession reaches the stage, they become the chorus.

The Chief Artisans wear cloaks over their costumes.

Boys and girls—about a third of each group are from the school choruses.

On Stage

E. The Celebrants—boys from the upper grade—they receive the first fruits and bless the bearers.

F. Assistants: "Acolytes"—seven pairs corresponding to the seven columns. They install the first fruit decorations of the lead pair in each column.

Buglers bearing long bugles adorned with the flags of the seven species.

G. "The Daughters of Zion"—a dance troupe for the dance of the first fruits. Each holds a scythe and a sheaf of wheat. Their costumes are girdled with leaves and flowers with which they festoon the "pedestal" and the "cornucopia of the seven species" on it.
Everyone on stage wears a stylistic costume.

H. The Master of Ceremonies. The Music Conductor. The Sentinel on the Watchtower.

> At central ceremonies—boys from the most senior high school chorus. Third and fourth grade boys.

II Selection of the First Fruits

On the first of Iyar, the classes go into their garden, find the fruit and vegetables that have ripened, mark them with a ribbon, place a sign reading "First Fruits," and recite the following:

"These are the first fruits! They are for redemption of the land!"

Throughout the month, the classes take particular care of their garden to ensure that the first fruits grow well. They make and decorate baskets for the first fruits and white clothes for the holiday.

III Preparation of the First Fruits

On the day of the first fruit offering the classes in the ceremony assemble and arrange themselves with their baskets in the schoolyard. At the appointed time, they all go into the garden singing:

> "And you shall observe the Feast of Weeks, of the first fruits of the wheat harvest" to the end of the verse . . .

> Each class separately.

In the garden, they circle the beds of the first fruits, the teacher recites and they repeat:

"First fruits, first fruits! Taken from our land, for its redemption you shall return!"

They immediately pick the first fruits and collect them in baskets, singing:

"The earth has yielded its produce, the land flowing with milk and honey!"

Festooned with flowers and leaves.

When the first fruits have been collected and decorated, they lift the baskets to their shoulders, rise and leave, singing:

"Our baskets on our shoulders, our heads garlanded . . ."

They return to the classroom, put on their white costumes, caps, and wreaths and wait for the time to offer the first fruits.

IV Offering of the First Fruits
— Program of the Ceremony —

The first fruits are offered on the day following the feast of Shavuot at sunset

4–4:30 in the afternoon.

1. Preamble.

The Columns of first fruit bearers wait outside the outer gate of the enclosure.
  The Artisans (who will welcome the first fruit bearers), arranged in groups, enter the enclosure. The groups converge and exchange holiday greetings:
  "Happy Holiday!"
  And questions:
  "Have you seen them? Have the first fruit bearers come?"
  The groups turn to look at the watchtower.

Several of the Chief Artisans step out and call to the sentinel on the tower:
  "Guard, what is happening? Have you seen them coming?"

The Sentinel answers:
  "I see a crowd. I will alert you when they arrive!"

The Groups of Artisans, as they wait for the first fruit bearers, sing and dance to the music of the drum and cymbals. Some organize games and contests among the groups.
—From afar, the shouts of the celebrating crowd are heard . . .

Exhibition games played at a swift, unceasing pace.

The Columns of first fruit bearers approach the gate. A flute and drum are heard, along with singing: "Hallelujah—Arise and let us go up."

The Lookout on the tower waves his banner and calls out:
"Go to the gate, they are coming, they are coming!"

2. Reception

The Groups of Artisans cease their singing and dancing and call to each other:
"Let us go and receive the bearers of the first fruits! Arise, let us go and meet our brothers who are coming!"

The Orchestra plays "With Flutes and Cymbals" for the reception.

Words and music continuous.

The Chief Artisans of each group step forward and walk toward the gate to receive the arrivals, coming together to form a single group as they all move toward the gate, skipping and singing while banging the cymbals and drums in their hands to the beat of the music.

Each group takes its predetermined place.

The Artisans also hasten to "find a place" along the path near the gate in order to greet the arrivals.

3. First Fruits Procession.

Orchestra: "Behold, how good it is"

Words and music continuous.

The First Fruit Bearers march through the gate column by column holding their baskets of first fruits on their shoulders, with a drum and flute leading the way.
The procession is led by the "symbol of the commemoration of the first fruits"—the seven species carried by a special group on a large flat cornucopia adorned with flowers.

Heaped up in the cornucopia.

The Greeters welcome them at the gate with cries of:
"You are welcome to enter by our gates!"
—They escort the columns in three groups: Group 1 at the head of the first column; Group 2 at the head

of the third column; Group 3 at the head of the sixth column.

The Columns of First Fruit Bearers stream in past the Artisans on the path circling the enclosure.

The Greeters, group by group, dance before them banging drums and cymbals.
When the first column passes before the Artisans, the greeters at the head of the column call out:
"You are welcome to enter by our gates!"

All the Artisans wave their banners and respond: Repeated several times. The greeters call out as they dance.
"You are welcome to enter by our gates!"
When the third column passes, the greeters at the head of the column call out:
"Make way, make way!"

All the Artisans call:
"Make way, make way!"
—and scatter flowers before the procession.
When the sixth column passes, the greeters at the head of the column call out:
"Surely rejoice, surely rejoice!"

All the Artisans clap and respond: Repeated several times.
"Surely rejoice, surely rejoice!"

Everyone sings "Arise and Let Us Go Up" and "Our Baskets" accompanied by the orchestra.

The Columns of First Fruit Bearers turn toward the first fruit gates—each column to its corresponding gate—and stand before them. At a distance of 5–6 steps from the gate.

The Chief Artisans escorting the columns separate into seven groups, one group for each gate, and then stand in place.

4. Decoration.
Two buglers appear on the central turret of the stage and play a fanfare.
—This is followed by soft rhythmic bells . . .

The Group of Acolytes appears at the sound of the bells from the sides of the stage, two abreast, carrying garlands with which to festoon the first fruits and walking up and down the ramps to the first fruit gates. Seven pairs for the seven columns of first fruit bearers.

The Orchestra plays "The Decoration Song." The first four bars serve as the cue for the children's singing. Words and music continuous. Sung once or twice, depending on the distance from the stage to the gates. After the singing, the clarinet continues playing the melody on its own until the decorators reach the gates.

The Columns of First Fruit Bearers with their escorts from among the Chief Artisans join the orchestra singing the first verse of the song.

The Acolytes, in pairs, walk majestically in a widely spaced forward-facing line, each pair walking on the path leading to its corresponding gate.

The Chief Artisans crowding around the gates go forward to meet the Acolytes when they reach the middle of the enclosure. When the two groups converge, the Chief Artisans make a path for the Acolytes and fall in behind them, following them up to the first fruit gates.

The Lead Pairs of the columns move toward the Acolytes from the other side of the gates as the latter approach the gates. The two pairs are meant to arrive at the same time and together climb the ramp to the gate, the pair of Acolytes from one side and the pair receiving decoration from the other.
When they reach the gate—the flute music stops.
Silence . . .

The Acolytes and Pairs Receiving Decoration climb the ramp in silence.

The Pairs Receiving Decoration hold out their baskets of first fruits to the decorators, who hold their garlands over the baskets and stand waiting.

The Orchestra plays the second verse of "The Decoration Song." Second verse: "This our basket let us raise . . ." Held out at an angle.

The First Fruit Bearers hold out their first fruits and respond to the orchestra, singing:
"And let us adorn it" to the end of the song.
When they finish, they stand at attention.

The Acolytes lower the garlands they have been holding aloft and decorate the baskets of first fruits held by the lead pairs in the columns.

The First Fruit Bearers lower the baskets they have been holding out to shoulder-level.

The Acolytes recite the blessing: "Adorn your year of plenty!"

The First Fruit Bearers respond: "A good year and adorned!"

The Acolytes and the Pairs that have been decorated descend backward down the ramp. They turn and return to their places.

A slow descent. They lower themselves and sit down slowly at the signal of the Column Leaders.

The First Fruit Bearers sit in line to rest, setting their baskets of first fruits down in front of them.

The Orchestra: "Halleluiah—Let Us Arise and Go Up."

The Chief Artisans pick up the ramps by their poles and place them around the foot of the stage in a half-circle. They ascend the platforms allocated to them at the sides of the stage and form the chorus for the ceremony. The Orchestra music stops.

5. Ascent to the Stage

The sound of a flute comes from one of the columns—"Rise Up My Brothers and Let Us Go Up" (first verse).

One or several flautists from the first fruit bearers. The leader of the middle column.

One of the Column Leaders repeats the verse, singing, while rising to his feet, pointing to the stage, and beckoning to the first fruit bearers.

The Columns sing "Rise Up My Brothers and Let Us Go Up," accompanied by the orchestra, from their seated position, while gesturing to each other to awaken and hasten.

The First Fruit Bearers, in their columns, rise to their feet singing the words "And Let Us Go Up to Mount Zion" a second time. They bend down and pick up their baskets of first fruits at the words "Baskets full . . . ," place the baskets on their shoulders, and stream through the gates walking excitedly toward the first fruits stage as they bow in greeting to each other with the music.

They rise slowly, and care should be taken that they do so in unison.

When they reach the borderline they stop. The music and singing cease.

The line is marked about 7.5 steps in front of the stage.

The First Fruit Bearers bend down at the signal of the conductor's baton and place their baskets of first fruits on the ground in front of them.

Order of Offering of the First Fruits

6. The Celebrants of the Ceremony.

The Group of Buglers ascends the stage by the two side ramps, bugling as they walk and heralding the arrival of the celebrants coming to begin their "work."

The buglers play "Look Down." See music.

The Celebrants walk toward the assemblage of first fruit bearers and extend their hands over them in prayer:
"Look down from your holy abode . . . "
When they complete the prayer, they hold out their hands toward the audience and greet them, saying:
"Our brothers, children of Israel, you have brought the first fruits—welcome!"

Words and music continuous.

The chorus assists the Celebrants in song.

The Columns respond:
"Peace on Israel"

The Celebrants: "You are blessed today in the name of Israel!"

The Columns: "May Israel be blessed now and forever!"

7. Blessing on the Seven Species.
The sound of bells . . .

The Bearers of the "Symbol of the Commemoration of the Seven Species" cornucopia ascend the stage and place the cornucopia on the pedestal reserved for it in the center of the stage, bow and descend.

The Chief Celebrant goes to the pedestal.

Two Celebrants standing at his left and right hold the cornucopia of the seven species out to him.

After counting off each species, he replaces it and takes another.

The Chief Celebrant takes one species at a time from the cornucopia, inspects it, holds it aloft, counting and saying:
"Wheat—one; and barley—two; and vines—three; and fig—four; and pomegranate—five; olives—six; dates—seven"—"These are the seven species with which our land has been blessed since the time of our forefathers, as it says in the Torah":—He holds his hands over the cornucopia and continues:
"For the Lord your God is bringing you into a good land, a land with streams and springs and fountains issuing from plain and hill; a land of wheat and barley, of vines, figs and pomegranates; a land of olive trees and honey."
(Deut. 8:7–8)

The Celebrants replace the cornucopia on the pedestal.

8. Dance of Praise.

The Orchestra and Chorus play and sing "They Who Sow in Tears," accompanied by the drums and cymbals.

A different song can be chosen, such as "With Flutes and Cymbals" (continuous), etc.

The Daughters of Zion Troupe performs a dance on stage before the pedestal of the Seven Species. Each holds a scythe and sheaf of wheat.

The Dancers perform the Dance of the First Fruit, reaping and sheaving: they collect the bundles of wheat into a single sheaf and place it on the pedestal beside the cornucopia, dancing around the pedestal, decorating it and the sheaf with the garlands of olive leaves and roses on their heads and around their waists and then taking their places at the sides.

One by one, the dancers remove the garlands from their heads and waists and use them as decorations.

9. Hymn to the First Fruits.

The Buglers play the melody of the verse: "You shall observe the Feast of Weeks" until the end . . .

The first verse of the hymn.

The Chief Celebrant and the Group around him (the chief celebrants) move in a half-circle to the pedestal and place their hands on the sheaf. All the celebrants sing:
"You shall observe the Feast of Weeks, of the first fruits of the wheat harvest"

Column 1 of the First Fruit Bearers sings:
"And to bring the first fruits of our soil, and of every fruit of every tree."

All the verses are conducted from the stage. The orchestra should accompany the singing where possible, especially the refrain: "The earth has yielded its produce . . ."

All the Columns and the Chorus respond:
"The earth has yielded its produce, the land flowing with milk and honey!"

Column 2 sings:
"You shall enjoy the fruit of your labors; you shall be happy and you shall prosper."

Column 3 sings:
"They who sow in tears shall reap with songs of joy."

All the Columns and the Chorus respond:
"The earth has yielded its produce . . . " to the end

Column 4 sings:
"Though he goes along weeping, carrying the seed-bag, He shall come back with songs of joy, carrying his sheaves."

Column 5 sings:
"They shall plant vineyards and they shall make gardens,
And drink their wine and eat their fruits."

All the Columns and the Chorus respond:
"The earth has yielded its produce . . ." to the end.

Column 6 sings:
"When the Lord restores the fortunes of his people, Jacob shall exult, Israel shall rejoice."

Column 7 sings:
"In days to come Jacob shall strike root, Israel shall sprout and blossom."

All the Columns and the Chorus respond:
"The earth has yielded its produce . . ." to the end.

The Celebrants place their hands on the sheaf, and toss it onto the cornucopia of the seven species.

10. The First Fruits Bible Passages.
A loud bugle call.

The First Fruit Bearers reach down and pick up the baskets by the rims.

Seven Pairs of Celebrants from the front row descend and stand on the platform above the lowest, each pair facing one of the seven columns.

At the sign of the conductor's baton, they slowly bend down sideways and outward, pick up the baskets and rise carefully maintaining unison in each movement.

The Acolytes, from their platform, rise and say:
"Remembrance of the first fruits in the Temple: Thus did our forefathers when the Temple stood, they would bring the first of the fruits of the land, raise them aloft and deliver them to the priest and thus would they say."

The Celebrants arranged in groups open scrolls removed from their pouches, show them to the group and respond, reciting in unison the First Fruits passages:
(reciting) "My father was a fugitive Aramean. He went down to Egypt with meager numbers and sojourned there; but there he became a very great and populous nation.
(reading) The Egyptians dealt harshly with us and oppressed us; they imposed heavy labor upon us . . .
"We cried to the Lord, the God of our fathers, and the Lord heard our plea . . .

Each group gathers for the reading around one scroll, and the readers sway slowly as they read. The Chief Celebrant starts with "My father" and the others continue from "went down to Egypt." The (reciting) He brought us to this place, and gave us this land, a land flowing with milk and honey." (Deut. 26: 5–9)

11. Raising the First Fruits.

The Lead Pairs of the Columns move forward and slowly ascend the first platform holding their basket out to the celebrants standing opposite them.

The Celebrants place their hands under the hands of the offerers, wait for the end of the recitation and together they raise the first fruits aloft,

All the First Fruit Bearers then raise their baskets and repeat after the Celebrants, word by word:

Celebrants: "And now / the Bearers: and now / Here / we have brought / here / we have brought / the first fruits of our land / the first fruits of our land / as a gift / as a gift / to redeem the land of Israel / to redeem the land of Israel. / When the recitation is completed, they lower the baskets to their shoulders and bow.

12. Blessing of the Celebrants.

The Celebrants raise their hands and bless the Bearers and their first fruits saying:
"Blessed shall you be in the city!"—Bearers: "Blessed!"
"Blessed shall you be in the country!"—Bearers: "Blessed!"
"Blessed shall be the fruit of your land!"—Bearers: "Blessed!"
"And blessed shall be the fruit of your labor!"—Bearers: "Blessed!"
"Blessed shall you be in your comings!"—Bearers: "Blessed!"
"And blessed shall you be in your goings!"—Bearers: "Blessed!"

13. Giving Thanks for the First Fruits.

The Orchestra plays the "Song of Thanks" as an introductory segment

All the First Fruit Bearers rise and recite the "Song of Thanks," singing the whole song once.

14. Delivering the First Fruits.

---

recitation is mannered, patterned on a Torah reading.

As the final verse of the Torah Portion is being recited: "He brought us . . ."

Bow by nodding their heads.

Music continuous.

Music continuous.

The Orchestra resumes playing from the beginning.

All Seven Columns stream at the same time toward the stage and deliver their first fruits to the celebrants standing in the front, who hand them to those behind them, who place them on the stage.

The Pairs of First Fruit Bearers in each column, after delivering their baskets, circle around—those on the right to the right and those on the left to the left—descending past the column and continuing until all the first fruits are delivered to the celebrants.

pairs
The Columns remain in line in reverse order, their backs to the stage.

The Orchestra stops playing.—All stand in place.

15. Joy of the First Fruits.

The Column Leaders meet in front of the central column, hold out their hands and declare joyously in unison.
"Our storehouses are full, affording all manner of store; Our flocks number thousands . . .
Happy are the people who have it so! . . ."

Standing on the stage platforms as the chorus.

The Chief Artisans from their place raise they hands and respond:
"Happy are the people who have it so"

One Bearer from the Columns cries out clapping:
"Rejoice in your festival! . . ."

Several others join in and repeat:

"Rejoice in your festival! . . ."

Another from the Columns leaps on the shoulders of other bearers, waving his hand and crying:
"And you shall have nothing but joy!"

They take hold of him and lift him up.

Several from each Column respond:
"And you shall have nothing but joy!"

They call out waving their hands.

All the Columns cry out:
"Nothing but joy! Nothing but joy!—Rejoice in your festival and you shall have nothing but joy!"

The Orchestra, after three beats of the large drum and cymbals, plays the dance melody from "Jeremiah" (or some other appropriate music)

As a cue for the dance. Music continuous. A general dance with several repeated movements in lines and circles.

The Columns dance to the music of the orchestra.

The Artisans and Chief Artisans, from their place, dance in the same movements beating their drums and cymbals.

16. Finale.

Bugle call: "For The Anthem"

All—"Attention!"

Orchestra: marching music

The Columns leave the enclosure in an orderly procession accompanied by cries of farewell and blessings from the Chief Artisans:

Chief Artisans: "May it be so next year!"   They call out and wave goodbye.

Columns (as they leave): "May it be so next year!"

Artisans—standing along the path: "Farewell!"

Columns: "Farewell, farewell, to near and far!"

(Arranged on the basis of the 1934 program by A. Shapiro, Secretary of the TC and prepared by the Arts Committee.)

Appendix 3

Planting on the New Year for Trees (Tu Bishevat), 1930s

The Location and Arrangements for the Planting

A well-fenced plot or boulevard prepared for planting.

A field for the festivity ceremony—next to the planting plot—fenced off with ropes and marked by chalk lines, flags, etc.

The platform for the saplings—at the top of the field—made of steps in the form of a natural hill with a square on top, on which there is the trunk of a almond tree, on its cloth branches, flowers (of plywood and cardboard) are blooming—a symbol of the festival of the tree. The entire platform is covered with greenery and the stairs are hidden by a green thicket of branches.

The saplings are in flowerpots ready to be planted, arranged in rows on the stairs of the platform and at its foot.

A mast for the national flag, as high as possible, is next to the platform at the head of the field.

The Participants

The audience—schools or one school with all its classes, who have come to partake of the joy of planting, assemble outside the festivity field and stand in two parallel rows, in threes or fours depending on the number of participants and the area of the field.

The planters—delegations of representatives of schools or classes, of the same number as the number of saplings to be planted. Every planter is accompanied by two helpers—one carrying a spade, the other a watering can. They are arranged in threes: the planter in the middle and his two helpers on both sides of him.

The planters and their helpers are wearing khaki trousers (skirts) and white shirts. It is a good idea for the entire audience to be dressed the same.

The head planter—a student from the highest class, holding a spade.

The planting honor guard symbolizes the care and maintenance of plants in nature—a group of 15–30 boys and girls from grades 7 and 8, fill all the roles on the platform:

Head of the guard—a pupil aged 14–17, with a nice appearance and good voice, and his four attendants, representing the four seasons of the year, all members of the higher school classes, dressed in long white shirts with wide sleeves, with colorful robes on them, in the spirit of the seasons. They have wreathes on their heads; in one hand, they hold a tall rod, in the other, a scroll bearing the verse of the day. *A group of flutists*—6–8 children dressed in striped shirts with skullcaps on their heads; *a group of girls -dancers and keepers of the seedlings*—wearing long white shirts decorated with greenery and flowers, with wreathes on their heads.

A group of heralds—4 boys and girls, dressed in white with hoops on their heads and wings (made of gold cardboard) at their sides, holding flowering almond branches.

Bearers of the "fifteen" fruits—4–5 girls (from the heralds and keepers of the seedlings) walk in front carrying a basket of flowers. The rest carry fruits from the "fifteen": carobs, almonds, dates, figs and citrus fruits, on large trays, made of straw. They wear white shirts with wide belts and have wreathes on their heads.

A group of drummers and trumpeters—carrying flags with national symbols and planting symbols.

An orchestra and choir—they stand alongside the platform.

The conductor of the ceremony—conducts the singing and playing of musical instruments.

Order of the Festivity

"Tu biShevat has arrived" (a herald)

A company of drummers and trumpeters come on to the field, playing their instruments. When they get to the middle of the field, they stand and play the melody of the day: "The almond tree is blooming"—the first stanza (twice).

(Standing—they raise their trumpets to their mouths in unison)

The orchestra replies by playing the second stanza.

The group of drummers and trumpeters march to the sound of the orchestra and arrange themselves alongside it.

The orchestra (and choir) open by playing "The Tu biShevat anthem".

The audience moves in two rows and take their places on the border of the festivity field on both sides of the sapling platform—*the rows of planters and their attendants*—before each school (class).

Note: The route of the planting procession should be decorated with ribbons and signs bearing inscriptions of Tu biShevat verses and slogans, which the schools or classes have prepared in advance. If conditions permit, they will be accompanied by large posters with symbols and drawings on planting and the forestation of the land, carried on their shoulders on litters adorned with chains of greenery and wild flowers.

The Message of the Day

A group of flutists goes up to the stage to play nature songs. They are followed by the heralds bearing flowering almond branches. The group of flutists remains in the place designated for it on the platform, at the side, on two of the stairs. They walk down to the first step and utter a proclamation. They are answered by a single voice, who then turns to the audience and says: "Rise and rejoice in the field, go out to meet the sun!"

The trumpeters in the orchestra play the melody "The almond tree is flowering" (first stanza). Then the entire orchestra plays the entire song. Everyone speaks a verse and an individual replies with another. Then they all turn and go down behind the platform.

Opening the ceremony with the raising of the national flag

The sound of a gong.

The conductor: On the day of our planting, we will raise the flag of Israel as a sign that we are planting today in this place for the sake of our land together with all our brethren in all the schools of the country. Skyward, the flag!

The audience of pupils stands at attention.

The orchestra—to the sound of a drum and trumpets—"Flying the flag."

The flag is raised on the mast.

Reading the [scriptural] verse of the day

The head of the honor guard and his four attendants climb on to the platform to the sound of a trumpet blast, and stand facing the heavens. They unroll scrolls and read the daily portion (in unison, or divided between the head of the guard and his attendants).

The crowd of participants responds by singing *Tichazekna*.

Song of the Day

—Dancing—

A group of flutists plays a shepherd melody. The "drowsy" seedling guard begins to wake up very slowly (moving to the rhythm of the flute music). As the orchestra plays "Song of the Day" the seedling guard awakens, arises and in a symbolic dance, expresses the awakening of nature.

—The choir—

The seedling guard recites a verse from Psalms and the audience replies, making appropriate gestures.

The orchestra, choir and seedling guard sing the first stanza of a song, and at the same time the planters, holding the saplings—leave their columns and take their place opposite the platform, leaving their assistants behind. They encircle the platform once, while the heads of the seedling guard walk in front of them, leading them. The audience responds by singing the second stanza of the song, while clapping their hands.

The groups encircling the platform walk at a slow pace, then they take their place in the columns of their assistants who are standing at the side and receive them with singing. The heads of the seedling guard, who led the circuit, return to the platform.

In the next party, the choir and the seedling guard alternately sing stanzas of songs.

This is followed by the recitation of blessings for the New Year of the Trees. At the same time, the group bearing the "fifteen fruits" comes on to the platform—three carrying trays of fruit and one in front carrying a basket of flowers. They stand on one of the steps, waving the trays and reciting a blessing. Then the planters wave their saplings. The orchestra bursts forth with a merry tune, and the bearers of fruits and flowers throw handfuls of fruit in the direction of the planters and flowers on the field at the foot of the platform.

The head of the seedling guard, with outstretched hands, speaks the blessing: "Happy New Year, trees!" and the audience repeats after him "Happy New Year" (2).

The head of the guard: "To a blessing and not a curse!"
The audience: "Amen!"
The head of the guard: "To plenty and not to want!"
Audience: "Amen!"

Head of guard: "To life and not to death!"
Audience: "Amen and amen!"
The head planter waves the "covenant-seedling" and calls out: "The time to plant has come!"
All the planters reply: "Here we are and we shall plant!"

The Planting Procession

To the music of the orchestra, the columns of planters and their helpers move merrily in a single file to the planting plot. There they go over to the rows of holes prepared in advance and each threesome—the planter and his helpers—go over to their hole. The audience and the orchestra accompany them with singing, waving their hands in greeting and cheering them on. After the planters have passed them, the schools (classes) follow them and encircle the planting plot. The orchestra stops playing and goes to the planting area.

A blessing on the planting

A trumpet blast.
The planters and their helpers bend over the hole, place the sapling in it and remain waiting.
The head planter stands in the middle on a high place, prepared in advance and blesses the planting:
"May the seedling be blessed, rise and grow!"
The planters and their helpers repeat the blessing and complete the work of planting, accompanied by the orchestra.

Reception for the planters

The orchestra plays a tune, and the audience sings. The planters and their helpers move into the middle and from there walk in a procession to the platform.
The reception party—a group of 8 to 12 girls—alights from the platform carrying palm branches, they bow, waving the branches up and down, receiving the planters with honor. When the second stanza of the song is being sung, they walk backward to the platform.
The planters and their attendants split into three columns and remain standing opposite the platform.

The covenant with the tree

The conductor: "Today, on this New Year for trees, we enter into a covenant with the trees and vegetation of our land."

Planting on the New Year for Trees

A loud trumpet blast.

The head planter climbs on to the stage when the blast is heard, his spade on his shoulder. The head of the honor guard takes a sapling handed him by one of his attendants, goes down to meet the head planter, who places his palm under the sapling handed him and says:

"With this seedling today we enter into a covenant with the tree of our land, to plant and care for it, and we shall fulfill the promise:

> I shall plant cedars in the wilderness,
> Acacias, myrtles and wild olives;
> I shall grow pines on the barren heath
> Side by side with fir and box tree (Isaiah 31:19)

(His four attendants, standing around him, repeat each line of the verse).

The head planter replies: Amen!

The audience—in unison: Amen and amen!

The head planter receives the sapling from the head of the guard, and turns to the audience, raising the sapling above his head:

"You have heard the words of this covenant. You are all witnesses today!"

All the planters reply in unison:

"Witnesses and witnesses! We, the children of Israel, today have given unto the trees this covenant: we shall plant them within our boundaries, we shall keep them alive and forever plant them in our midst!"

The audience calls out: "Forever, forever!"

The head planter descends from the platform and goes back to his place at the head of the column of planters.

A trumpet blast. The planters and the seedling guard sing, the audience responds with a song. At the same time, the planters draw closer to the platform and prepare to receive the saplings.

(Art Committee)

Appendix 4

Program for Purim Festivities in Tel Aviv, 1929

I. The objective

To improve the Tel Aviv Purim carnival, make it more beautiful, artistic and well organized.

II. The purpose
  (1) To continue the tradition, that has been followed for years, of celebrating Purim in a spectacular, festive manner.
  (2) To attract tourists from other countries by widely publicizing the Purim festival, with the aim of instilling the idea of building the country and familiarizing them with the new life being revived in it.
  (3) To artistically publicize and promote agricultural produce, industrial goods and local arts, as well as the aims of various organizations and institutions.
  (4) To improve the economic situation in the country through tourism, as a result of the enhanced income of hotels, shops, industry etc. throughout the country, particularly in Tel Aviv, and through tourists' investments in construction, agriculture, industry and commerce.
  (5) To increase the income earned by the Jewish National Fund from the Purim projects. The National Council of the Jewish National Fund feels committed to perpetuate this tradition, as it has done for several years, especially since this may increase the income gained from the Purim project, which is earmarked for purchasing land. However, the JNF calls on all interested national public institutions and other organizations and institutions, as well as commercial enterprises and industries, to assist with the project.

III. Organization of the Event

The National Council of the JNF undertakes the task of organizing the celebration, and is setting up a special committee for this purpose. The committee is composed of a representative of the JNF, a representative of the Municipality, and Messrs. Gefen, Fley and Aldema. It also is co-opting, for this purpose, representatives of the Manufacturers Association, the Chamber of Commerce, the Tourist Bureau, small tradesmen, hotels, artists from all fields, the Agricultural Center, sport federations, etc.

The Committee will be called "The Organization Committee for the Tel-Aviv Purim Festivities, 1929," part of the National Council of the Jewish National Fund.

(1) The Committee's functions include: approval of the festival program as prepared by various professional artists, and the execution thereof through sub-committees, each of which will function in its particular professional field according to an appropriate division of duties.

(2) The Committee is entitled to co-opt representatives of other institutions, as well as individuals, insofar as they are needed.

(3) All general questions relating to the festival program, the manner of execution, etc. will be decided by the Committee. Any disagreements between the National Council representative and the Committee will be resolved at a meeting of the Executive Committee of the National Council, with the participation of executive members of the Committee.

(4) A group of artists will work with the Committee, against payment, to prepare a full program of festivities, including the decoration of the entire length and breadth of the city, its neighborhoods, houses, public buildings and parks, from the banks of the Yarkon River to the last neighborhood. This group will also provide advice and guidance to the residents, exhibitors, factories, etc. so that every detail and exhibit in the procession will not only function as an advertisement but will also be aesthetically attractive.

(5) The festival will commence on the eve of Purim and last two-and-a-half days (March 25, 26, and 27), according to the program prepared by the artists and approved by the Committee.

(6) The festival program will include: Decoration of the houses with foliage, carpets, artistic drawings and various ornaments, confetti, electric lights, posters, slogans (both humorous and critical), a window shop competition, live pictures, processions, orchestras, athletic displays and competitions in the streets, plays at various times and places, pyramids, and scenery of Eretz Israel. All of the above should

be in keeping with the spirit of the holiday, to the extent possible, and stress the role of the JNF. The group of artists and engineers will be assigned the task of devising suitable artistic ways of combining all of these single impressions and turning all of the thousands of pictures and sights into one ensemble of a flourishing, developing city, intent on creativity, immersed in a sea of color and electric splendor—a complete portrait of artistic enterprise.

IV. The festival budget

The following entities will contribute to the budget: The Tel Aviv Municipality, Keren HaYesod, Jewish National Fund, the manufacturers, factories, shops, offices, etc.; hotels; export institutions; shipping agencies and other interested parties. In addition, money for the budget will be raised from the general public on two designated collection days, as well as from the sale of the festival newspaper and advertisements.

The carnival will take place on a Wednesday. The floats, automobiles, groups, processions, slogans and exhibits will pass through in a centralized fashion. All participants must inform a special committee of artists, set up for this purpose, of their subjects and the form of their exhibits.

Note 1: Participation in the carnival is subject to the permission of the committee.

Note 2: Non-artistic advertisement displays will not be included in the carnival.

The procession program and schedule, the order of appearance of the participants, location of open areas for dancing and additional orchestras, etc. will be determined by a special committee responsible for the parade, headed by a chairman.

Both sides of the main streets through which the procession will pass will be blocked by ropes and staffed by a group of ushers comprised of youth organization members.

V. Prizes

Prizes will be awarded for the best procession, best decorations, sport competitions, and the like. The first prize will be 25 pounds, the second 15 pounds, and the third 10 pounds. Manufacturers will distribute their own goods as prizes.

Judges from all fields of the arts will be appointed to choose the winners. All the prizes, including bank checks for the first three winners, will be placed on display in windows in city centers.

VI. The Committee's Plan of Action
1. Budget
   (a) Negotiate with the institutions regarding their participation in the budget.
   (b) Charge a fee to all manufacturers, hotels, drivers, institutions, schools, agencies, and all others having an interest in the festivities.
   (c) Designate two collection days to cover the expenses of the festival.
   (d) Negotiate with manufacturers and others about giving prizes to outstanding participants.
   (e) Set up an administration, an editorial board for the festival newspaper and organize sales.
   (f) Accept advertisements for the newspaper.

VI. Publicity
Publicize the festival and its program widely throughout the country and abroad by:
   1. preparing a poster;
   2. issuing a press release in various languages;
   3. sending notices through telegraphic agencies;
   4. releasing amusing news items about the ongoing work of the Committee, preparation of exhibits, plays, etc.;
   5. publishing the festival newspaper in Hebrew, English and German;
   6. advertisements in the cinema;
   7. a special postal stamp.

VII. Organization of the festival
   1. Negotiate with representatives of artists, manufacturers, farmers, sports clubs, orchestras, choirs, companies of actors, owners of automobiles and bicycles, shops, various youth organizations, etc. regarding their participation in the festivities.
   2. Establish a group of artists to prepare an artistic program for the festivities, decorate the city and provide advice and explanations to the participants.
   3. Conduct negotiations with youth organizations that will provide ushers, appoint an organization committee and a chairman to be responsible for the order and course of the procession and determine a location for each of the exhibits.
   4. Appoint a group of writers to prepare slogans, jingles etc. for the exhibitors, decorators and the institutions.

5. Appoint a committee to approve the exhibits' inclusion in the procession.
6. Appoint a panel of judges to award prizes.
7. Appoint an editorial board for the newspaper.

(Municipal Archive 4–32/8/A)

Appendix 5

A Citizen of Tel Aviv: A Proposal for the Organization of a Purim Carnival, 1931

I hereby submit to the Spring Projects Committee of the Tel Aviv Municipality our proposal for a "mass" pageant to be organized for the 1932 Purim festival, based on the following plan and description:

> The purpose of the pageant, other than to fulfill the requirements of a festivity, is to meet the demands of the hard times that have befallen our community and the entire [Jewish] people, to give some sort of historical lesson and to suggest some ways of organizing and coalescing into a nation in order to console our people in our times of suffering and to strengthen them in face of what the future holds.
>
> Below, we describe the pageant moving as a festive procession through the city streets. Throughout the description, we provide details about the arrangements and the costumes. This is to be followed by special remarks.
>
> 1. At the head [of the procession] two long poles are held aloft, to which a long, wide piece of cloth is attached, bearing the name of the pageant—ISRAEL AND HER ENEMIES—written in large letters. This mobile sign will serve as a gate for the pageant "scroll." Between the polebearers a line of people will pass. They will be a chorus, singing songs or just melodies without lyrics suitable for the occasion (after consultation with the conductor, see below). At the same time, they will give way to our procession.
>
>   At a considerable distance from the sign, an individual will march, in royal isolation. He will be a dignified elderly man, well built, energetic, but with a long white beard, dressed in a long

white robe and wearing a prayer shawl. In his right hand, he carries a wanderer's staff. He is Israel. . . .

2. Again, a considerable distance behind "Israel," groups will follow representing our enemies throughout our history. Each and every group, in chronological order, will depict the countries in which we have suffered. They will come one after the other, allowing some distance between them to leave an impression and to keep the concepts from becoming confused in the minds of the spectators.

Before each group, a white board in the form of a knight's shield will be carried, bearing the name and symbol of the country or nation and its motto as noted below. The members of the groups will wear some sort of "traditional" dress that they think symbolizes the period they represent. They will also carry a "weapon" typical of the country (of course, the weapons and clothing will be made of paper, plywood and the like).

The following is the order of the groups:

A. Egypt

The heading on the top of the board—**There was Egypt**
And the motto below—**Into the waters of the sea!**

A group of ancient Egyptians will appear, wearing white caps (like those worn by our hospital nurses) and white aprons. Their skin color will be dark brown. They are armed with a bow and arrow and are leading away several Jewish women holding their babies in small baskets. The Egyptians have the appearance of a cultured people, who know what they are doing. The women, their hair in disarray, project despair, slavery. The babies are being taken to the Nile . . .

B. Babylon

There was Babylon
Destruction

A company of Babylonian soldiers. In front, King Zedekiah and the Elders of Zion in Nehushtayim, being taken prisoner. Zedekiah's eyes have been pierced. Sorrowful singing . . .

C. Persia

There was Persia
Envy

Haman, leading his sons and men of the royal court, joyously exults, as the King has commanded, at the murder of the Jews. All of the Persians sing and play musical instruments, waving their swords as they go to the massacre.

D. *The Greeks*
There was Antiochus
Forced Conversion

Hannah and her seven small sons bedecked with doves are led to the gallows. . . . Hannah comforts the smallest of her children. They are followed by the Maccabees in a victory procession, Judah at its head, carrying the lit lamp.

E. *Rome*
There was Rome
Slavery

A company of Roman legionnaires, laurel wreaths of victory on their heads, carrying the lamp [of the Temple] upside down and a sign bearing the inscription: Judea Capta.

F. *Inquisition*
There was an Inquisition
Blood and Fire

A truck carrying a lit bonfire. On it is a beautiful young girl wearing a white robe, her hair disheveled. She is tied to a pillory, her eyes flashing sparks. From time to time, she murmurs the prayer "Oh hear me, Israel." Standing around the bonfire are hangmen dressed in red, medieval soldiers (landsknechts), other figures dressed in long, black clothing . . .

G. *Russia*
There was Russia
Killing

A group of rioters wearing red Russian shirts, Cossacks, soldiers . . . armed with lethal weapons—knives, axes, clubs . . . a mobile pogrom.

H.
There are still Bolsheviks
Exile

A group of "Chekhists" in leather uniforms lead prisoners of Zion, a map of the land [of Israel] and a Hebrew book into exile.

I. *There is still a Hitler*
Hunger

A company of brownshirts with the swastika insignia, holding clubs. They carry a salami and a huge bottle of beer along with a sign reading "Bread for the Aryans," "Death to Judah!"

J. And finally . . . carrying a blank board, with no name, motto or symbol on it, an orderly company of tall, slim men will pass, dressed in khaki wearing colonial summer hats also in khaki.

That is the end of the parade of enemies.

Bringing up the rear will be a group representing the rebirth of the Jewish people. A parade, arranged with military precision will march, composed of pioneers, armed with shovels and hoes, hammers and saws and other tools, singing a Zionist song, the words to which are on the sign they hold:

The Jewish People Lives
National Unity. Building the Land. The Revival of Israel
Everything bespeaks hope, will, strength!
(In front of this group—the national flag, in all its glory!)

Remarks:
1. Pupils of the upper classes in high schools should be encouraged to participate—about 200 in number (170 boys and 30 girls)
2. Work should begin early, organizing, rehearsing and preparing the people and the groups (as whole units). The participants will be divided into groups on the basis of their appearance.
3. The many types of "weapons" will be made of plywood and sticks according to the author's instructions. The same holds for the boards (the shields bearing the symbols).
4. Most of the costumes will be prepared by the participants themselves. We will have to see to the rest. The material—cheap cloth and paper (for the hats) and cardboard.
5. We will need the assistance of an artist and a make-up artist to work in concert with the author.
6. We need the help of a conductor to organize the two main choirs (one along with "Israel" and the second as a group of the Hebrew people). In addition, if possible, choirs of the groups of enemies. The choirs will sing in turn, no more than two at once (at the far ends of the procession). The songs will be chosen by the author together with the conductor.
7. Preparations should be started immediately, since there is a great deal to be done. The procession of this pageant should be a "moving show"

rather than simply walking. A lot of work has to be done in rehearsing the participants.
8. The author undertakes to do all the work of preparation and the procession, with the help of the committee.
9. The remaining details will be provided orally by the author. This proposal should be regarded as a general outline. Attached are two lists of "weapons" and "symbols."

Yoel Blanter
31.12.31
Address: a) Halfon 265, Government Survey Office until 2 P.M. b) 36 Bilu St., Apt. 5
Municipal Archive, ibid.

APPENDIX 6

LETTER FROM MEMBERS OF THE ATZ-KOTZATZ EDITORIAL BOARD, 1932

Atz-Kotzatz
Publishing House for Humoristic Literature
P.O.B. 389
Jerusalem

January 14, 1932

The Committee for Purim Festivities
Tel Aviv Municipality

Dear Sirs:

In response to the newspaper ad, we are hereby submitting several suggestions that we think could improve the Purim festivities and make them more pleasant and effective. The Purim festival is primarily a folk festival, and therefore we believe that the committee's activities should focus particularly on improving the festivities that take place in the streets of the city, without in any way interfering with the parties and festivities that are held in closed halls, although, of course, it can make its advice available to them as well.

These are our suggestions:

1. The most appropriate name for the carnival is *hilulah* ("merrymaking"). This is a popular Hebrew word, it has a nice ring to it and suits the concept of carnival, and the combination "hilulat Purim" also sounds good.
2. The order of the festivities:

A. The festival begins on Monday, March 20th, this year, at 5 P.M. The opening of the festival will be proclaimed by a siren throughout the city, and by trumpet blasts sounded from the roofs of the highest buildings in the city, and by runners.

B. At 6 P.M. the traditional reading of the Scroll of Esther will take place out of doors by the light of torches on a special stage constructed for this purpose, or on the steps of the Mograbi opera house. The building and the stage will be decorated with a blaze of colors and flags, the readers will be dressed in special costumes that suit the heroes of the Scroll.

C. After the reading of the Scroll, the Mayor will give the keys of the city to the queen who has been chosen. If there is no queen, then to the satraps, ministers, and runners in charge of the festivities. The orchestra will play a Purim song, the crowd will sing, there will be dancing, shooting, rockets, etc.

D. On Tuesday, March 21, from 8 to 10 A.M. all sorts of sports events will be arranged—competitions, running through the streets, parades, humorous games, and the like.

E. Exactly at 10 A.M. a procession of schoolchildren will set out, accompanied by an orchestra playing, the singing of children's songs, etc. (the details of the procession remain to be worked out).

F. Exactly at 3 P.M. the *hilulah* parade will begin, led by the mayor on horseback, followed by the satraps, and a company of riders wearing special holiday costumes, like those worn during the reading of the Scroll (the ten sons of Haman, Mordechai, eunuchs, etc.), and a special Purim orchestra, like the Histadrut band that plays at the "Ha-Ohel" parties. They will be followed by the masked participants in an order to be decided upon by the committee. The parade will go through the main streets of the city, and the committee must see to it that these streets are clean and decorated in honor of the festival. During the parade, confetti will be dropped on the city from aircraft. Negotiations will have to be held with the Eretz Israeli air corps command. A handbill is to be distributed to all the participants in the parade, asking them to wear at least a face mask.

Note: every mask, even if it is an advertising mask, must have a comic-caricatural nature. For example, the shoe company, Keter, could have a mask in the form of a huge imported shoe, its mouth wide open as it swallows Eretz Israeli currency notes, and on its back side, is spilling them out on to ships going abroad; and in contrast, a large shoe produced by Keter, and underneath or alongside it, all those who earn their living from its manufacture, thus helping to build the land and make it prosper—a shoemaker, a worker, manager and the like. Or for example, the Assis factory can appear with an advertising mask showing two dummies made of transparent material (celluloid, for example) which with the help of electric lighting, show the harmful effect of artificial syrups on the body, and another one showing the healthful effect of natural Assis juices.

These are only some examples, of course, and the committee has to set up an advisory bureau for commercial companies that want to take part in the *hilulah*, to advise them how to arrange their masks. It is desirable to avoid as far as possible the banality of having just a large shoe, a large bottle or a large package of cigarettes, that sort of thing. In this regard, a lot can be done and attention should be paid to it.

> G. In order to keep the crowd from getting bored for even one minute, small stages should be erected at various corners of the city, from which, on Monday or Tuesday evening, humorous pieces will be read, comical plays will be put on, in keeping with the spirit of the day, to occupy those attendees who are not participating in any parties, for either financial or other reasons.

The streets should be decorated with various comical slogans, lit up by electricity at night. As a matter of fact, all the streets should be lit up with colored lights, the more the better. At the entries to the city—Petach Tikvah Road, HaRekevet Road, etc., decorated gates of honor should be set up to welcome incoming guests. It's also a good idea to keep the custom of giving names from the Purim story to streets, but it's not enough to announce these names in the press; street signs made of cloth or paper should be put up.

> H. The committee should publish a humoristic newspaper called the official paper of the Hilulah, which in addition to the usual humorous material, will contain orders, proclamations, laws and bills issued by the committee—all humorous ones of course. We offer our complete services in this regard. The paper should be sold at a price everyone can afford, and it should be an organic part of the festivities.
>
> I. A lot of publicity should be given to the program of the festivities in the Jewish press throughout the world, and in all the various tourist bureaus. Contacts should be established with at least the

neighboring countries—Syria, Egypt, etc., so they will give discounts to tourists, and of course with the government of Palestine as well.

These are just a few sketchy ideas. Our suggestions have to be worked out in detail, expanded and perfected. We have a lot more to add, and would be very pleased if we were given the opportunity to do so, by adding us to the organizing committee, to work on editing the newspaper etc.
We hope that you will give serious consideration to our suggestions and reply to us at the earliest possible opportunity.

With best wishes and respectfully yours,
Members of the *Atz-Kotzatz* editorial board
[the names are illegible]

P.S. We are sending you under separate cover all of the humoristic newspapers published by us this year.

(Municipal Archives, file C 9/32–4)

APPENDIX 7

LETTER FROM YEHUDAH NADIVI OUTLINING PROPOSED PREPARATIONS FOR THE TEL AVIV JUBILEE CELEBRATIONS, 1924

11.4.1934
The Presidium of the Municipality
Tel Aviv
Re: *Preparations for the Tel Aviv Jubilee Celebrations*

Dear Sir:

    I am hereby submitting for your attention and decision, the proposals of the sub-committee of the expanded committee that was set up to plan a program for the Jubilee celebrations. The following participated actively in the preparation of this material: the artists Nahum Guttman and Glicksburg; Mr. Yaacov Gutman, representative of the Teachers Federation; Mr. Barham, representative of the physicians, Ms. Cheskin and Mr. Goldbross, representatives of the kindergarten teachers.

1. *Schedule of the Festivities*
    Monday, April 30 at 8 P.M.—the opening celebration
    Tuesday, May 1 celebration for native-born Tel Avivians
    Wednesday, May 2, A.M., celebrations in the schools and in the evening a ball for youth, and lighting [of torches].
    Thursday, May 3 (Lag B'Omer) Tel Aviv Day:
    Morning—assembly of Tel Aviv youth of all [political] streams, in the afternoon, a Tel Aviv procession and in the evening a festive ball.

2. *Opening celebration (Monday, April 30)*

The lower part of the stage of the Produce of the Land Palace [at the Tel Aviv fairgrounds] is adorned by a huge lighthouse adapted from the emblem of the Municipality. Chairs are prepared on the stage for the special guests listed below. After the opening of the celebration is proclaimed by trumpet blasts and fireworks, the gate of the lighthouse will open and the Mayor and the founders of Tel Aviv will enter the stage through it. (the proposal states that whenever the founders are scheduled to appear, those who are absent will be replaced by their eldest son). When the founders appear, their names will be announced one after the other and they will be shown to their seats. They will be followed by the members of the Tel Aviv municipal council. In addition to these, room will be left on the stage only for the representative of the Jewish Agency, the representative of the Knesset and of the Rabbinate. If it turns out to be possible to hold a convention of representatives of Jewish communities, they will come on to the stage in the same manner and each one will be presented to the audience and then take their places.

All the other guests will be seated inside the amphitheater in the front rows. It will be possible to invite representatives of all the federations, institutions, organizations, etc. up to 1,000 places or more. The fairgrounds management will be entitled to sell the remaining seats for prices approved by us.

As for the program, we propose an opening speech by the Mayor, brief greetings by the supreme institutions—the Knesset, the Jewish Agency and the Rabbinate. And if there is a convention of communities, one speech can be delivered in the name of the diaspora. Between these speeches, which definitely must be brief, there will be singing and musical pieces performed by the large choirs and orchestras. It was suggested that we ask Tel Aviv poets to write a special poem that can be recited by a choir perhaps accompanied by music.

3. *The Day of Native-Born Tel Avivians or the Tel Aviv Day of the Child (Tuesday May 1)*

On this day, the children born in Tel Aviv of kindergarten and elementary school age will be the guests of the Mayor. After consulting the representative of the kindergarten and school teachers, it was decided insofar as kindergarten children are concerned, no distinction should be made between those born in Tel Aviv and those born elsewhere, and they will all be brought. But as for the schoolchildren, a distinction can be made. According to the suggestion, they should be divided into two groups: the kindergarten children will come along at 8:30 A.M. and will stay until 11, and the schoolchildren will come at 11:30 and stay until 1 or 2.

The mayor will receive all of them at the entrance to the fairgrounds and will hand out flags bearing the municipality's emblem and postcards commemorating the event and the visit. On these visits the children will be accompanied by the kindergarten and schoolteachers of the relevant departments. There is also a suggestion to distribute to these children, free of charge, the tokens that are being prepared in honor of the occasion.

Another suggestion is to set up a large shelter inside the stadium to provide shade, under which tables and benches will be placed with refreshments for the mayor's guests. An orchestra should be playing throughout the visit. After the official reception by the mayor, the children will be dispersed in the fairgrounds and the visits will take place inside pavilions according to a special program that will be prepared by the representatives of the kindergarten and school teachers, and the management of the fairgrounds. Special arrangements should be made to enable these children to enjoy the facilities of the amusement park.

The kindergarten children should be brought in special buses especially decorated in honor of the event.

4. *Convention of Jewish Communities*

If it should transpire that a large number of representatives of Jewish communities from all the countries of the diaspora will participate, this convention can be arranged at 4 o'clock in the afternoon.

As in the opening celebration, here too the mayor and his aides will make their appearance followed by the representatives of the communities one by one, who will be introduced to the audience and then be seated in their places. The mayor will say a few special words of greeting directed to the diaspora and the representatives of the communities will reply. During this entire ceremony, orchestras will play and if possible, the large choirs will also participate. At the end of the ceremony, the speeches and the reception, a banquet will be held at 6 P.M. in the fairgrounds restaurant to which the members of the municipal council, the representatives of the national institutions and representatives of the various institutions representing the city will be invited.

5. *The Day of the Tel Aviv Schools*

In keeping with the existing custom, sports competitions will be held between the different schools in the city together with a general assembly of all the schools. This assembly will be opened by the mayor who will deliver a special speech.

According to the program, these festivities will continue in the morning and afternoon, and in the evening a party for the youth will be held according to a special program that will be planned, which will end with the traditional lighting [of torches]. All of this will take place in the stadium field.

6. *Tel Aviv Day*

In the morning, friendly competitions will be held in the stadium between the various sports associations in the city under jubilee flags. The same youths will participate in the afternoon in the jubilee procession as a homogeneous group, all wearing long, dark trousers and identical shirts, in blue with the municipality emblem. Every organization can walk alone under the municipality's jubilee flag. At the corner of the flag, the special emblem of each group can be added in a fixed place and standard size. The same group emblem can also be shown on the shirts, in a fixed size and place. The official group uniforms will not be worn in order to symbolize the unity of all the groups for the benefit of the city.

The Jubilee procession will be held at 4:30 P.M. and will begin at Dizengoff Circle. The circle will be divided in two, the right-hand part next to the center of Tel Aviv will remain completely empty, and on the left-hand part, on the silicate side, the main part of the procession will be arranged facing from north to south, and the participants will stand in the following order:

The Mayor—Tel Aviv grandchildren in strollers with their mothers (the strollers decorated with flowers).
Children born in Tel Aviv arranged by age, from 1 to 25, in rows of ten. The one-, two— and three-year olds will walk with their mothers in decorated strollers. The four-, five— and six-year old children will be taken from the kindergartens. The committee will choose three kindergartens and take 10 children of the same age from each. Children of school age will be selected by the same method. The committee will choose ten pupils of a certain age from each of the various schools. Together with the high schools, that will give us children up to the age of 18. In a newspaper ad, young people aged 18–25 will be asked to inform the municipality of their names and addresses so that they can be called on to participate.
Walking behind them will be the founders of Tel Aviv
Members of the municipal council
Representatives of the national institutions
Representatives of Jewish communities in the diaspora
A procession of Tel Aviv youth dressed as described above.
Representatives of the institutions, bodies and organizations of the city of Tel Aviv.
Followed by the public.

At the end of Dizengoff Street near the circle, from Carmel Street the street will be closed off by 25 blue and white ribbons symbolizing Tel Aviv's 25 years of existence. The Deputy Mayor will proclaim the opening of Dizengoff Street and the first row of the procession—the grandchildren of Tel Aviv in their strollers.

Accompanied by the orchestra, the procession will encircle the empty half of the circle and continue through it northward through Dizengoff Street. On its way, all those born in Tel Aviv will drive pegs into the corners of the streets on the circle, bearing the name of the street. A peg bearing its name will also be driven into the center of the square.

When the procession reaches Frishman Street, the kindergarten children will continue down Dizengoff Street until they reach the buses awaiting them. The rest of the procession will turn left into Frishman Street and continue through Frishman, Eliezer Ben Yehudah, Allenby and Bialik Streets past the municipality building. The entire procession will take its place around the garden in the municipality courtyard. Permission to enter the municipality building itself will be given *only* to the founders of Tel Aviv, members of the municipal council and representatives of the major national institutions. All of them will then appear on the balcony facing the crowd. The orchestra will take its place on the roof of the building and after a brief greeting by the mayor, it will play "HaTikvah" and the fireworks will be lit.

In the evening a jubilee ball will be held in the fairgrounds amphitheater, with the participation of the art and theater community of Tel Aviv, according to a program prepared especially for it. The proposals for decorating the city and other arrangements will be presented separately, as well as a budgetary proposal.

I would appreciate it if you would give these suggestions your consideration as soon as possible and let me have your instructions, taking into account the very short time at our disposal.

Sincerely yours,
(—)
Yehudah Nadivi
Municipal Secretary

NOTES

INTRODUCTION

1. Strong, *Art and Power*, 172.
2. See, for example, Wilson, *Folklore and Nationalism in Modern Finland*; Handler, *Nationalism and Politics of Culture in Quebec*.
3. See, for example, Andrews, "Making the Revolutionary Calendar"; Cressy, *Bonfires and Bells*; E. Zerubavel, "Easter and Passover."
4. It is important to note that the term "popular culture" often referred to the need to make "high culture" accessible to the entire public, not only to the elite.
5. See Y. Zerubavel, *Recovered Roots*; Gertz, *Captive of a Dream*; Abramson, ed., *Modern Jewish Mythologies*; Don-Yehiya and Charles Liebman, *Civil Religion in Israel*; Oahana and Wistrich, eds., *The Shaping of Israeli Identity*.

CHAPTER 1

1. See Lavenda, "Festivals and the Creation of Public Culture," 77. See also Errington, "Reflexivity Deflected"; Smith, *The Nation in History*, 53–54.
2. Sumner, *Folkways*, 19.
3. For example, a study on the evolution of national celebrations in the United States suggests that "Celebrations were no afterthought to Independence. They were anticipated deliberate, necessary responses to the Declaration of Independence." See Waldstreicher, *In the Midst of Perpetual Fetes*, 30.
4. Cressy, *Bonfires and Bells*, 68.
5. See Rearick, "Festivals in Modern France."
6. Newman, *Parades and the Politics of the Street*, 89.
7. MacAloon, *Rite, Drama, Festival*, 9. However, he adds that: "Yet, in other respects, performances are anything but routine."
8. Connerton, *How Societies Remember*, 51.
9. Lavenda, "Festivals and the Creation of Public Culture," 77–80. In an analysis of the festivities marking the three-hundredth anniversary of Yankee City, W. Lloyd Warner writes that one can reconstruct the way they were planned based on the minutes of the committee meetings. However, he merely describes the festivities without going into the deliberations of the Tercentenary Committee that planned, organized,

and produced them. In any case, this was only a one-time event, planned over a one-year period. See W. Lloyd Warner, *The Living and the Dead: A Study of the Symbolic Life of Americans*, 2nd ed. (New Haven: Yale University Press, 1965).

10. Clifford, "Introduction: Partial Truth," in *Writing Culture: The Poetics and Politics of Ethnography*, 19.

11. Davis, *Parades and Power*, 18.

12. Lane, *The Rites of Rulers*, 14.

13. Stites, "Bolshevik Ritual Building in 1920," 301.

14. Ozouf, *Festivals and the French Revolution*. Barbara Kirshenblatt-Gimblett writes about staging culture, but in the context of organizing folk celebrations and festivals for tourists. In this case it is clear that an institutional organizing force is behind the events. In any event, she abstained from describing the manner of organization, and focuses solely on the finishing product. See Kirschenblatt-Gimblett, *Destination Culture*, 17–128.

15. See, for example, Orgel and Strong, *Inigo Jones*; Strong, *Art and Power*, 153–70. These masters of ceremony created tournaments, ballets, state entries, water spectacles and "the most distinctive manifestation of the art of the festival"—the masque.

16. Hooke, "The Babylonian New Year Festival."

17. See Bar-On, "The Festival Calendars."

18. On the history of the Passover ritual see Tabory, *The Passover Ritual* (in Hebrew). The Passover ritual after the destruction of the Second Temple is a family holiday, conducted according to the rules in the Passover haggadah, which evolved throughout generations.

19. Burkert, *Greek Religion, Archaic and Classical*, 100. Fowler, who provides a detailed description of the system of festivals in Rome and the "endless but ordered variety of details, of prayers, processions and festivities," does not describe how and by whom they were organized. See Fowler, *Roman Festivals of the Period of the Republic*, 333.

20. Athina Kavoulaki, "Processional Performance and the Polis," in Goldhill and Osborne, eds., *Performance Culture*, 299.

21. Myliwiec, *Twilight of Ancient Egypt*, 159–62.

22. Smith, *To Take Place*, 91.

23. Wilkinson, *Egeria's Travels*, 163. We recall that in the processions in Athens as well, various locations are incorporated into the route, which is not simply linear and unidirectional; A. Kavoulaki, "Processional Performance and the Polis," 300.

24. Wilkinson, *Egeria's Travels*, 64–142.

25. Reiner, *Pilgrims and Pilgrimage to Eretz Yisrael, 1099–1517*; Reiner, "Destruction, Temple and Sacred Place," *Cathedra*, 47–64 (in Hebrew).

26. Burckhardt, *Civilization of the Renaissance in Italy*, 256–70. See also Muir, *Civic Rituals in Renaissance Venice*.

27. Dundes and Falassi, *La Terra in Piazza*. The rules were established by the *Regolamento per il Palio*.

28. See Ozouf, *Festivals and the French Revolution* and "Space and Time in the Festivals of the French Revolution." Also see Andrews, "Making the Revolutionary Calendar."

29. Rearick, "Festivals in Modern France"; Kertzer, *Ritual, Politics and Power*, 151–73. When Russian travelers, writes Lotman, "got to Paris after Tilsit [the peace treaty between Russia and France, 1807] they were struck by the ritualization and pomp of the court at the Tuileries, which was far removed from the calculated simplicity of court life at St. Petersburg under Alexander I" (Lotman, "Theater and Theatricity," 147). On revolutionary Russia, see Stites, "Bolshevik Ritual Building in 1920."

30. A. Ben-Amos, *Funerals, Politics, and Memory*. Arthur A. Goren describes the work of "arrangement committees" that organized various public events for the American community, but he also does not tell us what considerations guided the organizers in their work. In any event, there is a vast difference between "organizers" who primarily decide on the order of the event, the various arrangements, the sequence of its parts, etc., and the "stagers" in our case, who determined the full and exact content of public ceremonies and festivals. See Goren, "Pageants of Sorrow," and "The Rite of Community."

31. See Burden, *Nüremberg Party Rallies*. On the invention of local ceremonies in Germany, see Confino, *Nation as a Local Metaphor*.

32. Cannadine, "The Context, Performances and Meaning of Ritual." The fact that he fails to tell us the identity of the "masters of ceremony" who planned and staged the elaborate ceremonies is all the more striking because he does describe the manner in which the image of the English as a people that does not know how to conduct a splendid ceremonial performance changed to that of a people particularly good at ceremonies.

33. Among them, see Pieper, *In Tune with the World—A Theory of Festivity* (New York: Harcourt, Brace and World, 1965); Lane, *The Rites of Rulers;* Turner, *The Ritual Process;* Tambiah, "A Performative Approach to Ritual"; Kertzer, *Ritual Politics and Power;* Assmann, *Das Fest und das Heilige,* 13–30. See also the summary in Connerton, *How Societies Remember,* 48–61; and see Guss, *The Festive State.*

34. See, for example, the six characteristics suggested by Myerhoff and Moore: repetition, acting, special behavior, order, evocative presentational style (staging), the "collective dimension." Moore and Myerhoff, *Secular Ritual,* 3–24. See also MacAloon, *Ritual, Drama, Festival, Spectacle,* 1–15; Handelman, *Models and Mirrors,* 22–62. For more references on the subject see Waldstreicher, *In The Midst of Perpetual Fetes,* 10–11nn. 15–17, and Evan M. Zuesse, "Ritual," in *Encyclopedia of Religion,* Mircea Eliade, ed. (New York: Macmillan, 1987), 12:405–22.

35. Gluckman, *Essay on the Ritual of Social Relations,* 30. On categories of civic and religious rituals see Bocock, *Ritual in Industrial Society.* He defines ritual as "the symbolic use of bodily movement and gesture in a social situation to express and articulate meaning" (73) and distinguishes between four types of ritual action in industrial society: religious, civic, life cycle, and aesthetic (48). Stites defines ritualism as "the use of created forms of symbolic behavior for devotional and celebratory moments in life" ("Bolshevik Ritual Building in 1920," 295).

36. Kertzer, *Ritual, Politics, and Power,* 9. In "Religion and Rituals," Jack Goody defines rituals as "rigid acts of any kind," ignoring the crucial symbolic element in ritual and ceremony. See Bocock, *Ritual in Industrial Society,* 191–92.

37. Goody, "Against Ritual." Frank W. Young writes that "the very definitions of function and meaning are clouded. The usual distinction makes function an objective relationship between the rite and the social system, while meaning is the cluster of culturally ordered ideas by which it is summarized" (*Initiation Ceremonies*, 3).

38. See Turner, *The Ritual Process;* Bocock, *Ritual in Industrial Society.*

39. Turner, *Schism and Continuity in African Society*, 92.

40. See Singer, *When a Great Tradition Modernizes;* Redfield, *Peasant Society and Culture*, 92; Redfield, "Folk Society." And see the introduction to MacAloon, *Rite, Drama, Festival, Spectacle*. We believe that both rural and urban cultures consist of both traditions—the "Great," as well as the "Lesser." Obviously, different cultural performances have a different character, take place on different stages, different actors participate in them; hence they are performed according to a different set of rules.

41. See Goldhill and Osborne, *Performance Culture*, 1–29, and the bibliography on the topic cited there. Also see D. Ben-Amos, *Folklore*, 630–35.

42. Rappaport, *Ecology, Meaning and Religion*, 173–221.

43. Bauman, *Story, Performance, and Event*, 3.

44. Connerton, *How Societies Remember*, 59.

45. Huizinga, *Homo Ludens*, 11.

46. Kirshenblatt-Gimblett, *Destination Culture*, 61.

47. See Darnton, "A Bourgeois Puts His World in Order," 107–34.

48. On the case of visual arts and Hebrew culture see Mishory, *Lo and Behold* (in Hebrew).

49. Kluckhohn, "Myths and Rituals." On the diverse views in the field of myth-ritual study, see Segal, *Myth and Ritual Theory.*

50. See Fontenrose, *Ritual Theory of Myth;* Bell, *Ritual: Perspectives and Dimensions*, 3–22; Kluckhohn, "Myths and Rituals."

51. As a result, the intensive festive activity encouraged the development of popular Hebrew literature, mainly for young readers. See *Zionist Archive* (Jerusalem), kk15 2469, kk15 2473.

52. See Moore and Myerhoff, Introduction to *Secular Ritual.*

53. On the creation of the religious Jewish calendar see Gaster, *Festivals of the Jewish Year;* Greenstone, *Jewish Feasts and Fasts.*

Chapter 2

1. Hobsbaum and Ranger, *Invention of Tradition.*

2. On the re-invention and invention of religious folk culture in Israel, see Yoram Bilu, "Jewish Moroccan 'Saint Impresarios' in Israel," and Bilu and Ben-Ari, "The Making of Modern Saints."

3. See Meyer, *Response to Modernity;* Volkov, in *Studies in the History of Popular Culture*, 245–56 (in Hebrew; she deals mainly with the textual lesser tradition); and Mazor, *Hag and Moed in the Thinking of the Reform Movement* (in Hebrew). It is important to remember that a process of invention, as well as the dissemination and reception of the

resultant products, exists in all domains of culture and society, not only in the domain of rules and rituals that are symbolic in nature. Many innovations introduced into the existing system were portrayed, for various reasons, as a novelty or as the revival of old or ancient traditions even when they were manifestly new—in Jewish culture, for example, various literary genres, the development of the Hebrew theatre, or sports activities gained legitimacy by being presented as a revival of a long-enduring tradition, which had been discontinued for some reason.

4. Folk songs refer to songs intended from the outset to be sung at specific events and written specifically for them. These folk songs were sung by the public at various public events, and also at special events: "singing at public events" (group-singing). A brief piece printed in the newspaper *HaMagid*, signed "Chovev Zion," shows that the lack of Hebrew folk songs was already recognized at the beginning of the new Jewish settlement in Eretz-Israel. The author described how, in October 1889, young men and women from the moshavah Rishon le-Zion went up to Jerusalem on a "pilgrimage" in three wagons. He wrote, "On the way[,] they sang songs of Zion and then they all felt how sorely lacking we were in folk songs" (October 24, 1889).

5. See Shavit, "Supplying a Missing System"; and Shavit, "Warsaw/Tel Aviv—Yiddish and Hebrew" (in Hebrew).

6. See Shavit, "The Status of Culture in the Process of Creating a National Society in Eretz-Israel" (in Hebrew); Shavit, "The Yishuv between National Regeneration of Culture and Cultural Generation of the Nation" (in Hebrew).

7. Gellner, *Encounters with Nationalism*, 191.

8. Shavit, "Culture and Cultural Status" (in Hebrew).

9. Deshen, "Anthropological Study in Israel," 20. On the development of the mass pilgrimage to the graves of "holy persons" in Morocco from the 1930s onward, see Ben-Ami, *Saints Veneration*, 146–47.

10. Hirschberg, *In Oriental Lands*, 878–80 (in Hebrew). Hirschberg found some of these rituals excessive and extravagant.

11. Goren, "Pageants of Sorrow" and "Celebrating Zion in America."

12. Shmuel Navon, "Hachagim vehaChinukh" ("The Holidays and Education"), *Shoreshim*, 1937, 140–44.

13. See Cassar-Pullicino, *Studies in Maltese Folklore*, 39–67; Cremona, "Carnival in Gozo."

Chapter 3

1. See Yizhak Tabenkin's perception of culture as an "organic cosmos," in Chabas, *HaAliya Hasheniah* (Book of the Second Aliya) (Tel Aviv, 1947), 24.

2. Shavit, "Ahad Ha-Am and Hebrew National Culture."

3. Herzl, *Tagebücher, 1895–1904*, 49.

4. On nineteenth-century views that called into question the romantic assertion that oral traditions express collective sentiments see Linke, "Folklore, Anthropology, and the Government of Social Life." On the usage of folk culture in creating national

culture in Eastern Europe see Raum, *Estonia under Imperial Russia*, 74–80; Armstrong, *Ukrainian Nationalism*, 5–10; Vakar, *Belorussia: The Making of a Nation*, 75–92. For two other examples, see Wilson, *Folklore and Nationalism in Modern Finland*, and Handler, *Nationalism and the Politics of Culture in Quebec*.

5. See Lotman, "Theater and Theatricity."

6. Antoine Achard explained the motivation for organizing national festivals as follows: "The organization of a series of national festivals which brings the people memories that are connected to the existent political institutions is a necessity that all governments recognized and put into practice. . . . Moreover, not to create civic festivals that remind contemporaries of the greatness of their history and the heroic virtues of their fathers would mean failing to appreciate both popular instincts and needs" (A. Ben-Amos's translation of Rosemonde Sanson's "Les 14 juillet," in Ben-Amos, *Funerals, Politics, and Memory*, 157).

7. See A. Ben-Amos, *Funerals, Politics, and Memory*, 157.

8. Walicki, *The Slavophile Controversy*, 413–21.

9. A. D. Gordon, "Cheshbonenu im Atzmenu" (Our Reckoning with Ourselves), *Ha'aretz veha'Avodah* (Tel Aviv: 1914), 4.

10. On the same debate between those who believed in "spontaneity" and those who believed in "direction" see Lane, *The Rites of Rulers*, 57–58. Those who favored goal-directed rites argued that the rituals of Western civilization, namely Christian religious rituals, originated "as the result of controlled and consciously organized efforts on the part of the elite."

11. Yaacov Fichman, "Tarbut Amamit" ("Popular Culture") *Tarbut* 8, August–September 1923 (Warsaw):1–11.

12. Eliezer Steinman, "Hatarbut ha'Ivrit" (Hebrew Culture"), *Tarbut* 1 (November 1921):3.

13. Dr. Nisan Turov, "Al Tarbut veHaskalah: Chayim shel yofi" ("On Culture and Education: A Life of Beauty"), *Shai shel Sifrut*, a literary supplement to the weekly *Chadashot miha'aretz (Palestine News)*, September 27, 1918, 13–15. In the November 8, 1918, issue, Torov wrote about the "farmers festival" (la fête des pagans) held in French Switzerland once every twenty years, noting in particular that this was a huge, well-organized festival whose content was written and designed by artists. He was astonished by "such order, such style, such beauty!" Torov believed that the Jews in Palestine should organize popular festivities and fill them with content and order so that they might serve not only as an expression of national unity but also as a substitute for other types of entertainment.

14. Referring to the concept of an additional soul that God bestows upon the Jews on the Sabbath. Babylonian Talmud, Tractate Betza, 16A.

15. Jehudah Raznichenko (Erez), "Pirkei Havai Minisayon Achat Hapelugot" ("Aspects of our Life Style, From Experience in one of the Platoons") in *Gedud ha'avodah al shem Yosef Trumpeldor* (Anthology; Tel Aviv, 1931), 273–74.

16. Schohat, "In the Paths of Labor," 43 (in Hebrew).

CHAPTER 4

1. On the kibbutz see Near, *Kibbutz Movement.*
2. Ta-Shma, *Early Franco-German Ritual and Custom,* 41 (in Hebrew); Gutmann, "Jewish Medieval Marriage Customs in Art."
3. A historical example of the fact that not every "invented" festival was accepted and endured is a long list of festivals that were established during the Second Temple period but did not endure, contained in Talmud Bavli, Tractate *Ta'anit.*
4. Raznichenko, "Pirkei Havai Minisayon Achat Hapelugot," 275.
5. Aaronsohn, *Baron Rothschild and His Colonies,* 280 (in Hebrew). Also see Bartal, "Cossack and Bedouin"; Arye-Sapir, "The Lighting of Simhat Torah Bonfires" (in Hebrew).
6. See Pollack, *Jewish Folkways,* 174–77.
7. Freidhaber, "Wedding Ceremonies in the Jewish Yishuv" (in Hebrew).
8. Yigael, "Bimei haKibush" ("In the Days of Conquest"), *Kovetz HaShomer* (Tel Aviv, 1983), 108. And see Freidhaber, "Wedding Ceremonies in the Jewish Yishuv."
9. In an article sent by Haim Hisin in 1890 from Eretz-Israel to the Jewish-Russian journal, *Voskhod* ("Dawn"), published in Petrograd. Hissin, *Masa ba'Aretz hamuftachat* (A Journey to the Promised Land), trans. from Russian by C. Ben-Amram (Tel Aviv: Tel Aviv University, 1987), 392–93.
10. See Pollack, *Jewish Folkways,* 108.
11. Moshe Kalvary "Bechavlei Kismah shel ha'Ivrit" ("Enchanted by the Charm of Hebrew"), in Chabas, ed., *Ha'Aliyah HaSheniah* (Tel Aviv, 1947).
12. David Ben Gurion, *BeYehudah ubaGalil* (In Judea and in the Galilee), in *Anachnu veshecheinenu* (We and Our Neighbors) (Tel Aviv, 1931,) 280; excerpts from memoirs.
13. Katriel, "Rhetoric in Flames" (in Hebrew).
14. In the Second Temple period, in Jewish society, for example, adults' birthdays were not celebrated because of the distinctly pagan nature of such celebrations in the Roman world. Nonetheless, it is interesting to note that some of the customs observed in these ceremonies—candle lighting, a cake, crowns as adornment—came to European Christian society from the ancient world, and from there to birthday celebrations in modern Jewish society. See Ta-Shma, "On Birthdays in Judaism" (in Hebrew); Nitzche, *The Genius Figure in Antiquity and the Middle-Ages.*
15. The name kindergarten was given to the institution for children aged 3 to 6 established by Friedrich Fröbel in Germany in 1837, and after the 1860s it became popular as a private educational framework in Germany and other countries. The custom of celebrating birthdays was apparently first adopted by middle-class (bürgerliche Gesellschaft) Jews in Germany, as part of the new family culture. On the history of the kindergarten, see Allen, "Gardens of Children, Gardens of God"; Wollons, *Kindergartens and Cultures.*
16. See Sitton, "Between Feminism and Zionism" (in Hebrew).
17. Frykman and Lofgren, *Culture Builders,* 31–33.

18. C. Pinsod-Sukenik, "The Development of the Hebrew Kindergarten in Israel," *Hitpatchut Gan haYeladim Ha'ivri beYisrael* (The Jubilee Book of the Teachers Federation in Eretz-Israel) (Tel Aviv, 1928), 158–66. See also the two volumes of Elboin-Dror, *Hebrew Education in Eretz-Israel*, vol. 1: 1854–1914, vol. 2: 1914–20 (in Hebrew); and Doleve-Gandelman, "The Symbolic Inscription."

In 1883, two Jewish kindergartens had already been established in Romania. See Rotman, *Education as a Reflection of Society*, 198–200 (in Hebrew).

19. Tzviah Katerborski, *Benitivot hagan (In the Paths of the Kindergarten)* (Tel Aviv, 1962), 148–52.

20. It was also in Germany that the custom of lighting small candles to signify the child's age was first practiced.

21. Tova Haskinah, "Yom Holedet Bagan" ("A Birthday in the Kindergarten"), *Hed HaGan,* 5–6, year 5 (Center of the Kindergarten Teachers Association in Eretz-Israel, 1940):34–37.

22. See Shamgar-Handelman and Handelman, "Celebrations of Bureaucracy," *Ethnology*; Handelman, "Holiday Celebrations in Israeli Kindergartens."

Chapter 5

1. See, as one example, Mosse, "Mass Politics and the Political Liturgy of Nationalism."

2. Azaryahu, *State Cults* (in Hebrew).

3. Lowenthal, *The Diaries of Theodor Herzl*, 224.

4. Ibid. Nordau was persuaded and in a quarter of an hour returned wearing a frock coat.

5. *HaAretz,* 11 October 1920, *Doar HaYom,* 10 October 1920.

6. Dov B. Borochov, "Mah nishtana proletari?"("What has Changed, Proletarian?") in *Ktavim* (Writings), iii, 322–23 (Tel Aviv, 1960).

7. See Shavit, *Jabotinsky and the Revisionist Movement.*

8. See Aronoff, *Power and Ritual in the Israel Labor Party.* In this study of the ritual proceedings of the labor movement, Aronoff describes the practical and symbolic functions of the party rituals; he does not describe ceremonies, though, but rather the code of behavior at political gatherings and meetings.

9. Quoted by Isaac Rambah in "Religion and Tradition in the Life and Thinking of Zeev Jabotinsky," *Ha'umah* 3 (1963):149 (in Hebrew).

10. Zeev Jabotinsky, "Ra'ayon Betar" ("The Idea of Betar") In *Ba'derech La'Medina* (On the Way to Statehood), Jerusalem, 1953:321–23.

11. Zeev Jabotinsky, *She'lot haHaganah be'Eretz Israel*aH (Issues of Defense in Eretz-Israel), Jerusalem, 1929, 10.

12. Joseph Klausner, "Zeev Jabotinsky on Grandeur," in *Ha'uma* 1:9 (1964):149 (in Hebrew).

13. Frankel, "The 'Yizkor' Book of 1911."

14. See Rogel, *Tel Hai: A Front without a Rear* (in Hebrew) and the very detailed informative description of the genesis and reception of the "myth" in Y. Zerubavel, *Recovered Roots*.

15. Y. Zerubavel does include a description of a memorial ceremony in a kindergarten from a booklet of instructions printed in 1967, without tracing the evolution of memorial ceremonies from the thirties and thereafter (*Recovered Roots*, 94).

Chapter 6

This chapter is based mainly on Sitton, *Education in the Spirit of the Homeland* (in Hebrew). See also Sitton, "School Festivals and Ceremonies"; Shahar, *The Eretz-Israeli Song*, 33–58. We are grateful to Ms. Judith Shteiman of the Unit for Culture Studies at Tel Aviv University for allowing us to make use of her doctoral thesis prior to its completion. It deals with the way the image of the new Hebrew child was shaped as a planned part of Eretz-Israeli culture in the early twentieth century, and is based on the school's archives.

1. These numbers refer to the overall number of pupils each year; the number of graduates in the Hebrew educational system between 1920 and 1948 was more than a quarter of a million.

2. See Reshef and Dror, *Hebrew Education in the Years of the National Homeland*, 17–47, and Elboim-Dror, *Hebrew Education in Eretz Israel*.

3. Bar-Gal, *An Agent of Zionist Propaganda* (in Hebrew).

4. The ceremonies were meticulously organized and produced according to a uniform version. A student in a Hebrew school in Safed describes the Tu biShevat (the fifteenth day of Shvat, the Jewish New Year for Trees) festivities in the city this way: "To mark this special day, the whole neighborhood was decorated with flags and greenery which served as a walk of honor for the celebrants. Nearby a lovely, adorned gate was set up bearing an inscription in huge blue letters: from morning to noon, endless lines of students thronged to the area there carrying their school flags. The saplings and holes in the ground had already been prepared, and under the supervision of several kindergarten teachers, the children planted their saplings to the sound of the orchestra's playing" (Sitton, *Education in the Spirit of the Homeland*, 47).

5. The TC and the committee appointed for this purpose (Harari, Aldema, and Ben-Yehuda) solicited material from authors and poets and in May 1928 began to publish a pamphlet containing pieces connected to the holidays, as well as dramatization instructions (KKL: 2464).

6. It was a "ritualization of metaphor." See Marcus, *Rituals of Childhood*, 5–7.

7. Shahar, *The Eretz-Israeli Song*, 33 (in Hebrew).

8. Harari, *Writings* (Tel Aviv, 1941) (in Hebrew).

9. Among his books: *Hachag, haChagigah vehaMischak haDramati* (*Holiday, Festivity and Dramatic Acting*) (Tel Aviv, 1943).

10. He wrote that this documentation will enable us to know "how our fathers spoke in the various jargons; how they pronounced words, how they sang, how they

conversed.... The moving picture will convey this to the viewers as if they were alive, coming and going, sitting and getting up, praying and working, in the home and in the street, in the synagogue and the work shop, in the store and in the *yeshivah,* in all their movements, in the flicker of their eyelids, in their countenance" (Chaim Harari, "Between *Kinus* and Folklore," in *Writings* [Tel Aviv, 1941]), 212 (in Hebrew).

11. Chaim Harari, ed., *Mo'adim: Seder Sefarim leChagei ha'Am: Sefer haChanukah (Holidays: A Collection of Books for the National Festivals: The Chanukah Book)* (Tel Aviv: JNF and "Omanut" Co., 1938). 12.

12. Shmuel Navon, "Chagim veMo'adim beChayei haYeladim" (Holidays and Festivals in the Lives of Children), *Hed HaGan,* 7, Pamphlet 1–2 (Tel Aviv, 1942), 17–21.

13. In Baruch Ben-Yehudah, ed., *Hakeren haMechanekhet: Tenu'at haMorim lema'an Tzion veGe'ulatah beMeli'at Esrim veChamesh Shanah lepe'ulatah (The Educating Foundation: The Teachers Movement for Zion and Its Redemption on the Occasion of the 25th Anniversary of Its Activity)* (Jerusalem, 1952), 54.

14. Shmuel Navon, *Hachag be'avodat hachinukh shel haKeren haKeyemet le'Israel* (Festival in the Educational Work of the JNF). *Shoreshim,* 1, 1938.

15. Shmuel Navon, *Hachagigah beVet haSefer* (Festival in the School), pamphlet (Tel Aviv: Federation of Hebrew Teachers in Eretz-Israel, 1947), 14–39.

16. Ben-Yehudah, *Hakeren haMechanekhet,* 53–57.

17. A. Tubenfliegel, "Toldot hachinukh bevet hasefer" ("The History of Zionism in the School"), *Shoreshim* I, 1938.

18. A. Ben-Hillel, "HaBimah beVet-haSefer" ("The Stage in the School") in *Sefer Mo'adim,* Chaim Harari, ed. (Tel Aviv: JNF and "Omanut" Co., 1938), 419.

19. Architect Ben-Ora, "Keitzad Bonim Bimat-Teatron bishvil Mischakim-Chovavim" (How to Build a Theatre Stage for Amateur Plays), in *Sefer Mo'adim,* Harari, ed., 12.

20. Don Handelman describes in detail Purim and Hanukkah festivals in the Israeli kindergarten, but he does not describe the historical development of the festivals from the inception of kindergartens up to the present. See Handelman, "Holiday Celebrations in Israeli Kindergartens," 189–92. Also see Doleve-Gandelman, "The Symbolic Inscription," 264–66, 272–74.

21. Y. Alterman, "Al gan hayeladim ha'ivri" ("On the Hebrew Kindergarten"), *Hed haGan* 3–4 (1938):3–6. This statement was made at the first conference of Chovevei Sefat Ever in Moscow in 1917. See also Yehiel Heilprin, "Yesodot gan hayeladim ha'vri" ("The Foundations of the Hebrew Kindergarten"), *Hed haGan,* Year 8, 3–4 (1943):8, 23. Heilprin based himself primarily on Friedrich Fröbel's teaching. The article was first printed in the periodical *haGinah* that he edited in Odessa in 1918.

22. Chanah Rotenberg, "Tafkid hagan beyitzirat havai" ("The Role of the Kindergarten in Creating a Lifestyle"), *Hed haGan* 5–6, Year 3 (1938):41–44 (Center of the Kindergarten Teachers Association in Eretz-Israel). See also B. Ben-Yehuda, "HaKeren HaKayemet beGan haYeladim" ("KKL in the kindergarten"), *Hed haGan* 1 (1937):37–40; Tirzah Katinka, "Ha-Chagiga baGan" (Festival in the kindergarten), *Hed haGan* 1 (1935): 39–41.

23. Esther Rabinowitz, *Kavim: Takhniyot lechagim began hayeladim ha'ivri betziruf he'arot metodiot* (Introduction to the Booklet: Plans for Festivals in the Kindergarten along with Methodical Instructions) (Tel Aviv, 1953), 6–7.

24. Tirzah Katnika, "Chagigat haBikurim beganenu" ("The Festival of the First Fruits in our Kindergarten"), 52–54; and Leah Rokach, "Chagigat haBikurim beTel Aviv" ("The Feast of the First Fruits in Tel-Aviv"), 55–57; both in Rabinowitz, *Kavim*.

25. P. Schneurson, "Lap'sichologiah shel omanut hayeladim: Hachagigah ha'omanutit began hadati shel Zipora Wolfson" ("On the Psychology of Children's Art: The Artistic Festivals in Zipora Wolfson's Religious Kindergarten"), in A. Shapira, ed., *The Story of a Kindergarten*, 71–73.

26. Z. Wolfson, in Shapira, *Story of a Kindergarten*, 160.

27. Esther Rabinowitz, *Ba'ayot chinukh began hayeladim* (Problems of Education in the Kindergarten) (Tel Aviv, 1955), 223–27.

28. See, for example, Tovah Chezkinah, "Hanukkah Festivities in the Kindergarten," Supplement to *Hed haGan* (Tel Aviv, 1963), 49–57; Leah Rotstein-Yeshpe, *Be'olam gan hayeladim* (In the World of the Kindergarten) (Tel Aviv, 1960), 60–73; Tzviah Kartbursky, *Benetivot hagan* (In the Paths of the Kindergarten) (Tel Aviv, 1962), 126–85; *Chanukah letinokot* (Hanukkah for Babes) (Jerusalem, n.d., probably the end of the twenties).

29. Oliver Shaw Rankin, *The Origins of the Festival of Hanukah* (Edinburgh: T and T Clark, 1930); L. Finkelstein, "Hanukkah and its Origins," *JQR* 22 (1931–32).

30. Baskin, "Hannukah in the Zionist Discourse," *Zmanim*: 16:61; Don-Yehiya, "Hanukah and the Myth of the Maccabees," *The Jewish Journal of Sociology*; Don-Yehiya, "Hanukah and the Myth of the Maccabees," in Shlomo Deshen et al., eds., *Israeli Judaism: The Sociology of Religion in Israel* (New Brunswick, NJ: Transaction, 1995), 303–21. David Philipson writes that: "the truth of the matter is that reform Judaism has given the Hanukkah feast a place in the public religious life such as it never had in the heyday of rabbinical JudaismHanukkah was a veritable Cinderella" (Philipson, *The Reform Movement in Judaism* [London: Macmillan, 1907], 451–52). One can surmise that the reform Jews adopted the Hanukkah festival not because of its national heroic dimension, but because it is so near in time to Christmas.

31. As quoted in Sitton, *Education in the Spirit of Homeland*, 155.

32. *Gilyonot*, Book 5 (Center of the Kindergarten Teachers Association in Eretz-Israel, 1936). On torch races held in other cities of Greece in order to ignite the altars with fresh fire, see E. W. Gardiner, *Athletics of the Ancient World* (Oxford: Oxford University Press, 1930), 143.

33. *Shoreshim* 3, 1937, 111–13.

34. Gordonia archives/ Lavon Young Maccabee, Hulda.

35. A. Z. Ben-Yishai, "Taluchot ha'or" ("Processions of Light"), *Sefer Hamoadim/Hanukkah*, 214.

36. Circular 4:48, in Natan Slahar, *The Eretz-Israel Song*, 84.

37. See Y. Zerubavel, "The Forest as a National."

38. On the Tel-Hai incident and the legend created around it, see Nakdimon Rogel, *Tel-Hai;* On the genesis of the "myth" of Tel-Hai, see the detailed study in Y. Zerubavel, *Recovered Routes.*

39. *Leyom Tel-Hai: Choveret Ezer leGanenet velaMorah beKitot Aleph-Bet* (Tel-Hai Day: A Handbook for Kindergarten Teachers and 1st- and 2nd-grade Teachers), 2nd ed. (Center for Education of the General Labor Federation), 12–13.

40. A. Shapira, "Chag hachodesh Nissan: Hatza'at chagigah" ("The Festival of the Month of Nissan: A Suggested Festivity"), *Shoreshim,* 1938.

41. On the genesis of the "myth" of the Bar Kochba war, see Y. Zerubavel, *Recovered Roots,* 48–59, 133–96, 178–91.

42. The biblically mandated waving of the sheaves (Omer) signified the harvest of the first barley, and the Shavuoth holiday, falling seven weeks later, marked the harvest of the first wheat.

43. Rothchild, "Customs of the Shavuoth Festival in the Frankfurt Community," *Turey Yeshurun* (in Hebrew)

Chapter 7

The following dissertations were very helpful: Nili Arye-Sapir, "Stories of and about Ceremonies and Celebrations," and Anat Helman, "The Development of Civil Society and Urban Culture in Tel-Aviv during the 1920s and 1930s" (both in Hebrew).

1. Darnton, "A Bourgeois Puts His World in Order," 120. In ancient Egypt, the "Egyptian idea of the city was thus centered on and shaped by the religious feasts. The city was the place on earth where the divine presence could be sensed by everyone on the occasion of the main processional feast. The more important the feast, the more important the city." In Assman, *Moses the Egyptian,* 26.

2. Goren, "Pageants of Sorrow."

3. The summary is based on Shavit and Biger, eds., *History of Tel-Aviv.*

4. Chaim Arlosoroff, "Maskanot" (Conclusions), in Arlosoroff *Ktavim II* (Writings II) (Tel Aviv, 1934), 56.

5. Y. Lufben, "Tel Aviv," *Hapoel Hatzair,* May 11, 1934, 4–7 (in Hebrew).

6. Tel Aviv Municipality Archives, Section 4, file 2/5/2.

7. See Lavenda, "Festivals and the Creation of Public Culture."

8. The urban "middle class" was a major component of the urban society, and was not organized in a centralistic sub-society like the workers (many of whom were organized in the General Federation of Labor). The relatively large civil society in Tel Aviv led to the creation of a bourgeois European-style culture, which also strove to create European-style patterns of entertainment, leisure-time activities, and consumerism, and was largely free of the avowed normative cultural ethos, which regarded public festivals as "bourgeois culture" and "luxuries."

9. Harari, *Ben haKramim (In the Vineyards),* 95.

10. The name of the first suburb of Tel Aviv.

11. Uriel, *Three Generations,* 112 (in Hebrew).

12. Berkowitz, *Yemot haMashiach* (*Days of the Messiah*).

13. Moshe Smilansky, "*Tel-Aviviyut*" (Tel-Avivness) *Bustenai*, a weekly of Eretz-Israel Farmers, 6:11 (June 27, 1934):6.

14. Tel Aviv municipality archives, file C 3–142.

15. Harari, *Ben haKramim*, 108.

16. Sidro, *Le Carnaval de Nice et ses Fous Paillassou, Polcinelle et Triboulet*.

17. See the detailed and fascinating book by Batia Carmiel, *Tel Aviv in Costume and Crown: Purim Celebrations in Tel-Aviv, 1912–1935* (in Hebrew). Our description is much indebted to her study.

18. Written testimony in the Tel Aviv Municipality archives.

19. Tel Aviv Municipality Archives, Section 1, file 72.

20. Ibid; file A 4–3218.

21. On the Oktoberfest see Möhler, *Das Münchner Oktoberfest*.

22. Tel Aviv Municipality Archives, file A 4–3218.

23. Ibid.

24. About 5,000 U.S. dollars in 2000.

25. Based on the biblical Song of the Sea.

26. Tel Aviv Municipality archives, section 4, file 1/5/2.

27. Carmiel, *Tel Aviv in Costume*, 234.

28. Tel Aviv Municipality archives, file B 4–32/8.

29. On March 8, 1931, the mayor thanked the committee members for organizing the carnival, and mentioned the contribution of the various technical assistants: "Ordinary Tel Avivians filled various roles in organizing the carnival, and submitted their own proposals and plans." Municipal Archives B8/4–32.

30. Moshe Halevi, "Adloyada—Keitzad?" ("A Purim Carnival—How?"), Israel Museum of Theatre, Museum Eretz Israel: Tel Aviv.

31. Uriel, *Three Generations*.

32. In the Old City of Jerusalem.

33. *HaHerut*, 13 August 1913.

34. Municipal announcement no. 10, 28 April 1929.

35. Chaim Glicksberg, *Bialik Yom-Yom* (*Bialik Every Day*) (HaKibbutz Ha-Meuchad: Tel Aviv, 1945), 140–41.

36. For a detailed history of the Purim carnivals see Carmiel, *Tel Aviv in Costume*.

37. *Davar*, December 14, 1928. On torch processions on the Chanukah festival in Tel Aviv, see Arye-Sapir, "The Procession of Lights." She particularly emphasizes the motif of light and its symbolic significance in these processions, as well as the fact that these processions left a deeper impression in the memory of those who lived in the period than did other traditional customs, such as games with the *sevivon*, the Hanukkah top (dreidel), Hanukkah *gelt*, and the like. Her explanation for this seems somewhat exaggerated; she asserts that the traditional customs did not play an important role in people's memories, not because of their traditional nature, but rather because they were "taken for granted," while torch processions in the urban open space, and everything they involved, were a complete innovation.

38. Lewinski, *Encyclopedia of Folklore, Customs and Tradition in Judaism* (in Hebrew), 571–87. Public carnival festivals, which sometimes included dancing, were held in several cities in Christian Europe in imitation of the Christian carnivals. See Ahuva Belkin, *The Purimshpiel—Studies in Jewish Folk Theater* (Jerusalem: Mossad Bialik, 2002), 35–65 (in Hebrew).

39. Cohen, "Drama and Politics in the Development of a London Carnival," 83; de Matta, "Carnival in Multiple Planes," in *Rite, Drama, Festival, Spectacle*.

40. Sports Association of the General Labor Federation.

41. A sports association identified with the "civil" camp.

42. Betar—the youth movement of the Revisionist party.

43. Tel Aviv Municipality archives, Section 4, file 2/5/2.

44. Tel Aviv Municipality archives, Section 4–3320.

45. Tel Aviv Municipality archives, Section 4, file 2/5/2.

46. Carmiel, *Tel Aviv in Costume*, 140–51.

47. N. Alterman, *Ha-aretz*, March 6, 1936. See in Carmiel, *Tel Aviv in Costume*, 250.

48. Tel Aviv municipal archives, 2/4/2/4.

49. Carmiel, *Tel Aviv in Costume*, 250.

50. On the labor movement in Haifa, see De Vries, *Idealism and Bureaucracy in 1920's Palestine/The Origins of "Red Haifa"* (in Hebrew).

51. Program of the Bikurim Festivities in Haifa in 1932 (in Hebrew).

Chapter 8

1. A. Ben Gurion, "Tafkid hechag bechayenu" (The Role of the Festival in our Lives), *Yedion* 1:4 (December 1964):3.

2. At the end of 1945, the kibbutz society numbered 31,200 people (5.8 percent of the Jewish community).

3. See Near, *Kibbutz Movement*, Zeira, *Rural Collective Settlement and Jewish Culture*, 201–64 (in Hebrew).

4. He immigrated to Palestine in 1923, joined Kibbutz Beit Alpha in 1923, and then Kibbutz Ramat Yochannan in 1940.

5. The minutes of four such talks were kept in the Ein Harod archives.

6. Bomy, "Lidfusey haHag baKibutzim" (The Pattern of the Festival in our Kibbutzim), *Hedim* 2:3 (1943):22–26; see also Zeev Bloch, "Hagigim al hechag" (Reflections on the Festival) *Hedim* 2:3 (1943): 23–37.

7. Yitzhak Tabenkin, "Leorchot haChevra baKibuttz" (On the Lifestyle of the Kibbutz Society) *Mibifnim* 13, April 1949.

8. Mattityahu Shalem, "Hachag baYeshuv haKibuttzi" (The Festival in the Kibbutz Settlement) *Niv haKevutzah* 5:17 (1956):75–79.

9. D. Shmeterling, "Chagim" (Festivals), *HaPoel HaTzair* December 26, 1924, and "Chagei hateva" (Festivals of Nature), *HaPoel HaTzair*, February 12, 1926, 15–16.

10. Shalem, "Hachag baYeshuv haKibuttzi," 79.

11. David Meletz, "Al Avodatenu ha'Tarbutit" (On our Cultural Work) *Mibifnim* 10 (September 7, 1925):339–41.

12. P., "A member of Ein Harod" [in original], "Shivrei Tarbut" (Fragments of Culture) *Mibifnim* 3:39 (March 10, 1939):300.

13. See Keshet, "The Age of Innocence," 124.

14. *Ma Chidesh haKibutz beTfisat haChag?* (What was the Kibbutz's Innovation in the Perception of the Festival?) *Symposyon,* Newsletter of the Kibbutz Movement 4, December 1964, 2. Over the years, this division of roles gained legitimacy, and the active participants were described as representatives of the general community, while the latter was described as participating in the ceremony through its "psychological involvement in what was taking place in its presence and before its eyes."

15. Mattityahu Shalem, "Chageynu Hamehudashim" (Our Renewed Festivals: Passover/Omer) (Alliance of the Kibbutz Movement/Central Culture Committee, 1977):5–6. Some believe that the festival ceremonies in the kibbutz were *Festspiel*—a popular theater-festival held in a natural setting, inspired by, among others, Richard Wagner's idea of *Gesamtkunstwerk* (total artwork). However, none of the creators of festival ceremonies in the kibbutz or in the city explicitly referred to any Wagnerian influence, and the Wagnerian theatrical ritual was far removed from the festival ceremonies in the kibbutzim. See Gad Kaynar, "The *Gesamtkunstwerk* and Its Resonance in the Theatrical Text of Hanoch Levin and Others," *Zemanim* 20 (summer 2002): 54–62 (in Hebrew).

16. Nahum Benari, "Shabat veMoed" ("Sabbath and Holiday") (Center for Culture: Tel Aviv, 1967), 51.

17. She created more than 150 "folk dances."

18. Bet HaShittah archives, file 13.35.3.

19. See also Shaprut, *Festival as Theatre.*

20. Bomy, "Lidfusey haHag baKibutzim."

21. It is important to note that most of the documentary material preserved in the "festival archives" at Kibbutz Beit HaShittah relates to the period beginning in the fifties and thereafter.

22. *Ushpizin*—a sixteenth-century custom which originated among the kabbalists is still part of the religious observance in the sukkah. *Ushpizin* means "guests" and here refers to seven forefathers (Abraham, Isaac, Jacob, Moses, Aaron, Joseph, and David) who are symbolically welcomed into the sukkah, one each day.

23. N.A. "Chag haAsif veSimhat Tora" (The Harvest Festival and the Rejoicing of the Water-Drawing Ceremony in Ein Harod) *Mibifnim* 1 (1925), 188.

24. Shalem, "Chageynu Hamehudashim," 9–47. Also, Shalem, "Hirhurei chag" (Some Reflections on the Festival), *Shdemot* 42 (1971):15–18.

25. Newsletter 4, December 1964. Also see Aushalon Reich, *Changes and Developments in the Passover Hagadot of the Kibbutz Movement.*

26. The name "Festival of First Fruits" was given to the Shavuoth festival at a joint festivity held by three kibbutzim in the Jezreel Valley in 1924—Ein Harod, Geva, and Kfar Yehezkel—involving a procession of decorated horse-drawn wagons carrying "first fruits." In the following years, the festivity was celebrated by all the settlements in the eastern Jezreel Valley, as well as by the inhabitants of moshavoth in the Lower Galilee.

Because of its distinctly agricultural character, this festival was the first to assume its final form in the kibbutz society during the 1920s.

27. Yitzhak Michaeli, *Ein Harod 1928–. Newsletter,* Bet HaShittah archives, file 3.14.5.

28. *Journal of the General Labor Federation/HaKibbutz HaMe'uchad* (Ein Harod), no. 315, May 14, 1937.

29. *Journal of the General Labor Federation/HaKibbutz HaMe'uchad* (Ein Harod), no. 316, May 17, 1937.

30. Shalem, "Chageynu Hamehudashim," 55–126.

31. A. Ben Gurion, "Reshit Chag haBikkurim baEmek" (The Early Bikurim Celebrations in the Valley) Beit HaShittah archives, file 3.14.5.

32. "Tu beShevat," *Yedion* 87, February 17, 1936.

33. Eliezer Liebenstein, "Chagei haAvoda veMasoret Datit" (Labor Festivals and Religious Tradition) *Mibifnim* 35, November 25, 1925. And see Zeira, *Rural Collective Settlement and Jewish Culture,* 167–84.

Conclusion

1. On this, see Oz Almog, *The Sabra—The Creation of the New Jew.*

2. The high point of the Bikurim festival in Haifa (May 15, 1943) was when Menachem Ussishkin, president of the JNF, lifted a dove from a basket and said: "I have been given a Bikurim dove. You probably know that a dove symbolizes the Jewish people, its innocence, humility and beauty. The Jewish people in the Diaspora, and to a certain extent here in this land, is shackled, like this dove. I am releasing this dove from its shackles and giving it freedom. Fly away and be our symbol, for the time has come when we also will be given our freedom and the Israelite nation will be released from its shackles." Quoted in Menahem Regev, "The Bikurim Festival as a Means of Imparting Zionist and National Values," *Ru'ach Acheret (A Different Spirit)* (September 1998):66–67 (in Hebrew). And see Daniel Haag-Wackernagelm, *Die Taube*; Irit Ziffer, *O my Dove* (in Hebrew).

3. See Maoz Azaryahu, "Innovation and Continuity," in *On Both Sides of the Bridge* (in Hebrew).

Selected Bibliography

Aaronsohn, Ran. *Baron Rothschild and his Colonies: The Beginnings of Jewish Colonization in Eretz-Israel—1882–1890*. Jerusalem: Yad Izhak Ben-Zvi, 1990. (In Hebrew).
Abramson, Glenda, ed. *Modern Jewish Mythologies*. Cincinnati: Hebrew Union College, 1990.
Allen, Ann Taylor. "Gardens of Children, Gardens of God: Kindergartens and Day-Care Centers in Nineteenth-Century Germany." *Journal of Social History* 19 (spring 1986):433–50.
Almog, Oz. *The Sabra—The Creation of the New Jew*. Berkeley: University of California Press, 2000.
Andrews, George Gordon. "Making the Revolutionary Calendar." *American Historical Review* 36:3 (1931):515–32.
Armstrong, John A. *Ukrainian Nationalism*, 2nd ed. New York: Ukrainian Academic Press, 1963.
Aronoff, Myron J. *Power and Ritual in the Israel Labor Party: A Study in Political Anthropology*. Assen, Amsterdam: Van Gorcum, 1977.
Arye-Sapir, Nili. "The Procession of Lights: Hanukkah as a National Festival in Tel Aviv, 1909–1936." *Cathedra* 103 (March 2002):135–51. (In Hebrew).
———. "Stories of and about Ceremonies and Celebrations in Tel Aviv from 1909 to 1936." Ph.D. dissertation. Hebrew University, Jerusalem, 1997. (In Hebrew).
———. "The Lighting of Simhat Torah Bonfires in Gedera." In *Jerusalem Studies in Jewish Folklore* 19–20, 1997–98. Jerusalem: Magnes Press (1998):415–29. (In Hebrew).
Assman, Jan. *Moses the Egyptian: The Memory of Egypt in Western Monotheism*. Cambridge: Harvard University Press, 1997.
Assmann, Jan, ed. *Das Fest und das Heilige. Religiose Kontrapunkte zur Alttageswelt*. Guetersloh, 1991.
Azaryahu, Maoz. *State Cults: Celebrating Independence and Commemorating the Fallen in Israel, 1948–1956*. Sede Boker: Ben-Gurion Research Center, 1995. (In Hebrew).
Azaryahu, Maoz. "Innovation and Continuity: Jewish Tradition and the Shaping of Sovereignty Rites in Israel." In M. Bar-On and Z. Zameret, eds., *On Both Sides of the Bridge: Religion and State in the Early Years of Israel*, 273–294. Jerusalem: Yad Izhak Ben-Zvi Press, 2002. (In Hebrew).
Bar-Gal, Yoram. *An Agent of Zionist Propaganda: The Jewish National Fund, 1924–1947*. Haifa/Tel Aviv: Haifa University Press/Zemora-Bitan, 1999. (In Hebrew).

Bar-On, Simon. "The Festival Calendars in Exodus XXIII 14–19 and XXXIV 18–26." *Vetus Testamentum* 48:2 (1998):161–195.

Bartal, Israel. "Cossack and Bedouin: A New National Imagery." *The Second Aliya: Studies*, 482–93. Jerusalem: Yad Ben Zvi, 1997. (In Hebrew).

Baskin, Orit. "Hanukkah in the Zionist Discourse according to 'Seder Hamoadim' ('The Book of Festivals')." *Zmanim* 16:61 (1997–98):38–50. (In Hebrew).

Bauman, Richard. *Story, Performance, and Event: Contextual Studies of Oral Narrative*. Cambridge: Cambridge University Press, 1986, 1993.

Bell, Catherine. *Ritual: Perspectives and Dimensions*. New York: Oxford University Press, 1977.

Ben-Ami, Issachar. *Saints Veneration among Jews in Morocco*. Jerusalem: Magnes Press, 1984. (In Hebrew).

Ben-Amos, Avner. *Funerals, Politics, and Memory in Modern France, 1789–1996*. Oxford: Oxford University Press, 2000.

Ben-Amos, Avner, and Ilana Bet-El. "Ceremonies, Education and History: Holocaust Day and Remembrance Day in Israel." In Rivka Feldhay and Immanuel Etkes, eds. *Education and History: Cultural and Political Contexts*, 457–79. Jerusalem: Zalman Shazar Center, 1999. (In Hebrew).

Ben-Amos, Dan. "Performance." In Thomas A. Green, ed. *Folklore—An Encyclopedia of Beliefs, Customs, Tales, Music and Art*, 2:630–35. Santa Barbara, CA: ABC-CLIO, 1997.

Berkowitz, Y. D. *Yemot haMashiach* (*Days of the Messiah*), rev. ed. Tel Aviv, 1953. (In Hebrew).

Bilu, Yoram. "Jewish Moroccan 'Saint Impresarios' in Israel: A State Development Perspective." *Psychoanalytic Study of Society* 15 (1990):247–69.

Bilu, Yoram, and Eyal Ben-Ari. "The Making of Modern Saints: Manufactured Charisma and the Abu-Hatseiras of Israel." *American Ethnologist* 19 (1992):672–87.

Bocock, Robert. *Ritual in Industrial Society: A Sociological Analysis of Ritualism in Modern England*. London: George Allen and Unwin, 1974.

Burckhardt, Jacob. *The Civilization of the Renaissance in Italy*. Trans. G. C. Middlemore. Baltimore: Penguin, 1990.

Burden, H. T. *The Nüremberg Party Rallies: 1923–1939*. London: Pall Mall Press, 1967.

Burkert, Walter. *Greek Religion, Archaic and Classical*. Trans. John Raffan. Oxford: Basil Blackwell, 1985.

Cannadine, David. "The Context, Performances and Meaning of Ritual: The British Monarchy and the 'Invention of Tradition,' c. 1820–1977." in Hobsbawn and Ranger, eds. *The Invention of Tradition*, 101–64. Cambridge: Cambridge University Press, 1984.

Carmiel, Batia. *Tel Aviv in Costume and Crown: Purim Celebrations in Tel-Aviv, 1912–1935*. Tel Aviv: Eretz Israel Museum, 1999. (In Hebrew).

Cassar-Pullicino, Joseph. *Studies in Maltese Folklore*, 39–67. Msida: Malta University Press, 1992.

Chabas, Barcha, ed. *HaAliya Hasheniah*. (Book of the Second Aliya). Tel Aviv, 1947.

Clifford, James, and G. Marcus, eds. *Writing Culture: The Poetics and Politics of Ethnography*. Berkeley: University of California Press, 1986.

Cohen, Avner. "Drama and Politics in the Development of a London Carnival." *Man* 15:1 (1980):65–87.

Confino, Alon. *The Nation as a Local Metaphor: Württemberg, Imperial Germany, and National Memory, 1871–1918*. Chapel Hill: University of North Carolina Press, 1997.

Connerton, Paul. *How Societies Remember*. Cambridge: Cambridge University Press, 1989.

Cremona, Vicki Ann. "Carnival in Gozo: Waning Traditions and Thriving Celebrations." *Journal of Mediterranean Studies* 5:1 (1995):68–97.

Cressy, David. *Bonfires and Bells: National Memory and the Protestant Calendar in Elizabethan and Stuart England*. Berkeley: University of California Press, 1989.

Darnton, Robert. "A Bourgeois Puts His World in Order: The City as a Text." *The Great Cat Massacre and other Episodes in French Cultural History*, 107–34. New York: Basic Books, 1984.

Davis, Susan G. *Parades and Power: Street Theater in Nineteenth-Century Philadelphia*. Berkeley: University of California Press, 1988.

De Matta, Roberto. "Carnival in Multiple Planes." In John J. Macalloon, ed., *Rite, Drama, Festival, Spectacle*, 208–40. Philadelphia: Institute for the Study of Human Issues, 1984.

Deshen, Shlomo. "Anthropological Study in Israel: Involvement versus Observation." In S. Deshen and Moshe Shoked, *The Generation of Transition: Continuity and Change Among North African Immigrants in Israel*, 32–42. Jerusalem: Machon Ben-Zvi, 1977. (In Hebrew).

Deshen, Shlomo, and Moshe Shoked. *The Generation of Transition: Continuity and Change Among North African Immigrants in Israel*. Jerusalem: Machon Ben-Zvi, 1977. (In Hebrew).

De Vries, David. *Idealism and Bureaucracy in 1920's Palestine: the Origins of "Red Haifa."* Tel Aviv: Ha Kibbutz Ha Meuchad, 1999. (In Hebrew).

Doleve-Gandelman, Tsili. "The Symbolic Inscription of Zionist Ideology in the Space of Eretz Yisrael: Why the Native Israeli Is Called Tsabar." In Harvey E. Goldberg, ed., *Judaism Viewed from Within and Without: Anthropological Studies*, 257–84. Albany: State University of New York Press, 1987.

Don-Yehiya, Eliezer, and Charles Liebman. *Civil Religion in Israel*. Berkeley: University of California Press, 1983.

Don-Yehiya, Eliezer. "Hanukkah and the Myth of the Maccabees in Ideology and in Society." In Shlomo Deshen et al., eds., *Israeli Judaism: The Sociology of Religion in Israel*, 303–21. New Brunswick, NJ: Transaction, 1995.

Dorson, M. Richard. "History of the Elite and History of the Folk." In *Folklore: Selected Essays*, 225–59. Bloomington: Indiana University Press, 1972.

Dundes, Alan, and Falassi, Allesandro. *La Terra in Piazza: An Interpretation of the Palio of Siena*. Berkeley: University of California Press, 1983.

Elboim-Dror, Rachel. *Hebrew Education in Eretz Israel*, vols. 1 and 2. Jerusalem: Yad Izhak Ben-Zvi Institute, 1986, 1990. (In Hebrew).

Errington, Frederick. "Reflexivity Deflected: The Festival of Nations as an American Cultural Performance." *American Ethnologist* 14:4 (1987):654–67.
Finkelstein, L. "Hanukkah and its Origins." *JQR* 22 (1931/32): 169–73.
Fontenrose, Joseph. *The Ritual Theory of Myth*. Berkeley: University of California Press, 1966, 1971.
Fowler, W. Warde. *The Roman Festivals of the Period of the Republic* (1899) New York and London: Kennikat Press, 1969.
Frankel, Jonathan. "The 'Yizkor' Book of 1911—A Note on National Myths in the Second Aliya." In H. Ben Israel et al., eds., *Religion, Ideology and Nationalism in Europe and America*, 355–84. Jerusalem: Historical Society of Israel and Zalman Shazar Center for Jewish History, 1986.
Freidhaber, Zvi. "Wedding Ceremonies in the Jewish Yishuv in Palestine during the First and Second Aliya." *Jerusalem Studies in Jewish Folklore* 13–14 (1992):389–441. (In Hebrew).
Frykman, Jonas, and Orvar Lofgren. *Culture Builders: A Historical Anthropology of Middle-Class Life*. Trans. Alan Crozier. New Brunswick, NJ: Rutgers University Press, 1980.
Gaster, Theodor H. *Festivals of the Jewish Year: A Modern Interpretation and Guide*. New York: William Sloane Association, 1952, 1968.
Gellner, Ernest. *Encounters with Nationalism*. Cambridge, MA: Blackwell, 1994.
Gertz, Nurit. *Captive of a Dream*. London: Frank Cass, 2000.
Gluckman, Max, ed. *Essays on the Ritual of Social Relations*. Manchester: Manchester University Press, 1962, 1966.
Goldhill, Simon, and Robin Osborne, eds. *Performance Culture and Athenian Democracy*. Cambridge: Cambridge University Press, 1999.
Goody, Jack. "Against Ritual: Loosely Structured Thought on a Loosely Defined Topic." In Moore and Myerhoff, *Secular Ritual*, 25–34. Assen, Amsterdam: Van Gorcum, 1977.
———. "Religion and Rituals: The Definitional Problem." *British Journal of Sociology* 12 (1961):142–64.
Goren, Arthur A. "Celebrating Zion in America." In Jeffrey Shandler and Beth S. Wenger, eds., *Encounters with the "Holy Land": Place, Past and Future in American Jewish Culture*, 41–59. Philadelphia: National Museum of American Jewish History, 1997.
———. "Pageants of Sorrow, Celebration and Protest." *The Politics and Public Culture of American Jews*, 30–47. Bloomington: Indiana University Press, 1999.
———. "The Rite of Community." *The Politics and Public Culture of American Jews*, 48–82. Bloomington: Indiana University Press, 1999.
Greenstone, J. H. *Jewish Feasts and Fasts*. Philadelphia: Jewish Publication Society, 1945.
Guss, David M. *The Festive State: Race, Ethnicity, and Nationalism as Cultural Performances*. Berkeley: University of California Press, 2000.
Gutmann, Joseph. "Jewish Medieval Marriage Customs in Art: Creativity and Adaptation." In David Kraemer, ed., *The Jewish Family: Metaphor and Memory*, 47–62. New York: Oxford University Press, 1987.

Haag-Wackernagelm, Daniel. *Die Taube—Vom heiligen Vogel der Liebesgottin zur Stassetaube.* Basel: Schwabe and Com. AG, 1999.

Handelman, Don. "Holiday Celebrations in Israeli Kindergartens." *Models and Mirrors: Towards an Anthropology of Public Events,* 162–89. Cambridge: Cambridge University Press, 1990.

———. "Models and Mirrors." *Models and Mirrors: Towards an Anthropology of Public Events,* 22–62. Cambridge: Cambridge University Press, 1990.

Handler, Richard. *Nationalism and Politics of Culture in Quebec.* Madison: University of Wisconsin Press, 1988.

Harari, Yehudite. *Ben haKramim (In the Vineyards),* 1947. (In Hebrew)

Helman, Anat. "The Development of Civil Society and Urban Culture in Tel-Aviv during the 1920s and 1930s." Ph.D. diss. Hebrew University, 2000. (In Hebrew).

Herzl, Theodor. *Tagebücher, 1895–1904* Erster Band. Berlin: Judischer Verlag, 1922.

Hirschberg, A. S. *In Oriental Lands.* (Photocopy of the Vilna ed., 1910, with Indices). Jerusalem: Yad Izhak Ben-Zvi, 1977. (In Hebrew).

Hobsbaum, Eric, and Ranger, Terence, eds. *The Invention of Tradition.* Cambridge: Cambridge University Press, 1983.

Hooke, Samuel H. "The Babylonian New Year Festival." *Journal of the Manchester Egyptian and Oriental Society* 13 (1927):29–38.

Huizinga, Johan. *Homo Ludens: A Study of the Play Element in Culture.* New York: Bacon, 1955.

Katriel, Tamar. "Rhetoric in Flames: Messages in Flames in the Youth Movements." *Key Words—Patterns of Culture and Communication in Israel,* 116–30. Haifa: Haifa University Press, 1999. (In Hebrew).

Kertzer, David I. *Ritual, Politics, and Power.* New Haven: Yale University Press, 1981.

Keshet, Shula. "The Age of Innocence: 'My Glorious Brothers' at Kibbutz Givat Brenner, Sep. 1953." *Israel: Studies in Zionism and the State of Israel* 1 (2002):119–32. (In Hebrew).

Kirshenblatt-Gimblett, Barbara. *Destination Culture: Tourism, Museums, and Heritage.* Berkeley: University of California Press, 1998.

Kluckhohn, Clyde. "Myths and Rituals: A General Theory." *Harvard Theological Review* 35 (1942):45–79.

Lane, Christel. *The Rites of Rulers: Ritual in Industrial Society—The Soviet Case.* Cambridge: Cambridge University Press, 1981.

Lavenda, Robert H. "Festivals and the Creation of Public Culture: Whose Voice(s)?" In Ivan Karp and Christine Mullen, eds., *Museums and Communities: The Politics of Public Culture,* 76–104. Washington, D.C.: Smithsonian Institution Press, 1992.

Lewinski, Yom-Tov. *Encyclopedia of Folklore, Customs and Tradition in Judaism,* vol. 1–2. Tel Aviv: Dvir, 1975. (In Hebrew).

Linke, Oli. "Folklore, Anthropology, and the Government of Social Life." *Comparative Studies in Society and History* 32:1 (1990):117–48.

Lotman, Iurij M. "The Theater and Theatricity as Components of Early-Nineteenth-Century Culture." In Iurij M. Lotman and Boris. A. Uspenskij, *The Semiotics of*

Russian Culture, 141–64. Trans. G. S. Smith. Ann Arbor: University of Michigan Press, 1984.

Lowenthal, Martin, ed. *The Diaries of Theodor Herzl.* New York: Universal Library, 1962.

MacAloon, John J. *Rite, Drama, Festival, Spectacle: Rehearsals Toward a Theory of Cultural Performance.* Philadelphia: Institute for the Study of Human Issues, 1984.

Marcus, Ivan G. *Rituals of Childhood: Jewish Acculturation in Medieval Europe.* New Haven: Yale University Press, 1996.

Mazor, Yehoram, ed. *Hag and Moed in the Thinking of the Reform Movement.* Israel, 1988. (In Hebrew).

Meyer, Michael A. *Response to Modernity: A History of the Reform Movement in Judaism.* New York: Oxford University Press, 1988.

Mishory, Alec. *Lo and Behold: Zionist Icons and Visual Symbols in Israeli Culture.* Tel Aviv: Am Oved, 2000. (In Hebrew).

Möhler, Gerda. *Das Münchner Oktoberfest: Vom bayer Landwirtscaftsfest zum grössten Volksfest des Welt,* Munich: BLV Verlag, 1981.

Moore, Sally F., and Barbara G. Myerhoff, eds. *Secular Ritual.* Assen, Amsterdam: Van Gorcum, 1977.

Mosse, G. L. "Mass Politics and the Political Liturgy of Nationalism." In E. Kamenka, ed., *Nationalism: The Nature and Evolution of an Ideal,* 39–54. London: Routledge and Kegan Paul, 1976.

Muir, Edward. *Civic Ritual in Renaissance Venice.* Princeton: Princeton University Press, 1981.

Myśiwiec, Karol. *The Twilight of Ancient Egypt: First Millenium B.C.E.* Trans. David Lorton. Ithaca: Cornell University Press, 1993.

Near, Henry. *The Kibbutz Movement: A History.* 2 vols. Oxford: Littman Library of Jewish Civilization, 1994, 1997.

Newman, Simon P. *Parades and the Politics of the Street: Festive Culture in the Early American Republic.* Philadelphia: University of Pennsylvania Press, 1997.

Nitzche, Jane Chance. *The Genius Figure in Antiquity and the Middle-Ages.* New York: Columbia University Press, 1975.

Oahana, David, and Robert Wistrich, eds. *The Shaping of Israeli Identity: Myth, Memory and Trauma.* London: Frank Cass, 1995.

Orgel, Stephen, and Roy Strong. *Inigo Jones: The Theater of the Stuart Court,* vols. 1–2. Berkeley: University of California Press, 1973.

Ozouf, Mona. *Festivals and the French Revolution.* Trans. Alan Sheridan. Cambridge: Harvard University Press, 1991.

———. "Space and Time in the Festivals of the French Revolution." *Comparative Studies in Society and History* 17 (1975):371–84.

Philipson, David. *The Reform Movement in Judaism.* London: Macmillan, 1907.

Pollack, Hermann. *Jewish Folkways in Germanic Lands (1648–1806): Studies in Aspects of Daily Life.* Cambridge: MIT Press, 1971.

Rankin, Oliver Shaw. *The Origins of the Festival of Hanukkah.* Edinburgh: T and T Clark, 1930.

Rappaport, Roy A. "The Obvious Aspects of Ritual." *Ecology, Meaning and Religion*, 173–221. Richmond, CA: North Atlantic Books, 1979.
Raum, Toivo U. *Estonia under Imperial Russia*, vol. 2. Stanford, CA: Hoover Institution Press, 1982.
Rearick, Charles. "Festivals in Modern France: The Experience of the Third Republic." *Journal of Contemporary History* 12 (1977):435–60.
Redfield, Robert. "Folk Society." *American Journal of Sociology* 52:4 (1944):293–308.
——. *Peasant Society and Culture*. Chicago: Chicago University Press, 1956.
Reich, Avshalom. *Changes and Developments in the Passover Haggadot of the Kibbutz Movement, 1935–1971*. Austin: University of Texas, 1972.
Reiner, Elchanan. "Destruction, Temple and Sacred Place: on a Medieval Concept of Time and Place." *Cathedra* 97 (September 2000):47–64. (In Hebrew).
——. "Pilgrims and Pilgrimage to Eretz Yisrael, 1099–1517." Ph.D. dissertation, Hebrew University of Jerusalem, 1988. (In Hebrew).
Reshef, Shimon, and Dror Yuval. *Hebrew Education in the Years of the National Homeland (1919–1948)*. Jerusalem: Bialik Institute, 1999. (In Hebrew).
Rogel, Nakdimon. *Tel Hai: A Front without a Rear*. Tel Aviv: Hadar-Yariv, 1979. (In Hebrew).
Rosenau, William. *Jewish Ceremonial Institutions and Customs*. 3rd ed. New York: Bloch, 1925.
Rothchild, J. "Customs of Shavuoth Festival in the Frankfurt Community." *Turey Yeshurun* 1 (1966):19–21. (In Hebrew).
Rotman, Livio. *Education as a Reflection of Society: The Jewish Romanian School (1815–1914)*. Tel Aviv University, 1999. (In Hebrew).
Schohat, A. *"In the Paths of Labor," Chinukh vetarbut*. Tel Aviv: Am-Oved, 1967. (In Hebrew).
Schweid, Eliezer. *The Cycle of Appointed Times*. Tel Aviv: Am-Oved, 1984. (In Hebrew).
Segal, Robert A., ed. *The Myth and Ritual Theory: An Anthology*. Malden, MA: Blackwell, 1998.
Shahar, Natan. *The Eretz-Israel Song and the Jewish National Fund*. Jerusalem: Research Institute for the History of Keren Kayemeth leYisrael [Land and Settlement], research ser. 1, 1994. (In Hebrew).
Shamgar-Handelman, Lea, and Don Handelman. "Celebrations of Bureaucracy: Birthday Parties in Israeli Kindergartens." *Ethnology* 30:4 (1991):293–312.
Shaprut, Ezra. "Festival as Theatre" (Directing Bikurim Ceremonies in Eretz-Israel from the First Temple Period to the Present Day). M.A. thesis, Tel Aviv University, 1988. (In Hebrew).
Shavit, Yaacov, and Gideon Biger, eds. *History of Tel-Aviv*, vol. 1. Tel Aviv, 2000. (In Hebrew).
Shavit, Yaacov. "Supplying a Missing System—Between Official and Unofficial Popular Culture in the Hebrew National Culture in Eretz-Israel." In Binyamin Ze'ev Kedar, ed., *Studies in the History of Popular Culture*, 327–45. Jerusalem: Zalman Shazar Center for Jewish History, 1996. (In Hebrew).

———. "The Yishuv between National Regeneration of Culture and Cultural Generation of the Nation." In J. Reinharz, G. Shimoni, and Y. Salmon, eds., *Jewish Nationalism and Politics: New Perspectives*, 141–57. Jerusalem: Z. Shazar Center; Boston: Brandeis University, 1996. (In Hebrew).

———. "Warsaw/Tel-Aviv—Yiddish and Hebrew: Between Mass Literature and Mass Culture." *Ha-Sifrut/Literature* 3–4:35–36 (1986):201–9. (In Hebrew).

———. "The Status of Culture in the Process of Creating a National Society in Eretz-Israel: Basic Attitudes and Concepts." In Zohar Shavit, ed., *The Construction of Hebrew Culture in Eretz Israel*, 9–29. Jerusalem: Israeli Academy for Science and Humanities and the Bialik Institute, 1999. (In Hebrew).

———. "Ahad Ha-Am and Hebrew National Culture: Realist or Utopianist?" *Jewish History* 4:2 (1990):71–88.

———. "Culture and Cultural Status: Basic Developments in Hebrew Culture during the Second Aliya Period." In Israel Bartal, ed., *The Second Aliya: Studies*. Jerusalem: Yad Ben-Zvi Press, 1997. 343–66. (In Hebrew).

———. *Jabotinsky and the Revisionist Movement*. London: Frank Cass, 1987.

Sidro, Annie. *Le Carnaval de Nice et ses Fous paillassou, Polcinelle et Triboulet*. Serre: Nice, 1979.

Singer, Milton B. *When a Great Tradition Modernizes: An Anthropological Approach to Indian Civilization*. New York: Prager, 1977.

Sitton, Shoshana. "Between Feminism and Zionism: The Hebrew-Language Kindergarten Teachers' Struggle for Professional Recognition." *Zmanim* 16:61 (1997–98):26–37. (In Hebrew).

———. *Education in the Spirit of the Homeland: The Curriculum of the Teachers' Council for the Keren Kayemet (1925–1953)*. Tel Aviv University, 1998. (In Hebrew).

———. "School Festivals and Ceremonies: Transmitting a New Cultural Code in Israeli Schools." *Journal of Jewish Education* 62:3 (1996):54–62.

Smith, Anthony D. *The Nation in History: Historiographical Debates about Ethnicity and Nationalism*. Hanover, NH: University Press of New England, 2000.

Smith, Jonathan Z. *To Take Place: Toward Theory in Ritual*. Chicago: University of Chicago Press, 1987.

Stites, Richard. "Bolshevik Ritual Building in 1920." In Sheila Fitzpatrick, Alexander Rabinowitch, and R. Stites, eds., *Russia in the Era of NEP*, 295–307. Bloomington: Indiana University Press, 1991.

Strong, Roy. *Art and Power: Renaissance Festivals, 1450–1850*. Berkeley: University of California Press, 1984.

Sumner, W. G. *Folkways*. New York: Mentor, 1960.

Tabory, Josef. *The Passover Ritual throughout the Generations*. Tel Aviv: Hakibbutz Hamehuhad, 1996. (In Hebrew).

Tambiah, S. J. "A Performative Approach to Ritual." *Proceedings of the British Academy* 65 (1979):113–69.

Ta-Shma, Israel M. *Early Franco-German Ritual and Custom*. Jerusalem: Magnes Press, 1992. (In Hebrew).

———. "On Birthdays in Judaism." *Zion* 67:2 (2002):19–24. (In Hebrew).
Turner, Victor W. *Schism and Continuity in African Society*. Manchester, England: Rhodes-Livingstone Institute, Northern Rhodesia, 1957.
———. *The Ritual Process: Structure and Anti-Structure*. Ithaca: Cornell University Press, 1977.
Uriel, Gila. *Three Generations*. Tel Aviv: Resafim, 1995. (In Hebrew).
Vakar, Nicholas P. *Belorussia: The Making of a Nation: A Case Study*. Cambridge: Harvard University Press, 1956.
Volkov, Shulamit. "'To Invent a Tradition'—The Jews of Germany in the 19th Century." In Binyamin Ze'ev Kedar, ed., *Studies in the History of Popular Culture*, 245–56. Jerusalem, 1996. (In Hebrew).
Waldstreicher, David. *In the Midst of Perpetual Fetes: The Making of American Nationalism, 1776–1820*. Chapel Hill: University of North Carolina Press, 1996.
Walicki, Andrzej. *The Slavophile Controversy: History of a Conservative Utopia in Nineteenth-Century Russian Thought*. Trans. H. Andrews-Rusiecka. Notre Dame, Ind.: Notre Dame Press, 1985.
Wilkinson, John, trans. *Egeria's Travels*. Warminster: Aris and Phillips, 1999.
Wilson, William A. *Folklore and Nationalism in Modern Finland*. Bloomington: Indiana University Press, 1976.
Wollons, Roberta L., ed. *Kindergartens and Cultures: The Global Diffusion of an Idea*. New Haven: Yale University Press, 2000.
Young, Frank W. *Initiation Ceremonies: A Cross-Cultural Study of Status Dramatization*. Indianapolis: Bobbs-Merrill, 1965.
Zeira, Moti. *Rural Collective Settlement and Jewish Culture in Eretz Israel during the 1920s*. Jerusalem: Yad Ben-Zvi Press, 2002. (In Hebrew).
Zerubavel, Eviatar. "Easter and Passover: On Calendars and Group Identity." *American Sociological Review* 47:2 (1982):284–89.
Zerubavel, Yael. *Recovered Roots: Collective Memory and the Making of Israeli National Tradition*. Chicago: University of Chicago Press, 1995.
———. "The Forest as a National Icon: Literature, Politics and the Archaeology of Memory." *Israel Studies* 1:1 (1996):60–99.
Ziffer, Irit. *O my Dove, That Art in the Clefts of the Rock: The Dove-Allegory in Antiquity*. Tel Aviv: Eretz Israel Museum, 1998. (In Hebrew).

INDEX

Agadati (Koschinsky), Barukh, 91
agents of culture, 16
Agnon, Shmuel Yosef, 98
agriculture folk tradition, 19
Aldema (Eisenstein), Avraham, 91, 94, 96
Alliance society, 48
Alterman, Nathan, 103
Apollo cult, 7
Arab *fantaziah*, 31
Arab-Palestinian society, 20
Arab Revolt (1936–37), 74, 90, 103
Arab riots (1929), 101
Arnon, Abraham, 55
athlotheatati, 7

Babylonian new year rituals, 6
Baden-Powell's Boy Scouts, 9
Balfour, Lord Arthur, 66; visits Tel Aviv, 90–91, 95
Balfour Declaration day, 64, 66
Bar-Gal, Yoram, 51
Bar Kochba. *See* Shimon Bar Kochba
Bar Kochba revolt, 78, 79
Basel, 21, 42, 43
Bedouins, 113
Beit Alpha (kibbutz), 117
Beit HaShita (kibbutz), 106
Belinski, Vissarion, 24
Ben-Amos, Avner, 8
Benari (Bronsky), Nahum, 113, 115
Ben-Gurion, Arye, 106, 121
Ben haKramim (Yehudith Harari), 88
Ben-Hillel, A., 60

Ben-Yehudah, Baruch, 55, 57–59
Ben-Yishai, A. Z., 94
Ben-Zvi, Yizchak, 14
Berkowitz, J. D., 89
Berlin, 34
Bernstein, Leah, 113
Betar (the Yosef Trumpeldor Union), 45, 100
Bialik, Chaim Nachman, xiv, 56, 65, 94, 96, 101, 102; memorial day of, 64, 81–82
Bible, 6, 7, 74, 82, 91
bikurim, hag Ha-Bikurim 79, 117. *See also* Shavuot
birthday celebrations, 33–37, 62; elements and customs of, 34–36
Book of Esther (Megillat Esther), 94, 99, 101, 102
Book of Ruth, 81
Books of the Maccabees, 67, 69
Borochov, Dov Ber, 44
bourgeois culture, 17
Bukovina, 113
Burckhardt, Jacob, 8
Burden, H. T., 9

Cannadine, David, 9
canonical corpus of texts, 11
Carnot, Marie François Sadi, 23
Catholic Church, 108
Chag Ha'Omer. *See* Shavuot
Chagim uMo'adim leChagigot veNeshafim Bikhlal uleLag b'Omer befrat (pamphlet), 55
Chanukah. *See* Hanukkah

Chasidim, 72
childhood culture, 33. *See also* birthday celebrations
Christian liturgy, 7
civic culture, xi
civic society, 45
Clifford, James, 4
Cohen, Abner, 99
collective memory, xi, xv, 14, 54
Connerton, Paul, 4, 11
Crusaders, 8
cultural entrepreneurs, xiii
cultural revival, 125–26
cultural work, 17
Cyril, Bishop, 7

Daphnephoria, 7
Davis, Susan G., 4
Degania A (kibbutz), 109
Dewey, John, 53
Diaspora, 15, 18, 19, 25, 30, 45, 56, 66, 70, 71, 78, 81, 107
Dizengoff, Meir, 87, 89, 91, 93, 101
Droyanov, Alter, 85

East Europe, 20; Jews, 24, 45
Egeria, 7
Egypt: Exodus from, 6, 65, 78; Pharaonic period, 7
Ein Harod (kibbutz), 108, 111, 113, 115–16, 118–19, 122
English royal rituals, 9
Eretz-Israel (Jewish Palestine), xi, 18, 19, 32, 34, 45, 66, 70, 71, 78, 79, 81, 85, 106; British rule over (Mandatory period), xiii, 15, 41, 47, 50, 82, 125; educational network in (*see* Hebrew educational system);Hebrew culture in, xi, xii, xiv, 12, 14–18, 25, 37, 49, 64, 105, 125; Jewish immigrants in, 15, 86, 129; Jewish national home in, 66; Jewish settlements in, 25, 52; Jewish society in, xii, xv, 5, 13, 15, 20, 22, 24, 25, 30, 37,
41, 49, 52, 53, 54, 83, 107, 125, 127, 128, 129; Turkish rule over, xiii
etrog trees, 72
Europe, 62, 128. *See also* East Europe
Exodus, 6
Ezra Society *(Hilffsverehein der Deutschen Juden)*, 34

Feast of Tabernacles. *See* Succoth
Feinsod-Sukenik, Hasia, 34
Festival of the First Fruit. *See* Shavuot
Festival of the Giving of the Law. *See* Shavuot
Fest of Light. *See* Hanukkah
Festival of the new month, 64–65
Feuer, Johanes, 31
Fichman, Yaacov, 25
Finkerpeled-Amir, Anda, 71
Finland, xi
fire ceremonies, 33
First Temple period, 5, 16, 20, 113
Florentines, 8
"folk artists," 113
folk culture, xi, xii, xiii, 4, 15, 21, 25, 79, 85, 126; Hebrew folk culture, 37, 55
folk festivals, 22
folklore, 21, 127; Jewish folklore, xiv, 15
folk-ways, 4
formal popular culture. *See* official folk culture
French Republic, 8, 22
French Revolution, 5, 8
Froebel method, 34
funerals, 8–9, 13, 19, 96

Galilee, 77; Lower Galilee, 31, 32, 46; Upper Galilee, 31, 46, 72, 76
Gedera, 31
Gedud Ha'avodah, 26
Gellner, Ernst, 15
General Labor Federation, 104, 120
Genesis, 66
German Kinderfeste, 34

German language, 55
Germany, 14, 34; and Jews, 18, 30
ge'ulat ha'aretz, 51
Gluckman, Max, 9
Goody, Jack, 9
Gordon, Aharon David, 24–25
Gordonia (Zionist youth movement), 70
"Great Tradition," 10
Greek Orthodox Easter, 20
Guttman, Nahum, 94

hadar (grandeur), 44
Haggadah, 32, 78
Haggadah (kibbutz), 116–17
hag ha-Gez, 117
Haherut (newspaper), 95
Haifa, 104; ceremonies and festivities in, 104, 105; General Labor Federation, 104
Halevi, Moshe, 94, 95, 102
HaMizrachi party, 50
Handel, George Frideric, 68
Hanukkah (Feast of Light), 49, 55, 64, 66–71, 89, 97; candles, 67; *dreidel*, 70; Hanukkah money, 69; at the kibbutz, 116; motif of light, 70–71; songs, 67, 68, 69
HaPoel Hatzair (party), 28
HaPoel sport association, 100
Harari, Chaim, xiv, 55–56, 91
Harari, Yehudith, v, 88
Harvest Festival. *See* Shavuot; Succoth
HaTikvah, 32, 65, 66, 81
Hebrew calendar: new Hebrew calendar, 47, 53, 55, 61, 64; traditional Hebrew calendar, 128
Hebrew culture, xiv, 21, 24, 56, 64, 107, 110, 128; in Eretz-Israel, xi, xii, xiv, 12, 13, 14–18, 25, 37, 50, 86, 105, 125, 130
Hebrew educational system, 19 *(see also* kindergartens); schools and the JNF, 49–52, 61; Labor stream, 76
Hebrew language, 25–26, 53, 55, 63
Hebrew literature, 20, 82

Hebrew poetry, 74
Hebrew revival, 24
Hebrew Teachers Federation of Eretz-Israel, 50
Hebrew village, 19
Heimat, 16, 86
Herzl, Benjamin Zeev (Theodor), 21–23, 26, 29, 42–43, 52; memorial day of, 64, 81–82
hieropoie, 7
high culture, 16, 24, 25, 127
Hirscberg, A. S., 18
Holocaust Day, 129
Hovevei Zion, 18, 48, 67
Huizinga, Johan, 11

Independence Day, 105, 129
integration, 29, 30
Isaiah, 74, 116

Jabotinsky, Zeev, 44–45
Jaffa, 48, 49, 67, 86; Jewish community in, 85
Jawitz, Ze'ev (Wolf), 72
Jerusalem, 6, 8, 20, 43; the Hebrew University, 91; pilgrimages to, 20, 79, 117; Rothschild School for Girls, 34; Sephardic community, 18; the Temple, 6–7, 79, 81, 120; Via Dolorosa, 73
Jewish National Fund (JNF, *Keren Kayemet le'Israel*), 35, 49–52, 61, 90, 93, 104, 121; the "birthday" of (the 18th of Tevet), 64, 71; the Blue Box, 51, 65, 67, 70
Jewish revolt against Roman rule, 78
Jewish tradition, 24, 108
Jewish Yishuv, xiii, 20, 29, 46, 48, 50, 51, 52, 81, 82, 99, 101, 123, 129; absence of public political performative lore in, 41–42; educational network in (*see* Hebrew educational system); first elected assembly, 43; political culture of, 41, 47

Jewish-Hebrew culture, 21
Jezreel Valley, 115, 117
Joshua, 66
Judah the Maccabee, 68

kabbalat shabbat, 31–32, 65–66
Kabbalists, 71
Kaddish prayer, 82
Karni, Yehudah, 94–95
Katriel, Tamar, 33
Keren Kayemet le'Israel. *See* Jewish National Fund (JNF)
Kerzer, David I., 9
Kfar Giladi, 46
kibbutz, kibbutzim, 32, 106, 114, 122; Chagigat Zikhron haBikurim, 120 (*see also under* Shavuot); communal stagers in, 112; culture committees in, 112–13, 114; Festival of Tabernacles, 115–16, 119; festivals and ceremonies in, 106–23; hag ha-Gez, 117; Hanukkah festival, 116; kibbutz community, 106, 107, 110; kibbutz lifestyle, 107; kibbutz movement, 104, 107, 108, 109, 111, 113, 114, 117, 120, 122; kibbutz society, 28, 29, 106, 107, 110; Passover seder, 116; Purim festival, 116; "return to the land" ideology, 107; Shavuot (Chag Ha'Omer), 117–21, 123; *tarbutnikim*, 112; Tu BiShevat, 117, 121, 122–23
Kibbutz HaMe'uchad movement, 122
kindergartens, 19; birthday celebrations in, 33–37, 62; festival and ceremonies in, 62–63, 105, 123; first kindergarten in Eretz-Israel, 34; Hebrew kindergarten, 33, 34–37, 63; Jewish kindergarten, 34
kindergarten teachers, 5, 19, 34, 35, 50, 62, 63
Kindergarten Teachers Association, 36
Kipnis, Levin, 68
Klausner, Joseph, 45
Kluckhohn, Clyde, 12

Knesset, 43
Krishavsky (Ezrachi), Mordechai, 48

labor movement, 24, 44, 45, 47, 86
Lag ba'Omer, 20, 78–79
Lavenda, Robert H., 4
"Lesser Tradition," 10, 18
Levites, 5
Leviticus, 6
Libensteinn (Livne), Eliezer, 121

MacAllon, John, 4
Maccabees, 68, 79
Maccabee sport association, 91, 100
Maccabiah games, 42, 96–97
Matman-HaCohen, Judah Leib, 67
May Day parades, 44
Megillat Esther. *See Book of Esther*
Meletz, David, 111
Melnikov, Abraham, 46
memorial ceremonies, 46–47, 96
Meshcha (Kfar Tabor), 31
Middle Ages, 8, 30, 31
Mishna Yoma, 6
mitzvah, 51
Mo'adim — Seder Sefarim Lechagei Ha'am (Festivals — Book of Folk Holidays), xiv
moledet (local geography and history), 53
Morocco, Jews in, 18
moshava, 31, 32
moshavim, 32
Mt. Meron, 20, 78
Muscular Judaism, 42

Nadivi, J., 94
Namirovsky (Namir), Mordechai, 94
national ceremonies, xi, 22
national culture, xiv, 11, 22, 23, 25, 85, 126
national festivals, 23
nationalism, xii, 14, 72; Jewish-Hebrew nationalism, 93; Jewish nationalism, 21, 126; modern nationalism, xi

national life, 44
nation building, xii, 14, 17
nation of culture *(Kulturnation)*, 16
Navon, Shmuel, 55, 56–57
Nazi parades, 9
Nebi Mussa festivities, 20
Neue Freie Presse (newspaper), 22
Newman, Simon P., 4
Nice carnival, 91
nigunim, 32
Nisan (Hebrew month), 64
Nordau, Max, 43

official folk culture, xii–xiii, 15, 123, 125, 126, 129, 130
official popular culture, 28, 36
official public culture, 23
official state ceremonies, xiii
organized public performance, 3
Oriel, Gila, 89, 95
outdoor public space, xi, 84–86
outdoor spectacles and festivals, 9, 20
Ozouf, Mona, 5
Ozravokitch (Ezariyahu), Yosef, 48

Palm Sunday procession, 7, 73
Passover, 6, 18, 64 (*see also* Haggadah); at the kibbutz, 116–17; the seder, 28, 32, 78, 116–17
performance: definition, 10–11; texts and rituals, 11–13; performative language, 17
Pestalozzi-Froebel Hause, 34
political culture, 23; performative political culture, 41
Political parades, 44, 45
political rituals, 41, 42
popular culture, xii, 16, 27, 55; Jewish popular culture, 18
"Popular Culture" (article of Fichman), 25
Psalms, 81
public sphere, 11, 45; open-air memorial ceremonies, 46–47; open-air performances, 87, 90; open-air political events, 42–46; open-air public culture, 87, 88; open-air public sphere, 18–20, 84–86
Purim, 64, 78, 85, 105; *Adloyada,* 98, 101, 103; balls, 103; Carnival in Tel Aviv, xiii, 19, 86, 89, 91–95, 97–104; "Dionysian" character of the Carnival, 99, 103; at the kibbutz, 116; masquerade, 78, 103; parade of "Queen Esther," 92, 99–101, 102; *Purim Schpiel,* 98; songs, 102

Queen Esther, 91 (*see also Book of Esther*); Tel Aviv parade of "Queen Esther," 99

Rappaport, Roy A., 10
Reform movement, 14
Rehovoth, 32
Renaissance, 8
Revisionist movement, 44, 47
Rishon-Le-Zion, 31, 34, 67
Rosh HaShanah, 28
Rosh Pina, 31
Rothschild, Baron Edmond de, 95
Rousseau, Jean Jacques, 22, 52
rural-agriculture society, 107, 110
rural communities, 6, 19
rural environment, 85
rural society, xv
Russian Salvophiles, 24

Sabbath, 28, 59, 64. See also *kabbalat Shabbat*
Sabbath book *(Sefer Hashabbat),* xiv
Schatz, Boris, v
schools, 19; boys' school in Jaffa, 48; festivals and ceremonies in, 6, 48–62, 63–83, 123 (*see also under specific festivals and ceremonies*); girls' school in Jaffa, 48, 49; Hebrew schools, 26, 47, 48, 49, 52, 63, 80; "Herzliya" Hebrew

schools (continued)
  gymnasium, 55, 67, 91, 95–96;
  Mikveh Israel, 117; study of
  agriculture, 80
schoolteachers (mechanekhim), 19, 26, 48, 50, 52
Second Temple period, 5, 16, 19, 20, 113, 118
Seleucid empire, 68
Sephardic community, 18
sesgallu (head priest), 6
Shalem, Mattityahu, 108, 109, 111, 113, 117, 120
Shapira, A., 73–74
Shapira, Eliezer, 55
Sharet, Yehuda, 113
Shavit, Yaacov, xi
Shavuot, 56, 58, 62–63, 64, 75, 79–81, 97–98, 104, 129; "first fruit field," 80; at the kibbutz (Chag Ha'Omer), 117–21, 123; the seven species, 80
Shihman, J., 94
Shimon bar Kochba, 79. *See also* Bar Kochba revolt
Shimon bar Yohai, Rabbi, 78
Shmeterling (Gilad), David, 109
Shochat, Eliezer, 28
Shoreshim, 51
Shturman, Rivka, 113–14
Sifrei HaMo'adim, 51
Sillman, Kadish Yehudah, 102
Simchat Torah, 31
Sitton, Shoshana, xi
Sitz im Leben, xv, 28, 34, 74
Song of Songs, 65
State of Israel, 130
Steinman, Eliezer, 25
Stites, Robert, 5
Strong, Roy, xi
Succoth, 31, 64, 73; at the kibbutz, 115–16; *succah*, 115; *Ushpizin*, 115
Sumner, William Graham, 4

Tabenkin, Yitzhak, 108–9
Talmudic (Sages'), literature, 19, 79
Teachers' Council (TC), 49, 50–83, 93, 97, 104; Art Committee, 53, 57; Literary Committee, 57
teachers' organization in Palestine, 48
Tel Aviv, xiv, 55, 63, 75, 81; ad hoc committees for festivities, 90; *Adloyada*, 98, 101, 103; Ahuzat Bayit, 88; as a center of performative culture, 88; as a city of festivities, 88–90, 104, 105; the Committee for Purim Projects, 93–94; demographic growth, 86; the first Hebrew city, 85–88; the Great Synagogue on Allenby Street, 102; "Herzliya" Hebrew gymnasium, 55, 67, 91, 95–96; Jewish immigrants in, 86; Maccabee Stadium, 87; the middle class in, 88; municipality of, 87, 90, 95, 97, 99; occasional ceremonies, 95–96; Ohel theatre, 94; parade of "Queen Esther," 92, 99–101, 102; public funerals in, 96; public sports events in, 96–97 (*see also* Maccabiah games); as a public stage, 84–85, 90; Purim Carnival in, xiii, 19, 86, 87, 91–95, 97–104; schools in, 87; the "Tel Aviviya," 99; twenty-fifth anniversary (1934), 96; the working class in, 88; Tel Hai, 46–47, 76, 77; the "Roaring Lion" (sculpture), 46–47, 76; Tel Hai day (the 11th of Adar), 64, 76–78
Torah Laws, 81
Torov, Nisan, 25
traditional festive calendar, 15, 30
traditional-religious Jewish society, 107
tradition invention, xi, 17
Trumpeldor, Yosef, 26, 76, 77
Tubenfliegel, A., 59–60
Tu biShevat (the 15th of Shevat), 49, 64, 71–75, 88, 97, 98, 129; almond tree

(shekedia), 49, 74; at the kibbutz, 117, 121, 122–23; planting ceremony, 72–75
Tukchinsky, Rabbi Yehiel Michal, 72

United States, xi, 4, 44; Jews, 18
urban communities, 19, 85, 86, 87
urban lifestyle, 86, 89
urban patriotism, 87
urban society, xiii, xv, 19, 85, 86, 87, 106, 107
Ussishkin, Menahem Mendel, 50

Vaad Leumi, 50
Valry, Paul, 11

wedding ceremonies, 13, 30, 31
Wissman-Dizengof, H., v
Wolfson, Zipora, 63

Yadin (Sukenik), Yigal, 34
Yavetz, Zeev, 122
Yediot Tel Aviv (Tel Aviv News), 94
Yehieli, Yehiel, 48

Yemot haMaschiach (Berkowitz), 89
Yesod Hama'alah, 72
yiddishkeit, 24
Yizkor, 81
"Yizkor" Book, 46
Yudilewitch, David, 67

Zeev, Aharon, 75
Zerubavel, Yael, 47
Zichron Yaakov, 122
Zionism, 24, 86
Zionist Congresses, 21; First Congress (1897), 21, 42–43; Fifth Congress (1901), 51
Zionist education, 56–57, 58
Zionist Federation, 50, 51, 66
Zionist ideology, 53, 54
Zionist Marxists, 44
Zionist movement, 23, 25, 43, 46, 66
Zionist propaganda, 51
Zionist youth movements, 70, 72
zmirot, 32
Zuta, Haim Arie, 48